Murder On A Horse Trail

Murder On A Horse Trail

✦

The Disappearance of Chandra Levy

Ralph Daugherty

iUniverse, Inc.
New York Lincoln Shanghai

Murder On A Horse Trail
The Disappearance of Chandra Levy

iUniverse, Inc.

For information address:
iUniverse, Inc.
2021 Pine Lake Road, Suite 100
Lincoln, NE 68512
www.iuniverse.com

ISBN: 0-595-31847-9 (pbk)
ISBN: 0-595-66433-4 (cloth)

Printed in the United States of America

Many people spent countless hours posting on the internet about Chandra, discussing pro and con every possible aspect of her disappearance. This informed those of us whose imaginations are not nearly as active as some, but for all of us our sympathy for the Levy's loss was always uppermost in our hearts. This book is dedicated to the Levys in the loss of Chandra, and the continued work they do for others who have also suffered the loss of a loved one.

Contents

Acknowledgements

To all the many Chandra posters on the internet, whose comments, insights, breaking news alerts, online reporting of cable tv interviews, arguments, support, passion, and concern for Chandra Levy and her family made this a life affirming journey in the midst of death.

A special thanks to the members of www.justiceforchandra.com, whose perseverance and skill in seeking the truth about Chandra's disappearance and murder is truly appreciated, and to phpBB for the message board software which along with Google made it all possible.

Hunting Turtles

You would never believe you were in Washington, D.C. The road winds through a steep valley in perpetual twilight under a canopy of trees. Walking along it is to take your life in your hands. A car whizzes around the curve in its pursuit of a Grand Prix win, or at least getting somewhere in a hurry. You jump aside and cling to a hill that forms a wall, hopeful you don't lose your footing and join a dead deer lying next to the road, a deer who had infinitely surer footing than you do.

The car races by, and you venture back out on the road and continue your walk through the primeval forest. Across the narrow two lane road is a creek, the Broad Branch tributary of Rock Creek for which this road is named. Large boulders line the creek bed providing ways to get across for someone who can get to the bottom from the road. The more venturesome can try tightrope walking across a giant fallen tree to get to the other side, although few would find the steep tree covered mountainside across the road very inviting.

It was on the morning of May 22, 2002, reports Michael Doyle of the Modesto Bee, that a man was walking along the side of this road hunting turtles with his dog. According to the report, the dog crossed the road and up that uninviting mountainside, attracted to something. The turtle hunter followed and looked where the dog was sniffing 125 yards up the hill. What the dog had sniffed out and the man found was a skull, buried in leaves with dirt on it.

The unidentified turtle hunter made his way back to the road and found some workers remodeling a house. He alerted the U.S. Park Police with a call at 9:29 a.m. and within 20 minutes a Park Police sergeant arrived, followed soon after by the Washington police. The Washington Post notes that when he showed the sergeant the site where he found the skull he pointed out other items scattered about.

The skull turned out to be Chandra Levy's, identified through dental records provided by the family. The nation had been captivated the summer before by the mystery of her disappearance on May 1, but the greater horror of 9/11 diverted the nation's focus away from the tragedy of a missing intern. Now she was found, but as in almost every other aspect of this mystery, under questionable circumstances.

I would normally expect that he would be walking along the side of the road where the creek was to look for turtles, but he was across the road from the creek and the hillside where Chandra was.

Why would somebody walking along the side of the road say he was hunting turtles? True, he might have been, but wouldn't most people say they were walking their dog if walking along the side of the road? Did he feel it necessary to explain why he would follow his dog up the side of the hill and dig around where the dog was sniffing?

The only presumption one can make is that the dog runs alongside the road and when he detects a turtle he barks and paws and his owner comes and retrieves the turtle. Otherwise it is a very strange story as reported.

I have to think that Michael Doyle was right in describing how the man got to the area, by walking down Broad Branch, but I can't imagine the turtle hunter noticing this about his dog from the road, can't imagine that he follows the dog anytime it runs up a hill, and can't imagine the dog being lured up the hill by the smell of the year old skull buried under a foot of underbrush.

It only makes sense to me if he walked up the hill hunting for turtles, and then the question remains. Is this the first time he or anyone else and their dog walked in the area? Why didn't a dog notice her remains anytime in the previous year?

Also troubling is the refusal to identify the turtle hunter. Some people who watched news reports heard him described as a boy, but was someone who sounded older. He was not shown. Others think he was not identified because he was a juvenile but press reports consistently identified him as a man. For some reason, he remains unidentified.

A turtle hunter's dog being attracted to the site of her remains is very difficult to reconcile with Chandra's body lying there a year. Whether reconciled or not, this is just one of many mysteries surrounding Chandra's disappearance and murder. There is much written here to make sense of this murder on a horse trail, and much that remains to be unraveled.

A powerful Congressman to whom the murdered Chandra was a mistress is part of that mystery, but only part. This is not about getting a powerful politician with secrets. This is about shining a light on a great mystery made more mysterious by what appears to be a coverup, not an explicit coverup, but an implict decision not to pursue a murder investigation into the very halls of Congress itself.

Should the mystery be solved and the murderer found to be only a drifter in a park, it still will be a great mystery and a very public demonstration of the influence wielded by the powers that be to be shielded from what we all would face, and a demonstration of what we would experience if it were one of our loved ones caught in a web of power and deceit.

It is a story whose ending is as yet unknown, a story yet to be told. But in the end the telling of this story will rival the most complex murder mysteries ever told. The search for Chandra had ended, and now the search for justice for Chandra begins.

Paid Intern

Chandra Ann Levy was a bright, inquisitive 23 year old when she came to Washington, D.C. in September of 2000. She had come to take her final semester to complete her master's degree in public administration at USC in California, where she had grown up in Modesto. Friends and neighbors of Chandra described her as strikingly diminutive, perhaps smaller than her official 5 foot 3, 110 pound size, but with curly brown big hair that made her look taller.

She had a small rose tattoo placed above her right ankle in college that her mother was not too pleased about but, being an artist, she did at least try to see the beauty in it. Susan Levy, Chandra's mother, and her husband Dr. Robert Levy, are Jewish but Susan combined Jewish, Christian, and Buddhist teachings in her own beliefs, inspiring Chandra to name her pet parakeets Christmas and Hanukah. Some sense of Chandra's thoughts on her heritage were captured through her interest in journalism in this piece for the Modesto Bee when she was in high school:

HOLOCAUST MEMORIAL: A student's view of Wiesenthal Center
By CHANDRA LEVY
SOPHOMORE, DAVIS HIGH SCHOOL
(Originally published August 27, 1993)

As I began walking through the Simon Wiesenthal Museum of Tolerance in Los Angeles, I had a feeling that I would have a lump in my throat and a big headache when the tour would be over.

I was right.

People just coming from the last tour had disturbed looks on their faces. Some, I think, even were crying.

The museum itself was big and beautiful; the outside had a big monument showing where some of the concentration camps were. It was very peaceful. But on the inside, it was quite a different story. it was dark, dreary and cold.

4

In the beginning of the tour there were different exhibits to see. One particular exhibit was a dark hall that you would walk down and hear different racial slurs whispered at you. It seemed quite normal because you can hear many of these words used toward people every day in many situations.

There were many films to see, such as one called "Genocide" which showed graphic pictures and told chilling facts about different genocides throughout history. What I found weird was that there was a phrase from the Declaration of Independence, "All men are created equal," in the beginning and end of the film. It reminded me of the first rule in the book "Animal Farm" and how their rule was suddenly changed. It seems like our first Declaration was never really true and, in some ways, it still is not true.

As we moved on in our tour, we were guided into a replica of what Germany looked like in the 1930s and '40s. There was a replica of a German concentration camp, along with films of how the camp was run, and life in those camps.

We were each given a little card with a picture of a concentration camp survivor and told to stick them in a machine. When we did, a photocopy came out with a story of the survivor's personal history. We were then told to keep the copy as a reminder of that person's ordeal.

In the last part of the tour, there were exhibits of items crafted by people in the camps. One item was a little handmade guitar made from some sheets of a holy book.

There were many pictures all over the place. Some were cheerful, but most were sad and horrifying. Certain pictures stood out in my mind, such as a picture of a father holding his little girl as they were shot to death. Other pictures showed many different human torture techniques and how fragile many people looked after being treated like old rags. Some pictures were just plain disgusting such as a man's cut-off head, shrunken for medical purposes, and many young children withering away from human medical experiments.

While I am writing this, just thinking about these things makes me want to smash the keyboard with my fists. The Holocaust is a very hard subject to think about, much less to write or talk about.

My mother came from the tour just shaking her head in disbelief. My father couldn't even go on the tour because it brought back too many bad memories. My brother asked why we had to go to see the center anyway (I wouldn't recommend letting younger children see the center) and I told him that we went there to see what happened to these people, to realize how thankful we should be, and to prevent anything like the Holocaust from every happening again.

Anne Frank thought that in spite of all the bad in the world, people are basically good. I agree with her. Hey, even Hitler was a good person some time in his life. But people also make big mistakes about judging others at one time or another. This is a fact of life and it is all in the course of human nature. [1]

What talent and passion Chandra had. She took that passion for writing to San Francisco State to major in journalism and work on the school paper as reporter and sports editor. She had also displayed an interest in law enforcement by volunteering in high school for the Modesto Police Department, but between the disenchantment from her experience with reporting in college and the strong love she had for a Modesto police officer she dated when she came home on weekends, somewhere along the way her interest shifted to law enforcement and a minor in criminal justice. When she graduated in only three years, she returned to Modesto for a year and worked for the police department during the day and on the sports desk for the Bee at night.

That love affair with her policeman boyfriend ended in heartbreak, however. In 1999 after over two years of dating Mark Steele ended the relationship, but at ten years older encouraged Chandra to seek a life outside Modesto. She was devastated, pursuing Mark with a bombardment of phone calls before finally accepting it, and he married someone else a year later. A train trip through the Rockies with her mother gave her time to deal with the disappointment, and according to her mother, they had a great time and bonded. However, when Chandra went to Los Angeles in August to pursue a master's degree in public administration at USC, a friend in LA said Chandra was "shattered" by the breakup. [2]

Chandra recovered though, living in a small graduate student apartment in LA with a fold down bed, no TV, and a gym in the apartment building to work out in. She interned during the fall semester, from September to December, for LA Mayor Richard Riordan working in the lobbying office. For the winter 2000 semester she moved to Sacramento and took classes at the USC Sacramento branch, interning for Gov. Gray Davis' legal staff from February to June.

Even as she was getting over Mark Steele, Chandra's friends knew that she preferred older men to those closer to her own age. The London Daily Mail quoted one friend, Michael Vanden Bosch, as recalling that she called them "hunks with power". The Washington Post quotes him: "She wanted a guy who was concerned, dignified, stable, respected, and a guy who was headed somewhere in his field." So friends were not surprised when they believed that she was involved with a married doctor while in Sacramento.

A friend from San Francisco State in 1997, Jakub Mosur, told The New York Post: "She certainly wasn't into college guys, that's for sure. She was very mature for her age, and didn't date college guys. She was ambitious in a quiet, but very serious, way."

Her intern work for Governor Gray Davis' legal staff included helping to process death row pardon applications. Out of that came a tour of Folsom Prison and attending a parole hearing, and Susan Levy recalls that was the impetus for Chandra to apply for an internship at the Federal Bureau of Prisons (BOP) public affairs office. [3]

Chandra called a BOP manager, Daniel Dunne, from California and told him she didn't want just any job, she wanted one that would "teach her something, advance her career". Dunne hired her on the spot for a $27,000 a year paid internship taking phone calls and doing computer research. [4] Chandra was on her way to Washington.

Her mother was protective as parents are wont to be. "Don't you become a Monica Lewinsky," she jokingly warned, as she related later to Newsweek along with an apology to Monica's mother, Marcia Lewis. Chandra left California that summer and got an apartment in Arlington, Va. Her classes started in September but her internship at the BOP was not to start until late October. She moved into an apartment building in downtown Washington just off Dupont Circle sometime before her internship started and took the Metro train to work.

The Dallas Morning News quotes the recollection of a friend from the USC graduate school, Matt Szabo: "She loved it in D.C. It was the excitement of being in the capital and around the centers of power that we read about in books."

One of her USC graduate program classmates she met in Sacramento was Jennifer Baker, who grew up near Modesto. Jennifer also went to Washington with Chandra for the fall 2000 semester. The USC graduate program was an intensive mix of internships and ten hour days on weekends, so time consuming that a dissertation was not required for the master's degree in public administration that they were pursuing.

They palled around, doing "touristry things", according to Jennifer. [5] They also took "political field trips" and it was on one those visits to government offices that they dropped by Rep. Gary Condit's office, Chandra's own local congressman.

Jennifer describes the visit as impromptu, with neither knowing Congressman Condit, but Condit spotted them, posed for a picture with them, took them to the House gallery to watch him vote, and offered Jennifer an unpaid internship in his office for the semester, but when she left Chandra stayed behind in Condit's office. [6]

The LA Times further quotes Jennifer Baker: "As far as I knew, that was the first and last time Chandra ever met him. She came over to meet me at his office once or twice a week so we could go out for lunch, but I never saw them together again. If there was a relationship, she never told me about it."

Condit's staff stated that he knew Chandra through his intern Jennifer Baker. [7] Numerous news reports described Jennifer as introducing Chandra to Condit. Yet they walked in together, Jennifer was offered an internship on the spot, and Chandra stayed behind with Condit. Who introduced whom to who?

Vince Flammini had been Condit's staff driver in California for almost ten years. In an Geraldo Rivera interview, Flammini relates Condit describing a girl to him who matched Chandra perfectly, but describing her to him earlier during the summer:

> He said that she had "melons" for breasts and had the greatest body he'd ever seen. And that she had curly hair but she was dark complected. I thought maybe she might have been a black girl. And he did talk about her but he didn't give me a name. But he talked about her even before that time. That's why I was wondering if he knew her before. You know, before September 2000. [8]

Flammini elaborates further on Hannity & Colmes:

> He explained to me—it was way before December. I left in September. And June, July, and August, he was telling me about this girl that he met. And he described Chandra to the tee. And then it comes out that he said didn't meet

her until December. And here she worked in the governor's office with his son and daughter and sister. And he said—and they all said they didn't know her. Well, I don't believe that. [9]

And he adds another corroboration for Greta Van Susteren:

…like he was seeing a girl that her ex-boyfriend was a police officer. That's the first time. And Chandra's ex-boyfriend was a police officer. [10]

The son and daughter working in the governor's office that Flammini refers to are Chad Condit, a $110,000 liason for Governor Davis to California's Central Valley, and Cadee Condit, a $52,000 special assistant to Davis. Dennis Cardoza, a former Condit aide and later elected to Congress himself, described the bond between Gray Davis and Gary Condit "as close a bond as any politicians have". [11]

So Condit was extremely close to Governor Davis and his staff by virtue of his relationship with Gray Davis and the positions his grown children had on his staff. However, Governor Davis' office pointed out that Chandra did her internship in an office building three blocks from the state Capitol building. [12]

Did Condit know Chandra in Sacramento and help arrange for her BOP internship? Did he arrange for Jennifer Baker's internship in his office as cover for Chandra to visit? Condit did seem to have known who Chandra was. The Modesto Bee reports that he helped her obtain her BOP internship. Oddly, this is in conflict with what the BOP says. Daniel Dunne, the manager who hired her, said no congressional office "intervened on her behalf". [13]

The Bureau of Prisons internship in the public affairs office certainly seemed to be worth some intervention. It was a prestigious and valuable internship for someone seeking a career in federal law enforcement, a paid internship at $27,000 per year handling press inquiries. Chandra described it to her parents as "the best internship I could possibly get". [14]

It may have been a total coincidence that she was in Sacramento working on the legal staff of Condit's ally, Gray Davis, whose staff included Chad and Cadee, before serendipitously wangling a coveted paid public relations internship position in D.C. with a phone call from California. But Condit described her to his driver Flammini in the months before she went to D.C. while she was working for the governor. Was she secretly seeing her congressman before she even started work for the BOP?

If so, Chandra didn't make an announcement to friends and family of a new boyfriend until shortly after her visit with Jennifer to Condit's office to meet him. Chandra told Jennifer in November about having a new boyfriend. AP quotes Jennifer: "She never told me what his name was or what he looked like." Chandra's mother recalls: "I do know that she had mentioned to me that she had a boyfriend in November. Actually, I don't know of any particular boyfriend." [15]

To friends back home, she told of dating someone in politics and to one friend even said that he was a member of Congress. To Jennifer, who was interning for Condit, she said her boyfriend was in the FBI. However, Chandra wrote to another friend that she had lied about that. According to AP, her e-mail read: "Don't tell her who I am seeing, since" she "thinks that I am dating an FBI agent (which is obviously not the case but I lied to her so she wouldn't ask any questions)."

USC classmate Michelle Yanez said Chandra was so secretive about her boyfriend that "it worried us". [16] The Los Angeles Times: "She couldn't say who it was. "'Couldn't,' that's how she put it," Yanez said. "She was also extremely excited about whoever it was that she was seeing. She said it was 'someone in politics.'"

An argument can be made that Chandra already knew Condit when she and Jennifer walked into his office, that Jennifer Baker was cover for her to know Condit, and that the married doctor earlier in Sacramento may have been Condit. Whether that is true or not, James Lau, the USC classmate who introduced Chandra and Jennifer, sums it up best in the Daily Telegraph: "She was very mysterious about who she was dating." Did that mysterious boyfriend help her get a paid internship? It is a critical question in that the ending of her internship is even more mysterious than the beginning.

Secrecy

While Condit was describing a dark curly haired girl with a great body to Flammini in the summer of 2000, Vince was driving him to see another woman, a 39 year old red haired stewardess, he was to find out. The Modesto Bee quotes Flammini recalling the incident. They were going to a 19th Avenue mall in San Francisco and Condit told him to wait, he had to meet someone. Flammini asked who, and Condit told him a stewardess. Then Flammini saw her and Condit meet at a small cafe in a bookshop.

Another time he took Condit to meet her at a motel in Los Angeles. At some point during these rendezvous Flammini met the stewardess. Within a couple of months Condit told Flammini to find another line of work. Flammini had ridden motorcycles with Condit, roomed with him on the road, lifted weights with him in Flammini's gym, and even gardened together, but Flammini had done something to end a thirty year relationship and ten years as Condit's driver and security. Flammini isn't sure why, but he thinks he knew too much. [1]

And there was a lot to know. Condit was now dating Chandra in D.C. and the stewardess, Ann Marie Smith, in both D.C. and San Francisco. Ann Marie was a San Francisco based stewardess for United Airlines working a cross country flight between San Francisco and Washington. They would meet in Washington at his apartment or her hotel, or in San Francisco she would pick him up at the airport on his flight home from Washington and go to the Hyatt. She would then drop him off at a Starbuck's or other locations and his California chief of staff, Mike Lynch, would pick him up to drive him home to Modesto, an hour and a half drive or longer.

One time Condit came to see her on his Harley he had at home in Modesto and gave her a ride to a hotel in Livermore which, perhaps as cover, was next to a Harley shop. Condit didn't take the risk of going to Anne Marie or Chandra's apartments. Ann Marie had roommates sharing her apartment in San Francisco.

Chandra lived alone at the Newport in Washington, but security was such that he would have had to be buzzed in at the front door, and he was never seen there.

Congressman Gary Condit had reason to avoid risk. He was married, very much so in Modesto, more questionably so in Washington. For years congressional colleagues had been led to believe that Condit's wife Carolyn was an invalid. As journalist Lisa DePaulo points out, Condit was the only congressman whose Web site or personal bio info doesn't mention their wife.

Fellow California congressman Dave Dreier is quoted in Newsweek as saying: "I was told early on that his wife was ill, and that he went out. I'd heard she'd been ill for 30 years. This is a guy who's active, and if his wife can't do much of anything with him, that's sad and unfortunate, and if he ends up seeing other women, it couldn't come as a humongous shock."

Cal Dooley, another California congressman, had seen her "maybe once". Carolyn rarely went to Washington, and the former mayor of Modesto, Dick Lang, had not even seen her attend public events in Modesto much in the past 30 years. [2]

Condit's wife Carolyn had been married to him for 34 years and had two children with him, Chad and Cadee, who both worked for Governor Gray Davis of California. She did suffer from migraines, but friends described her as "bubbly", "outgoing", and "a live wire", hardly an invalid. [3]

But Condit cultivated the image of not exactly being married. When another stewardess that he told he was divorced checked up on him with the League of Women Voters and found out he was married with two kids, he responded that his wife was "terminally ill". He told Anne Marie that his wife was extremely ill with encephalitis of the brain and that it was more a marriage of friendship than husband-wife. Because of that, he would not get divorced, was "not pulling a Newt", referring to Newt Gingrich divorcing his wife while she was in the hospital and the political fallout that came with that. [4]

Anne Marie started seeing him in July, and by November Condit was mentioning the prospect of a vacation with her in Palm Springs. Coincidentally, Chandra was telling her Aunt Linda Zamsky at Thanksgiving of the same thing, the possibility of taking a vacation with her boyfriend to Palm Springs. It had been a month since Chandra and Jennifer Baker had visited Condit's office. On Thanksgiving Chandra journeyed up to Maryland's Eastern Shore to visit her uncle, Paul Katz, a doctor who was Susan Levy's brother, and his wife, Linda Zamsky. Chandra took the train from D.C. and Linda picked her up.

Chandra was excited about telling her aunt, at 40 a little older than Chandra but still someone she shared girl talk with, about her new boyfriend in politics. In Linda Zamsky's own words, she describes what Chandra told her:

> I've known Chandra's uncle for eight years. I've known her for eight years. We were rather close from the very beginning, actually. She would talk about her boy friends and school and just what was going on in her life. The few times that we would chat, most of the time it was through family affairs, bar mitzvah—her brother was bar mitzvahed, I was there. We had a family reunion down at our condo that we used to own in Florida, we had a big family reunion there, and she spoke to me there about a boy friend that she was dating, a guy that was about 10 years older than she, and they were in love and whatever, and—so she started confiding in me from almost the very beginning of having this girl talk.

> Then she came to Washington, I think in September or October, and she gave me a call and she said, "Hey, Lynn, I'm out on the East Coast, let's get together, you know, when can we get together?" I said you can come up any time you want, I'll pick you up at the train station…you can spend the weekend at my house, whatever you want to do, she said, "Okay, I'll let you know," and we chitchatted on the phone, nothing significant that I can remember, just girl talk. She was excited about her job, being here in Washington was something she'd dreamed about for quite a while, working in a government position was something she wanted to do. So she felt that she was on her way to where she wanted her career to take her.

> She came in on Thanksgiving. I invited her to Thanksgiving dinner…she wasn't going back West, and her grandmother, Paul's mother, was going to be in for Thanksgiving. So she came in Wednesday night, the 22nd of November, and she told me—I think on the 20th or the 21st of November, she said, "Oh, I can't wait to see you, I have a lot to tell you about, a lot has happened here in Washington, my job, yada yada," and so I said great…she said, "I can't talk"—it's not like I was trying to say, well, what's going on—she said, "No, I'll talk to you when I get there."

> So I picked her up at the train station on Wednesday night, and we came back to the house and her grandmother was up for the first hour or two so it was idle chitchat, and then we had our girl talk and that's where she first mentioned that she was dating a man that was married and quite a few years older

than her. And I said, "Well, how old?" and she said he was in his 50s, he was "fiftyish." And I said, that's interesting. And I said, "Well, who is he?" She said, "He's married...Well, he's here in Washington and he goes home occasionally."

She said, "He's in the government." She didn't say he was in the FBI or this—Congress or Senate, or she didn't say that that particular evening. She mentioned he had two kids...

And she was just, you know, it was a new relationship, she had met him a couple weeks prior. She kind of referenced like either four or six weeks, and I don't remember exactly, but she'd been dating him for four to six weeks prior to Thanksgiving. And—Thanksgiving. Thanksgiving Day came. That night happened. I don't think we did a lot of speaking Thanksgiving.

The next day was Friday. We went to the mall with the grandmother, we talked about—she did talk about the boy friend then, how, you know, she wanted to spend time with him, how they'd spent time with each other.

I asked her, "How do you get in touch with him if it's so secretive, this relationship?" And she said, "Well"—and this is when she came and accidentally said his name to me, okay? That she would dial a number, it would play music, and she would leave a message. And she said she would also call his office. She said, "And I would also call the office and he would—you know, they'd answer, "Gary Condit," and that's how his name came out, "Congressman Condit's office." "Congressman Gary Condit's office," that's how the name came out.

And she goes, "Oops." She says, "Oh, you didn't hear that, did you?" And I said, "No." And of course I did, but I didn't—I always wanted to make—well, anybody, I like to make them feel comfortable when they talk to me. As I expect them to do with me, speak with me. So she said his name, and then she continued with how she would get in touch with him.

He would call her back after she would leave a message on the number she would dial, she would leave a message and he would call her back, 'cause she would say, "My cell phone will be on between this time and this time, you can reach me, call me if you can." She was very patient. That was something he liked about her...He said that, "It's nice to see someone that's willing to be flexible with my schedule and my lifestyle. You know, I haven't had that in a relationship before."

So Chandra was aware...that he had had previous relationships. She didn't say that there were relationships, just that's how she knew of them. Because she was being very flexible. She was being easygoing. She didn't make demands on him.

I said, "Well, what do you guys do, if it's such a secret, what do you guys do?" And she said, "Well, most of the time, because he's so busy in his job and his political career, that he—you know, he goes to a lot of dinners, a lot of luncheons, a lot of benefits, he just—when we're together, we just like to hang out at his place and be together, and we can cook in or we'll go get a bite to eat and we go out." I said, "Well, how do you go out if it's such a secret?" and she said they would take a taxi…she would come out the door, grab the taxi, and then he would come out, baseball cap, jacket, kind of a little incognito, and he would get in the cab with her.

I said, "Well, wasn't he afraid that the cabby was going to, you know, know who he was?" And she said no, she said they didn't do a lot of talking in the cab, they kept everything very, you know, quiet.

And these were the rules, these were rules that she had to follow for this relationship to be flow and to be all right. He wanted, you know—no one could know about this.

She—I mean, when she told me his name, she was really—I mean, I made real light of it and I kind of dummied up because I wanted her to feel comfortable, I didn't want her to be a nervous wreck talking about her boy friend. Obviously, I was one of the few people that she—one or maybe a few people that she could talk to about this, so I wanted her to feel comfortable.

When she would go to his apartment—she also told me this at Thanksgiving—she would go in, go into the elevator, and if someone was in the elevator or got in the elevator with her she was to push another floor. She could not get off that floor. If someone asked her, "Oh, you look new in the building," or, "Did you just move in?" she would say, "No, I'm not new here, I'm visiting a sick friend." So these are all little details that she had worked out with him, that kind of, you know, really shows how serious this relationship was and how serious it was that it had to remain a secret.

We also watched—and I guess this was Friday night we watched C-Span or C-Span II, Bloomberg, wherever the Senate and the Congress go on, and she was, like, watching it—and I know very little about politics, well, then I knew very little about politics, and she was explaining the Senator's role and the Congressman's role and who has more power and, you know, what kind of guy this was—and then she described him then, when we were watching TV. I don't know, I don't remember if he ever came up on TV. I really—I don't believe he did, because I think she would have gotten a little bit more excited and then I would have seen what he looked like, because she did describe him as looking a little bit like Harrison Ford. And she said he was lean, good shape, worked out, very conscientious about his body for 53 years old, and that's when she told me his age…I knew he was fiftyish, but she said 53.

My husband has a Harley Davidson. And we go in and out of my house most of the time through the garage into the mud room, and our Harley's parked there, and she didn't—she's never seen Paul's Harley. So she saw the bike and she said, "Oh, my guy drives a bike too." And I said, "He does?" I said, "Is it a Harley?" and she said, "Yeah, it's great." I said, "You know, maybe in the spring we'll get together, you guys can come out here, I don't know who he is, it wouldn't matter, you could tell me his name was Tom Jones, I wouldn't know who he is, and we can go for a bike ride together. You know? You can come out on a bike or he can rent one, whatever."

And she said, "Yeah, because his bike's not here, it's at home in California." And I said, oh, okay. And she said, "But he would never do that because he wouldn't want to be seen, you know, Paul might know him or you might—you know, it's just that's not something he would do." I said okay, well, you know, the offer's there. If you want to come out here and spend the weekend, you're more than welcome. I mean, I said you two can go upstairs and have your privacy, it'll be your little bed and breakfast, and you don't have to see me at all, you know, if you just want to get away and be together.... [5]

The Washington Post quotes Linda further on the secrecy demands Condit made of Chandra: "He was emphatic. It had to remain secret. If anybody found out about this relationship, it was done, over, kaput." Chandra couldn't call him directly. She called a private answering service and left a message for him to call her back on her cell phone. When they went out to dinner, she would go down and hail a cab, get in, then he would come down with a cap pulled down over his face and get in. Condit told her he "admired" her for her skill at secrecy, and Chandra actually relished the intrigue. [6]

Condit lived in the Adams Morgan section of D.C., described in the press as bohemian, trendy, and hip, with the Tryst coffeehouse and restaraunt nearby. He met Chandra there once, but when they went to dinner they would take a cab to the suburbs, Chandra recalling to Linda that it was often for Thai food. The rest of the time when she saw him they stayed in his apartment, sometimes all weekend with hot oil messages and Ben and Jerry's low-fat chocolate chip cookie dough ice cream being favorites. He never came over to her apartment on Dupont Circle, about a mile and a half away.

A very controversial rule, that she had been instructed not to carry any identification when meeting her unnamed secret boyfriend in Congress, was told by Chandra to her parents. It is not intuitively clear why such a demand would be made, and the rule was not mentioned along with the others that Linda initially described from her talks with Chandra over Thanksgiving. Also, Anne Marie never mentioned any similar rule in her descriptions of secrecy in her relationship with Condit. Was Chandra given this demand to carry no id when she was with Condit, and if so, why?

As with Anne Marie and other women, Condit told Chandra that his wife never came to visit because she's "sickly". [7] Chandra saw this as a long term opportunity for them and told her aunt of a five year plan for her to live with Condit secretly and then get married and have a baby.

Linda suggested there would be problems but was not surprised Chandra was seeing someone older. She told Larry King: "Because Chandra was a very, very mature, independent individual. She is a very independent individual. So I—it didn't surprise me that she was in love or having a relationship with someone that was much older than her."

Anne Marie at 39 was much closer to Condit's age, but she describes the same rules of secrecy as Chandra would relate to Linda Zamsky. She told Rita Cosby of Fox News: "He was very adamant about it: 'Don't talk to anybody about this. Don't talk to other flight attendants. Don't talk to your friends. Totally keep it a secret.' And so, you know, I tried to, as best as I could." [8] "The secrecy was huge. He, you know, forbade me to talk to other flight attendants, family, friends. I mean, it was supposed to be totally kept secret…" she told Hannity and Colmes. [9]

Condit stood behind the door when letting her in his apartment so that nobody in the hallway would be able to see him. Anne Marie also went downstairs out of his apartment building ahead of him, wait for him to catch up to her with sunglasses and a hat pulled down low, and go out to dinner incognito. Calling an answering service and leaving a message for Condit to call her back worked the same way as with Chandra as well.

Not being able to call Condit directly was not limited to his girlfriends. A former legislative director for Condit, Joe Thiessen, recalls that Condit never carried a cell phone or pager. Associated Press quotes Thiessen:

> Clearly there were times that he didn't want anyone to know where he was—and he was quite successful at it. We would be scrambling to find him.

He would frequently borrow a car from someone on the staff and take off for extended periods of time throughout the day. He liked to be invisible in lots of ways. But it was not my experience that there was a dark side. [10]

The LA Times reports that Condit just dropped out of sight from his staff during the day. He would go to the gym or go get a tan on the Capitol balcony. According to the San Francisco Chronicle, he kept a bicycle in his office and rode off to Rock Creek Park during lulls.

One would think that Condit could be e-mailed, but there has never been an indication that he had a computer or used e-mail. Thinking about it, things like e-mail, a cell phone number you hand out, or having information on a laptop that someone may get a look at are not compatible with having multiple girl-friends who spend time with you at home. Everything was a secret. Chandra was to keep that secret, or, as she told Linda Zamsky, it was "done, over, kaput". How kaput remained to be seen.

Friendships

"Yeah, it's great," Linda Zamsky recalls Chandra saying. Chandra was talking about her boyfriend's motorcycle when she and Linda walked past husband Paul's bike in the garage during the Thanksgiving visit. The Washington Post quotes the exchange between them:

> As they walked past a motorcycle in Zamsky's garage, Levy commented, "Oh, my guy drives a bike, too."
>
> "He does? Is it a Harley?" her aunt asked.
>
> "Yeah, it's great," Zamsky recalled the young woman saying. [1]

This from a picture, or what? Having only been dating Condit four or six weeks, as Linda recalled later, with Condit's Harley back home in Modesto, Chandra would seemingly not have seen his bike.

It's possible she thought it looked great in a picture, but it's odd that Condit described someone resembling her to Flammini the previous summer, that she had one of the most prestigious paid intern jobs which the Modesto Bee reported Condit helped her get, and that she started a relationship with him as soon as she met him with Jennifer Baker. That visit was in October, four to six weeks before Thanksgiving, the same amount of time that Chandra had a new congressman boyfriend.

Chandra had arrived in Washington in September and got an apartment in Arlington. Her parents came to visit in October and were concerned about her security in Arlington and the noise of the airport, and she moved to the nicer Newport apartments off Dupont Circle, only ten blocks from the Capitol.

Coincidentally, the move to the Newport put her within walking distance of Condit's residence in Adams Morgan, about a dozen blocks away. The move close to Condit's condo was just before starting her internship but also just before her visit to Condit's office and a relationship with him. If the visit with Jennifer Baker was arranged, the move to another apartment close to him may have been suggested as well.

Denis Edeline was the co-owner of Chandra's Newport condo. The landlord recalled to the Modesto Bee: "She really wanted the apartment, but she first wanted her parents to see it, because they were concerned for her safety." She had found the apartment and was ready to move before her parents visited from California, so it may not be just a coincidence that she moved close to Condit before she was supposed to have even met him.

Chandra and Jennifer Baker continued getting their political feet wet in Washington during their internships. They attended the vice presidential debate at Georgetown University, and Jennifer was in the spotlight to ask a question. Chandra went to a breakfast for Senator Barbara Boxer of her home state of California. In November they watched election 2000 results at the Hawk and Dove on Pennsylvania Avenue where capitol hill staffers gather. Then they moved on to a Xando coffee bar to talk more election night politics.

At night Chandra stayed home and researched on the internet, according to Jennifer. [2] Her Newport neighbors rarely saw her, and never with anyone else. Chandra worked out regularly at the Washington Sports Club just a few blocks away on Connecticut Avenue. She was always friendly and pleasant, but kept to herself.

Chandra, Jennifer, and the other USC graduate students in Washington for the semester worked hard with classes and internship jobs. Finals for the semester were back in California before Christmas, and the students returned to Sacramento to take their tests. Chandra passed hers and in December completed requirements for her master's degree in public administration from USC.

But Chandra had a round trip ticket back to Washington, provided by Condit. In an e-mail to a friend:

> My short trip to California wasn't much fun, I was sick when I was in Sacramento, and I only got to go home for one night before I flew back to D.C. The nice thing is that the man I'm seeing took care of my plane ticket for me! [3]

On her visit home during the trip, she also talked to her parents about the man she was seeing, and told them he was a congressman. Her father, Bob, is captured on videotape, joking that "Chandra told us all about her adventures in D.C., the Bureau of Prisons, and her congressman friend". [4] As far as they knew, the congressman was a divorced congressman in his "late forties" from southern California. [5] Susan recalls: "She kept telling me she had to keep it secret, that in five years she could make it public, that I would understand." [6]

Her mother also was, puzzled by Chandra making a tape of Frank Sinatra's 'Fly Me to the Moon' even though she normally listened to classical rock. She says "Chandra said he listened to it". [7]

Jennifer Baker and her other USC classmates were home to stay, but USC friend Michelle Yanez said Chandra wanted to stay in Washington and extend her stay beyond her internship because of her relationship, but her parents wanted her to come home. [8] Despite that, Chandra visited one night and was on her way back to D.C.

With her friends back home and Condit home in Ceres as well, Chandra spent Christmas in Washington alone. She did get a gold bracelet from Condit for Christmas, but unknown to each other identical to Anne Marie's Christmas gift. First the promise of Palm Spring vacations, then gold bracelets. Identical gifts certainly made the logistics of handling two mistresses easier, one may presume.

Condit had a campaign expenditure disbursement on January 18, 2001 for $830 to Neiman Marcus in Washington, D.C. that probably would have covered the pair of very nice double clasp bracelets he got Chandra and Anne Marie for Christmas. [9] But then again, maybe not. The Neiman Marcus purchase was described as gifts to contributors, and Chandra Levy and Anne Marie Smith weren't listed as contributors to Condit's campaign. Still, he paid for them somehow.

Chandra was even more disappointed to find out Linda was ill for the New Year's visit she was going to make to Paul and Linda's. Linda says "she was kind of sad because she had spent Christmas by herself, and she hadn't gone home to the West Coast. So I could see—I could hear that she was disappointed, but I was feeling lousy…". [10] Chandra recovered well, going to a black-tie affair on New Year's Eve with a friend.

But she was waiting for her man to come back to Washington. She e-mailed one friend: "Everything else here is going good. My man will be coming back here when Congress starts up again. I'm looking forward to seeing him." [11] And in January, Chandra was in the VIP section for the Bush inauguration.

According to Linda, Chandra was organizng her evenings to be available for Condit, avoiding making plans because she was waiting to hear from him and never knowing what he was doing. She frequently went to Condit's apartment straight from work, although Condit says that she didn't have a key and he always admitted her with the security system. [12] This is hard to believe based on a Washington Post interview with Linda Zamsky. Linda describes one phone call she had with Chandra who was whiling away a Saturday alone at Condit's apartment:

> But over the winter, Levy lamented that she was having trouble filling her long hours alone at Condit's apartment, Zamsky said.
>
> Her aunt asked what the apartment was like.
>
> "Well, he grows cactus…. "Levy said, according to the aunt.
>
> "Well, get a terrarium, you know. Go to a craft shop, get some colored sand…get him little cactus and plant them in the terrarium," the aunt said she offered.
>
> The aunt suggested that the young woman, a vegetarian, try "The Moosewood Cookbook." Make dinner for him. Be helpful.
>
> "Organize his closet," she suggested.
>
> "It's pretty clean," Levy said.
>
> "Well, color-coordinate everything, you know, put all the long sleeves by color…" [13]

With her classes ending in December and no more ten hour classes on Thursday through Saturday when she returned from taking finals, the change for her after Christmas must have been dramatic. In January, Chandra told Linda she had discussed moving in with Condit. She said she could save money on rent, keep up his apartment and be there for him. She even checked with her landlord on breaking the lease to move in with her boyfriend. He offered to let the boyfriend live with her, but she paused and said that was not an option.

By February however, she told her landlord that "it didn't work out". [14] She did get Godiva chocolates and a card for Valentine's Day though.

By now Anne Marie was ironically getting suspicious about another woman. She "poked around" once in his condo to look for signs of someone else to see if he was two, make that three, timing her, but she didn't find anything.

Still, she found him very caring, thoughtful, and concerned as a boyfriend. He called her nearly everyday and wanted her to call him on layovers, or when her trips were over, and let him know she was ok. Occasionally on visits to Washington he would drive her around in an older red Ford he borrowed from his aide Mike Dayton, the rest of the time they would take cabs.

The pure duplicity of having two mistresses and a wife, none of whom know of each other, is illustrated aptly here. Condit was controlling and would get upset if Anne Marie wasn't available to him, even when he had no intention of showing up. He would tell her not to go somewhere she was thinking of going, such as Seattle, saying that he would be in San Francisco that weekend, and then not show up. One weekend Anne Marie went to Telluride and Condit got upset. He said "you know, if you want to have an open relationship, if that's how you're going to be about it..." [15]

Meanwhile, Chandra's dreams of a career with the FBI were getting closer as her work continued at the Bureau of Prisons. She was doing Internet searches and preparing daily news summaries, answering phones and mail, and working on special projects such as working with the media for the execution of Timothy McVeigh.

Jennifer Baker talked with her quite a bit about becoming an FBI agent. "That's her goal, her dream," she said. [16]

Her mother says "she thought maybe down the road, go into law school, but her dream, I think, was to go into FBI work. She wanted to go to the FBI Training Academy in Quantico…" [17] Chandra applied to the FBI in March for an analyst job.

At work, Chandra became friends with a fellow Californian, Sven Jones, 37, who had just started in public affairs at the BOP in February, sharing the same subway ride and talking. They would talk politics at Starbucks and he would walk her home at night. It is reported that he was also a member of the Washington Sports Club, but they did not work out together as she was always seen working out alone in the gym. She soon tapped into all of Sven's knowledge acquired from two degrees in psychology to share her thoughts and plans with her man in politics, without breaking the rules of secrecy and naming him.

Susan was wondering who that man in politics was that her daughter was so secretive about. When she saw a newspaper article that said their own local congressman, Gary Condit, was a teetotaler, she remembered that Chandra said her boyfriend didn't drink. But Chandra also said her boyfriend in Congress was divorced and in southern California, and Condit was very much married and local.

The Levys were soon to be making a trip east to visit Chandra, Susan's brother Paul and Linda, and Chandra's godparents, Fran Iseman and her husband, also in the Washington area. The trip was for getting together at Paul and Linda's for the Jewish Passover holiday, on April 7 in 2001, and then to stay and visit a week with the Iseman's and celebrate Chandra's 24th birthday on April 14.

Her daughter continued to worry her, and one day in late March to early April she sat in her backyard talking to her gardener, a Pentecostal minister, part-time gardener, and friend of four years, Otis "OC" Thomas. The conversation would prove to be pivotal in their lives and the lives of those they loved. It is a conversation that defies belief, yet created its own reality once it occurred.

Susan and her gardener friend the minister were discussing their daughters and, concerned about Chandra secretly dating a congressman, Condit's name came up, although Susan tells Newsweek she didn't say he was dating Chandra because she didn't know. OC recalls the remarkable conversation to the Washington Post:

> Thomas, who has parlayed his weekend groundskeeping at his Modesto, Calif., church into a weekday freelance gardening business, has done work at

the Levy home for about four years. He had a conversation with Chandra's mother, Susan Levy, in April while he was tending roses in the back yard. The conversation continued by the pool, where Susan Levy brought him a cold drink. The two often talked about their children, and Thomas said he asked Susan Levy how Chandra was doing in Washington.

Susan Levy replied that Chandra was doing well and that she had befriended a congressman, Gary Condit.

"Mrs. Levy asked me if I know Gary Condit and asked me what I think about him," Thomas said. "She said she was asking about him because her daughter was friends with him in Washington."

Thomas said he remembered that his daughter had asked him for advice about seven years ago, when she wanted to break off a bad relationship. He said he had been shocked when she told him the man she was seeing was Condit, whom she said she met at a political rally.

"Lord have mercy, I told her she has to be around men her own age," Thomas said.

He said he advised her to end the liaison immediately. She did so, and the two never spoke of it again, he said. "I didn't really think much about it since then, until Mrs. Levy asked me about him," Thomas said.

At the Levy house that day, Thomas said he and Susan Levy talked about Condit, gingerly at first. "Then Mrs. Levy asked me if I've ever heard anything about him and other women," Thomas said. The two eventually confessed to one another that both their daughters had relationships with Condit. "I told Mrs. Levy that with my daughter, it ended badly, that I think her daughter should end the relationship with him right away," Thomas said.

He remembers that Susan Levy then got on the phone and called Chandra in Washington. He said he heard the mother argue with her daughter. "Mrs. Levy talked to Chandra about it, but Chandra told her mother to mind her own business, that she was a grown woman who could deal with it," Thomas said.

Susan Levy confirmed that she had the conversation with Thomas and said she had sparred with her daughter about the relationship with Condit over the phone. [18]

OC said his daughter Jennifer met Condit at a California State local campus political rally in 1993 or 1994 when she was 18 or 19 years old. But he says she became distraught over his sexual demands and ended the relationship in a tense breakup. OC says it ended badly. Susan was then told by OC that his daughter Jennifer was warned by Condit not to tell anyone about it.

During the two year affair OC told Susan about, in September of 1994, Jennifer had a mixed-race son. It so happens that the minister and his family are African-American, and Jennifer told neighbors that her son was Mexican. No one would know otherwise. The Modesto Doctors Medical Center birth certificate has the word "withheld" written in where the father's name goes.

The emotion of sharing the story of his daughter with Susan was intense. Susan told the Modesto Bee: "I had him in my living room and he was full of tears," she said. "...I've never seen a man broken up like that." He sat with Susan in her living room as she called Chandra to pass on his warnings to her. For all their emotion and concern, Chandra told her mother to mind her own business.

Surely just as Susan believed her friend, Chandra could not have given it any credence. Her mother was telling her the man she loved, a congressman, had an affair with a black teenaged daughter of a local minister, and that it ended badly. Mind your own business? Could there be any reason to think she believed it?

1994 was a watershed year for congressional politics, with a Newt Gingrich led House running on the conservative morals and economics of the Contract with America platform. Condit supported that agenda with the Blue Dog coalition of conservative Democrats, and even was rumored to be switching to the Republican Party that year, but it didn't happen.

However, the family values that Condit espoused as a congressman were falling apart at home. Carolyn was said by friends to have returned to her parents home in Tulsa in 1994 for awhile, perhaps to help her mother move to Tampa near another sister, but even after returning to Ceres friends say she asked for a divorce as early as 1996. [19] It is during these tumultuous two years that OC told Susan that Condit had an affair with his daughter. Susan would not have known that, and it is doubtful that OC did either. Is it just a coincidence?

What would normally be inconceivable with Carolyn home becomes at least possible with her out of town. The Ceres street Richard Way conveniently runs between OC Thomas' apartment and Condit's house on Acorn Lane about a mile away. Was Condit a name picked up by OC from empathizing too much with Susan or was Condit someone who had an affair with his daughter Jennifer?

Whatever the answer, friendships had unleashed forces that no one would comprehend.

Explanation

Chandra developed a close friendship with Sven Jones at the Bureau of Prisons after he arrived in February of 2001. They worked in public affairs together and Sven considered her a "computer whiz" who helped him with technical problems at work. They spent a lot of time together, riding the subway to work, talking after work at Starbucks, and discussing at length her career and over time her boyfriend problems. Jennifer and her other USC friends had stayed in California after taking finals. Only Chandra had returned to be with her man in Congress.

She had become much more serious about Condit through the winter. Linda Zamsky had noted it as they kept up on the phone. Neighbors at the Newport didn't see her at all in March and most of April. According to CNN:

> A neighbor who lives three doors from the apartment Chandra Levy rented in the Dupont Circle area told CNN Thursday she thought Levy did not actually live in the building, but just maintained a residence there.

> The resident, who wished to be identified only as "Karen," told CNN she shared her observation with police during the six times she was interviewed.

> "She never carried laundry, or got packages, or took out any trash," said the woman. "And I live three doors down" from the unit Chandra rented. [1]

Chandra had become totally engaged in the process of becoming engaged, to become Mrs. Condit. She still talked to her aunt Linda and now her friend Sven of a five year plan to marry and have children, but the urgency to get a commitment from Condit was increasing. She discussed this at length with Sven without revealing her boyfriend's name to him as she had to Linda. Sven didn't think it was necessarily important anyway to know exactly who it was for him to offer feedback. He told the New York Daily News: "She was very private about that. Always."

Lisa DePaulo captured the essence of that dialogue between Chandra and Sven in a Talk magazine article:

"I tried to tell her," says Jones, "that if you push a man like that too hard, he's going to feel as if he's lost some self-control. I said, 'If you really want to hook this guy, you should lay low and let him feel like he's making the decisions.'"

But Chandra was beyond lying low. She'd been down this road before with older married men—her weakness—who promised her the world and abandoned her. Friends from pre-Washington days knew how devastated she had been in the past and worried that if it happened again she would, as one put it, "do something drastic. You know, call the wife or something".

As Levy told Jones: "I've invested too much in this." And this time the stakes were much higher, as they often are the third or fourth time around, particularly with a man she considered the ultimate catch. Despite her appearance—she was a tiny little thing, much more petite than her photos suggest—"Chandra could be a pretty forward person," says Jones. "She was not the type of woman who was going to be the little mistress waiting home on the couch."…

She was determined to "have this confrontation", he says. Jones, who has two degrees in psychology, knew to tread lightly. "Sometimes men do leave their wives," he told her. But did she realise how many other hurdles she'd face down the road by being with a powerful man 30 years her senior? And if he cheated on his wife…

Over those last months in the spring, as her romance seemed to be reaching a crescendo, Levy "vacillated between being angry with him and feeling placated by him", says Jones. Her Man knew how to talk her off the ledge, at least temporarily. Then the drama would repeat itself. "It was cyclical and predictable," says Jones. Compounding the emotional drama was the sex. Levy was not a kiss-and-tell woman, but she made it clear that "when they were together it was pretty intense", Jones says. [2]

Sven asked her about the wife, and Chandra replied "it was not really a major issue". [3] But there was some problem. In early April she mentioned she had a problem, and when Sven asked her about it she said it was a "female problem", something she "needed to take care of" but "could handle". [4] She wasn't very comfortable talking about it, so Sven didn't pursue it. He got the impression she was going to go to a doctor about it.

DePaulo and Sven later discussed what the female problem could be. Lisa told Roger Cossack on Larry King Live:

Well, you know, women don't usually refer to pregnancy as a female problem. Especially women who want to be pregnant, which she did. She would have been very happy if she was pregnant with Gary Condit's child. So I don't think it was pregnancy. That doesn't mean that she—I've discounted totally the possibility that she could have been. But I think it was something else.

I think it might have been some kind of sexually transmitted thing which, by the way, would have been extremely upsetting to this woman if it were true, because she really believed he wasn't having sex with anyone else. And if it weren't for Anne Marie Smith being brave enough to come forward, we might not know that. But she believed that she was the only sexual partner Gary Condit had. [5]

Chandra's father, Dr. Robert Levy, usually handled any medical needs she had. He prescribed her birth control pills. No appointments for a doctor in the Washington area were ever found to be made by Chandra for her problem. What was the female problem that she needed to take care of, and how was she going to handle it?

Her parents would be arrivng in a few days for a visit at her aunt's over the Passover weekend and then staying a week for her birthday. She did not discuss a female or medical problem with them during the visit, or with her aunt, whom she had been confiding her secrets. Her father is a doctor, and she didn't discuss a medical problem with him.

The Levys didn't think she was pregnant, in fact, are certain that she wasn't from their visit. It is believed based on their statement that Chandra may have mentioned she was having her period to one of her relatives. A cynical view of that is that she may have deliberately misled her family about a pregnancy by mentioning she was having her period. That implies she would be getting an abortion she didn't want her family to know about. But DePaulo points out above that Chandra would have been happy to be pregnant with Condit's child, and her parents told Larry King that they didn't think Chandra would even consider an abortion:

Larry King: Did you ever think she was pregnant?

Bob Levy: Oh…

Larry King: It has been reported she's got some great news to tell her aunt.

Bob Levy: No. I didn't really think so but, you know…

Susan Levy: Who knows?

Bob Levy: We don't know. You know, we don't know what's—you know, she—I guess she could have been, but we just don't know. She's not a—you know, she wasn't favorable of abortion at all. So, you know, she wouldn't do that.

Susan Levy: And if she was pregnant, we would love her and her grandchild just—our grandchild just the same no matter who…[6]

Chandra went through the whole visit, with her parents and everybody else, dreamy eyed in love and making phone calls to her secret boyfriend. She hardly acted as if she had a medical problem or a problem pregnancy, especially a problem caused by Condit. The fact that she didn't want to talk about it is strange in that she brought it up to start with. "I have a problem." "what kind of problem?" "a female problem, but I can handle it".

Sven may take that as a medical problem, and with two degrees in psychology and being her best friend he's a better judge of that than anyone, but it is strange she brought it up but didn't want to talk about it, strange that one would refer going to a doctor as something she "could handle", and strange that if she had a medical problem she neither talked to her doctor father nor made an appointment with a doctor.

One other possibilty of a female problem is another woman. She had told Sven that her boyfriend's wife was "not a major issue", but she had just received the call from her mother and OC about OC's story of a past affair between Condit and OC's teenaged daughter. Her mother and her had argued about her secret boyfriend, whom Susan was beginning to suspect might be Condit, and Chandra had told her mother she was a grown woman and to mind her own business. It is possible the female problem was her mother, or Condit's wife, but it remains a mystery as to how she was going to handle it.

Chandra was calling Condit every day in early April, but Condit says they "never had a cross word". [7] According to Condit, Chandra was prone to call him to discuss politics; such things as to tell him she saw a new federal prison was going to be built back home or "What's going on with that crazy mayor in Modesto? He sounds nuts. Let's talk about it". [8] She wanted to talk about federal prisons topics like the upcoming executions of Tim McVeigh, the Oklahoma City bomber, and drug trafficer Juan Raul Garza, a lot more than he wanted to talk about them, he says. [9]

He also says he had family in town in early April, who that might be and whether they were staying with him he doesn't say. Congress adjourned for Easter-Passover recess on April 7 and Condit says he returned home to California. [10] Yet Chandra was still making dreamy eyed calls to her boyfriend while visiting with her parents the next week, "a lot of phone calls", according to her parents. [11]

Linda was trying to arrange when to pick up Chandra at the train station, but they played phone tag for a few days because Linda wasn't able to find Chandra home. Linda continues with Chandra's visit to her home for Passover:

> So I picked her up...she called, I called, we played phone tag for a couple of days prior to Passover, because she wasn't in her apartment. I called her a couple of evenings, she wasn't there. And finally she called me from work one day and we made arrangements to pick her up the Friday before Passover, which was April 5th, I believe it was. And I picked her in Perryville at the train station, and we went and her grandmother was with us...And her parents weren't arriving till Saturday morning, on a red-eye, and then they were going to, they were staying at a hotel, and they were going to sleep and then they'd come out to the house Saturday, early evening. So Chandra and I had all Friday night to talk, and part of Saturday to talk before the parents got in.

> And we were at the...pizzeria for dinner, we had pizza, we chitchatted. It was idle chitchat, nothing, we weren't discussing the boyfriend then because the grandmother was there, and she kind of she didn't care if she spoke in front of the grandmother, she just preferred not to. She did mention her boyfriend, you know, that she had a nice Valentine's Day and that was it, like in front of her, because the grandmother would ask hey, what was going on, you know, 'Are you still seeing him, I don't think you should be seeing a married man, you better be care'—you know, grandmother wisdom words.

> And then we spoke, I don't know if it was Friday night or Saturday morning, but we started to talk about...just went blank.

> She showed me the bracelet. We were in my living room. And this was Saturday morning. Grandma was still sleeping, the husband was still sleeping. And she showed me the bracelet on her right wrist, a gold bracelet. A chain bracelet, a very nice piece of jewelry, double clasp, and she said that he bought her this. [12]

When they went out for pizza and ice cream, she told the Washington Post:

We bought Ben & Jerry's chocolate chip cookie dough. We didn't buy the low fat. She said that's what they eat. She didn't use his name. She said her 'boyfriend, my guy.' Most of the time she referred to him as 'my guy.' [13]

Chandra's parents, worried about her secrecy and OC's warning, not knowing if her boyfriend was Condit, tried to coax it out of her when they arrived. Chandra's 19 year old brother Adam recalls to the LA Times: "At one point, my sister said she had a 'friend in government.' I joked with her and asked it he was a 'boyfriend,' but she said, 'No, just a friend.'" Her dad is heard asking her about her friend while shooting a home video, and she brushes him off with "Dad, it's none of your business". [14] She can be seen wearing the gold bracelet in the video. [15]

After Passover, the Levys moved on to visit their good friends, Fran and Charles Iseman, Chandra's godparents, who also lived in the Washington, D.C. area. Chandra was with them to celebrate her 24th birthday that weekend and called her boyfriend on Friday. Her mother describes her calls to Stone Phillips of NBC News:

Mrs. Levy: "She was in love. Happy."

Stone Phillips: "Dreamy eyed?"

Mrs. Levy: "Dreamy eyed, definitely. Calling. A lot of phone calls back there."

Stone Phillips: "You were aware that she was using your cell phone to make calls back to Washington to a boyfriend."

Dr. Levy: "That's right."

Stone Phillips: "When you later looked at the phone bill, after Chandra disappeared, did you recognize the number she called?"

Dr. Levy: "No. We didn't know what number it was. We just saw it on the phone bill several times." [16]

According to Jeff Jardine of the Modesto Bee, Chandra's mother says that during the visit Chandra told her she had talked to Condit about the affair Susan and OC Thomas had called her about, and told her mother he had "explained it all" to her. Her uncle, Paul Katz, told Larry King that Chandra had told her mother "don't worry, mom, I talked to him about it and there's nothing to worry about".

Chandra made a call to Condit on Friday, April 13th, the day before her birthday. After that, they "tail off", according to Michael Isikoff of Newsweek. What would cause a cessation of dreamy eyed phone calls to her boyfriend the day before her birthday?

She celebrated her birthday with her family and, as Donna St. George, Allan Lengel and Petula Dvorak of the Washington Post report:

> ...she celebrated at the home of her godparents, surrounded by her family and presiding over a chocolate cake with flowers that read, "Happy Birthday, Chandra. We love you."
>
> Her godparents gave her a silver ankle bracelet and a check for $54—"triple chai," her godmother called it, referring to the Hebrew letters that represent 18 and translate to "life."
>
> The birthday honoree mentioned the congressman that day—happily—but discreetly avoided using his name. "She was very much in love and had stars in her eyes," said the godmother...[17]

Susan and Chandra celebrated by sharing a visit to the Hershey, Pa. spa. As Frank Murray of the Washington Times reports:

> ...The family drove to Hershey, Pa., to celebrate her 24th birthday—Saturday, April 14—at the end of Passover week. "Chandra and I did the Hershey spa treatment for her birthday," Mrs. Levy said. Other such mother-daughter outings included world travels, concerts by Paul Simon and Bob Dylan and a trip by train and car to Canyonlands National Park. "We travel together. We laugh together. We argue together. We share opinions, not always agreeing. Mother and daughter," Mrs. Levy said, never losing her composure as she reviewed memories. "We try to be always nice to each other," she added...[18]

It would be the last time the Levys saw Chandra.

They flew back to California on Sunday. Chandra returned to focusing on her career, according to Sven Jones, submitting multiple federal government applications for a permanent job, although she could see potential in returning to California. [19] She was hoping her internship would lead to a permanent job at the Bureau of Prisons.

For that or some other reason, Chandra made a last visit to the Congressional office of Condit, her friend, her mentor, her secret lover, and someone she sought help and advice for her career. The last visit, Condit aide Michael Dayton told Fox News, occurred five weeks before the May 18, 2001 article. This would seem to be during the Easter recess with Condit reportedly back home in California. Was Condit actually in California the previous week with Chandra talking to him every day? Was he there when Chandra made her last visit to his office? What was Chandra checking on?

More importantly, just what had he explained?

BOP

It was Friday, just a few days after Chandra's parents had spent a week with Chandra, celebrated her birthday with her, shared a spa visit to Hershey, Pa. with her, and been reassured that Condit had explained it all, not knowing what it was and suspecting but not knowing that he was Chandra's secret boyfriend in Congress. Chandra shared her thoughts and career plans with her family that week as she looked forward to transitioning to a full time job in law enforcement with the federal government. She had told her BOP supervisors she wanted that, maybe with the FBI. She had recently applied to the FBI for an analyst position and didn't expect it to be acted upon for awhile. She also told family and friends that she liked her internship so much she hoped to be hired full-time by the BOP when it ended.

But on Friday, April 20, she was to be in for a shock. Here are two accounts of it, first from Donna St. George, Allan Lengel and Petula Dvorak of the Washington Post:

> Barely a week later, Levy found herself out of a job.
>
> Government regulations that covered her position require that internships end within 120 days of graduation. Levy had told the agency that she was graduating in May. She apparently had not thought to point out that because she had attended summer school, her official graduation date had been the previous December.
>
> Talking to a personnel officer April 20, she mentioned the official date.
>
> The personnel officer balked.
>
> Levy's last day, she was told, would be Monday, April 23—several months sooner than she expected. A month earlier, Levy had applied for an analyst job at the FBI, but she knew it would take weeks or months to hear back. [1]

and another similar account from Mark Hosenball and Michael Isikoff of Newsweek:

Chandra Levy didn't realize it, but she'd just talked herself out of a job. Last spring the Washington intern was so happy with her temporary post at the Federal Bureau of Prisons that she'd told friends and family she hoped to be hired on full time after getting her master's degree in public administration from USC. Then one day she offhandedly mentioned to a personnel officer that, officially, she'd graduated last December. She just needed to pick up her diploma at the May graduation ceremony back home in California. The officer was taken aback. Levy's internship was supposed to expire four months after graduation. Now she would have to leave. Her friends and family told police that she was upset at her sudden dismissal, NEWSWEEK has learned, and hastily prepared to return to California. [2]

Also, Fox News' recounting of Newsweek's report:

Levy had told friends and family that she hoped to be hired full-time with the Bureau when her internship ended, but a casual remark to a co-worker ended her aspirations. Although she was planning to attend commencement ceremonies at the University of Southern California in mid-May, Levy mentioned to a personnel officer at the Bureau that she had technically completed her master's degree in public administration in December 2000.

This new information, Levy was told, meant that her internship was invalid. She was asked to leave. [3]

Both the Washington Post and Newsweek report that Chandra's internship had a limit of four months after meeting graduation requirements and that a BOP personnel manager just happened to be conversing with her, four months after she took her finals. The supposed offhand remark from Chandra to an HR manager that she had met her graduation requirements in December and was attending the upcoming commencement ceremony in three weeks resulted in the HR manager telling her on the spot that her internship was over. Isn't that rather odd?

Helen Kennedy of the New York Daily News obtained an e-mail Chandra sent to her landlord from which she describes the sudden loss of her internship:

This was not the way the program I was in was supposed to work, someone in the human resources office of the agency I worked for didn't do their job very well. [4]

Sven Jones recalls that she was surprised by the news that she could no longer be considered a student intern and began considering other agencies where she could apply. [5] CBS News obtained an e-mail that Chandra sent to a friend describing her disappointment:

> I haven't had too much luck lately. I'll probably eventually move back to DC, if I can get another federal job that's worth it, or I may work in Sacramento for the state again. I'll let you know more later on. [6]

Chandra expressed her surprise and disappointment to her friends and landlord but also started planning her next options. She described in detail to her family what she thought was a chance encounter with someone in human resources, someone who was prepared to end her termination on the spot when Chandra said she met her graduation requirements in December but was not getting her diploma till May. DePaulo even reports that Chandra was informed she had been violating bureau policy by remaining an intern after finishing classes.

This is in stark contrast to what the Bureau of Prisons had to say. Her manager at the BOP, Traci Billingsley, says "It was a 180-day internship, and it ended on schedule. Believe me, we would have loved to keep her on. She was a very good worker. [7] An internship just can't be extended." [8]

Condit, through a spokesman, said that Chandra came to Washington to serve a six month internship with the Bureau of Prisons. The USC Trojan school paper also reported she was completing a six month internship.

It had been six months after she started her internship in October. Her exact starting date had never been given by the BOP but based on their statement that it was a 180 day internship that ended April 23, an October 23 starting date has been used in a Washington Post timeline.

It was also four months after Chandra finished her last semester in December. She flew back to Sacramento with Condit's frequent flier miles and took her finals December 13. She returned to Washington on December 14 expensed on Condit's House office account as Gary Condit.

So it was a six month internship that ended on schedule when a supervisor heard that Chandra was graduating?

It doesn't seem possible that it was a six month internship that was part of her graduation requirements. She had supposedly completed her graduation requirements in December after only two months of the internship.

Was it a two month internship with a four month post-graduate extension? How is that described as a six month internship completed on schedule, as the BOP described it? Wouldn't Chandra know if she applied for a four month post-graduate extension?

The change from being an intern while a student to being an intern after completing classes is a major change that would have affected Chandra, the Bureau of Prisons, and the University of Southern California. Her schedule changed drastically after December. For two months during the fall semester she attended classes ten hours a day on Thursday, Friday, and Saturday at the USC center.

How could the BOP not be aware that she was now working all week from January on and that her classes had ended? How could the supervisor not know she was no longer signing off on USC intern hours for Chandra? How could USC not know she was no longer in a graduate program internship?

The odds of a random conversation with someone from human resources on the six month anniversary, or four month extension date, take your pick, are too high. There is something very strange about why the BOP told the public she was wonderful and they would have loved for her to stay on, but told her to clean out her desk and leave.

It is strange that the Washington Times reports that Chandra's internship ended abruptly over a technicality, that she never applied for a permanent job at the BOP even though she expected to be kept as a full-time employee when her internship ended. What is even stranger is that Time reports that the FBI could not find the electronic record of her application for an FBI analyst job, although they did find the paperwork. The missing FBI record of her application would certainly delay her application, possibly keep it from being processed altogether. Was Chandra being run out of town?

The Modesto Bee reports that Condit helped Chandra get the internship. For some reason, the BOP never acknowledged this in their statements from former

Chandra supervisors Dunne and Billingsley, and insisted it was a normal six month internship. However, it is completely abnormal in all respects.

The USC intern syllabus for the related subject of Political Science spells out some of how an internship works:

> ...
>
> Course grades will be based on your satisfactory completion of the required number of hours at the internship, your supervisor's evaluation of your performance, and your completion of the above requirements. Your final grade for the course will be based approximately 50% on your supervisor's evaluation and 50% on your final policy paper.
>
> ...
>
> **Student Intern Agreement Contract**
>
> This form reflects the understanding between you and the supervisor at your internship office of your start date, ending date, and your weekly work schedule. Please note that your supervisor must clearly state exactly which hours you are expected to work each day at the bottom of the contract. Simply checking the boxes is not sufficient.
>
> ...
>
> You are responsible for working out a schedule with your supervisor that permits you to work the number of hours per week required for the units for which you have enrolled. (See the chart at the end of the syllabus.) It is especially important that the beginning and ending dates of your internship be clearly understood and agreed to by you and your supervisor. You are expected to start your internship by the add/drop deadline and to work through the last day of classes.
>
> **The Internship**
>
> The primary requirement of the internship course is to work in the office of your choice for the required number of hours per week. It is vitally important that you act in a professional manner at all times. Please remember that you are a representative of USC. You must be punctual and notify your office supervisor if you are unable to work because of serious illness or emergency. If, after consultation with your supervisor, you make any changes in your work schedule, you need to inform the [USC] Unruh Institute in writing. If your supervisor changes, or is not the person listed on your job agreement, inform the internship coordinator. We will contact your supervisor midway through the semester to check on how your internship is going and again at the end of the semester to ask him or her to fill out an evaluation of your performance. You should feel free to contact the [USC] Unruh Institute at any time if you

have any concerns or questions about your internship.

…

Internship Hours Per Units of Credit

Units
2 3 4 5 6 7 8

Hours per week at internship
8 12 16 20 24 28 32
…[9]

Chandra's supervisor changed from Dan Dunne to Traci Billingsley. When did that change take place? USC was to be notified of any change in supervisors if it was during the internship, which the BOP insists was a six month internship that ended on schedule.

Who was the personnel officer that terminated her the same day she casually talked to her about her graduation requirements? What kind of termination takes place in a government bureaucracy within hours on the same day a personnel officer finds out that Chandra technically met her graduation requirements in December but was getting her diploma in May?

An internet poster, H.F., puzzled at the reported abruptness of Chandra's internship, had this to say:

> …I heard that Chandra had been abruptly terminated from her job at the Federal Bureau of Prisons and that she was soon to return home to receive a Master of Public Administration degree from USC. The report about the abruptness of the termination bothered me.
>
> While most federal agencies have one sort of intern program or another, very few of those programs are so open-ended that an intern would be abruptly terminated in the manner in which the news stories would have us believe. The standard story says that her internship allowed her to work 4 months after she completed her degree requirements. We are supposed to believe that she completed her degree requirements last December but her supervisor in the Bureau of Prisons only realized in late April that she had done so and the 120 day grace period was about to expire so the supervisor ran a Standard Form 50 (Request for and Record of Personnel Action) through the system to terminate her employment. But that story is not plausible.
>
> Only an extremely poorly run internship program would not have clear dates for specific personnel actions to be accomplished. Since it usually takes two to

four weeks for an SF50 to make it through the personnel mill, the termination would have been abrupt only if Chandra had been dishonest with her supervisor and/or her supervisor was an incompetent dolt. (Okay, so we can rule neither possibility out!)

But we also know that Chandra was an intern during the fall semester of 2000 and we have been led to believe that she did not finish her degree requirements until December 2000. What's the logical conclusion we deduce from that information? That Chandra's internship was part of her degree requirements. If so, her supervisor should have been providing some sort of written evaluations to USC probably on a monthly basis. If the internship was part of her degree program. The USC website shows that an internship can be 12 credit hours or one full semester of work toward the degree requirements. While it is possible that the internship was completed in one semester, it is also possible that Chandra signed up for 6 credits each of two semesters and that her termination from her internship at the Bureau of Prisons would have been tantamount to her not receiving her degree on May 11, 2001. If that's the case, she could well have decided simply to disappear rather than show up at graduation with her parents and be humiliated by not receiving a degree.

Someone needs to know what the SF50 that terminated Chandra's employment said and what courses she took during the Fall and Spring semesters at USC. [10]

Good questions then, still good questions now that need to be answered. Chandra knew she could convert to a permanent employee, and they said she was a great employee and they wished they could keep her, so what was the problem? The studentjobs government site states:

As a Student Career Experience appointee, you may be eligible to convert your position into a permanent job. [11]

Another related government web site states:

U.S. Marshall Service (USMS) Student Career Experience Program, a cooperative education program, targets college students pursuing criminal justice or political science degrees. It is used as a recruitment tool, targeting schools with significant minority populations and women to increase diversity in the [BOP] workforce....

This is a student employment program whereby, when all of the program requirements are met, students may be non-competitively converted to career-conditional appointments in the competitive service within 120 days. [12]

Here the 120 days, or four months, is mentioned. This is a time period during which the federal government has an aggressive program for non-competitively converting women and minority student interns to full-time positions.

A different type of internship is described on another BOP site:

> Another option is to serve as a student volunteer. As a student volunteer, your service is performed without compensation and an agreement is established with your educational institution. You can perform the service for a period not to exceed six months on a full-time or substantially full-time basis. Extensions may be authorized. [13]

Here the six months internship is mentioned, but it is volunteer, Chandra's was paid, and an extension can be requested. The internship program seems more proactive in converting to full-time employment and much more flexible than the BOP would have the public believe.

Did the BOP get a leak that Chandra was technically not in compliance with internship regulations by listing a May graduation date? The behavior Chandra described indicates that. An HR person would do what they did, raise the issue casually and gather from her what the situation was. When she told them, she thought let it slip, because she was nudged toward divulging it and didn't know she was being questioned, the BOP manager responded right there on the spot, "wait a minute, then it's been past 120 days, we'll have to end it".

If there was an anomynous call to the BOP that caused Chandra to lose her internship, it has important implications. It means that someone didn't want her around, and it means they were intimately familiar with the details of her BOP internship.

Lisa DePaulo writes in the Talk article that Chandra was understandably bitter and that her friends think her disappointment deepened when her boyfriend did nothing to help her find another position. She told friends "He promised". She saw him the next day, April 24, when she went to his apartment.

There are a lot of questions when a government intern doesn't show up for work, a nod of the head when said intern disappears after her internship ends because she was distraught over, among other things, someone she was said to be obsessed with who didn't arrange for a new job for her. The questions didn't come till later though, much later.

Big News

As Chandra talked to Sven in March and April about getting her guy to make a commitment to her, to keep his promise, she was spending more and more time at Condit's condo. One neighbor was quoted in the New York Daily News: "When they came to change the [air conditioning] filters, I asked if Chandra had moved out," said a woman who lives in an adjacent apartment. "I hadn't seen her for so long." However, another neighbor who hadn't seen Chandra for most of March and April noticed hearing her inside her apartment the last week of April, the week after losing her internship. Was she just more noticeable around the Newport now that she was not at work all day, or was there another change, something even more substantial than losing her internship at work here?

Anne Marie had also noticed a change earlier, at the end of March, signs of another female in Condit's condo apartment. She found long brown hairs on the floors of both of Condit's bathrooms. She told Rita Cosby of Fox News:

> I found some hairs in his bathrooms. And you know how girls are; I was very suspicious and I asked him, like, "Whose hairs are these?" And he said, "Well, they're yours." And I said, "No, they're not. They're way too long for me." They're not my hairs and they were like long brown hairs. And I think that was, kind of, the end of the discussion. He kind of just brushed it off, like, "Oh, they're yours." [1]

She saw some female toiletries that Susan Levy later identified as the kind of toiletries that Chandra used. And strangely, Condit forbid Anne Marie to use the bedroom closet. She was told to use the hall closet. Her lawyer Jim Robinson related to Paula Zahn for The Edge what she said:

> Well, I usually hung up my coat in his closet in the bedroom. And the last time I was there, he didn't want me going near that closet. I had to hang up all my clothes in the hall closet by the front door. [2]

She was too jet lagged to question why, but questions started forming in her mind the next morning when she noticed a newly opened bottle of massage oil and "neckties tied together that were tied to the feet of the bed and shoved underneath the bed. They looked like they'd "been there awhile" and used as restraints during sex. [3] She told Hannity & Colmes of Fox News:

> I confronted him. And he was very frantic and pulled them out and started untying them and putting them away in his closet and asked me why I was snooping, and I said, "I wasn't snooping. I just saw them sticking out from under the bed". [4]

Condit made a joke of it, "Oh, oh, honey, I was just thinking about doing that with you", but she didn't believe him. [5] She got nervous and thought, "This is not the guy I know". [6] She was tying together what she had seen with a sexual fantasy that Condit often mentioned to her but she had passed off as a joke.

Condit had been urging her in one-way phone sex talk throughout their relationship to participate in sex with him and other guys, Robinson told Paul Sperry of WorldNetDaily.com. "I have a fantasy about a bunch of guys and one woman, you," Condit told her. He said it would probably make her cry. She was now convinced he was serious about his sexual fantasy and worried, "oh, my God, I could have been hurt". [7] That didn't stop them from continuing to talk daily and her suggesting they get together, but whether inadvertent or not, they were to never get together again after she confronted him about what she had seen.

Robinson goes on to suggest to Paul Sperry that Anne Marie was told not to use the bedroom closet because bondage and discipline apparatus that Condit would not want her to see might have been kept there, but it is more likely given the hair on the bathroom floors, female toiletries in the bathroom, and neighbors of Chandra who never saw her that Chandra had clothes in the bedroom closet that Condit didn't want Anne Marie to see.

How moved in was she? She had asked her landlord a couple of months earlier about breaking her lease to move in with her boyfriend, but her aunt Linda thought it might have been wishful thinking on her part since Condit was married. She later told her landlord it didn't work out. And in April, Congress was in Easter-Passover recess from April 7 to April 22, with Condit saying he had family in town the first week of April and was home for Easter recess the next two weeks, so he hadn't seen Chandra for much of April. [8] Yet her neighbors thought she had moved out and didn't see her again until the last week of April, the same time as Chandra lost her internship and Condit returned from Easter recess. If she wasn't at Condit's, where was she?

Along the same lines, how was Chandra having dreamy eyed phone calls with her secret boyfriend in Congress after he went home to Ceres for Easter recess? Was he checking his messages from California and calling her back? And why did the calls stop midway through the Easter recess, the same time as Chandra told her mother that he had explained it all? For that matter, the calls from her cell phone to his message line never did resume, even after Condit returned to Washington, according to Michael Isikoff of Newsweek. Chandra was still calling her answering machine on the phone line in her apartment to check for messages as if she were expecting them. Did she start calling him from a local untracked line, and, if so, why?

She was apparently not concerned about OC Thomas' story. As Susan Levy told Newsweek, Chandra told her, "Everything's OK. He knows everything". But from that point on everything in Chandra's life changed, and not for the better.

Her last day at the Bureau of Prisons was Monday, April 23. She had believed herself to have been abruptly dismissed the previous Friday due to a technicality concerning her graduation date. Congress was also returning from Easter recess at that time. According to Condit, the next morning after cleaning out her desk she showed up at his condo to ask for assistance in getting another job, annoyed but not distraught. [9]

Condit says he remembers offering to help her get another job but Chandra indicated to friends that he apparently did nothing to help. Friends were told, "He promised". Instead, a neighbor started hearing Chandra in her apartment again.

Condit recalls with his lawyer Abbe Lowell to Newsweek's Michael Isikoff:

> NEWSWEEK: You mentioned I think the last time you saw her was [April] 24 or 25.

CONDIT: Actually, I don't know if it was the 24th. That's my understanding.

NEWSWEEK: But she came to your apartment that morning.

CONDIT: Right.

NEWSWEEK: How did she come to come to your apartment? How was that meeting set up?

CONDIT: Well, she knew I was there because we were working late. I went in late that day and that's why I think it might have been the 24th.

NEWSWEEK: Had there been a prior-

CONDIT: I can't recall. Maybe we talked earlier. I would have thought she would have been at work. I may have said I was going in late. She buzzes the door. She comes in and then we start to talk. So that's basically-

NEWSWEEK: But you were expecting her?

CONDIT: No, I was surprised to see her because I figured she'd be at work. This was the time she told me that she had lost her prospects on the job with the Bureau of Prisons.

NEWSWEEK: So it was a surprise visit?

CONDIT: Yes.

NEWSWEEK: Prior to that, when was the previous visit?

CONDIT: I can't recall. I mean, a couple of days before that maybe.

NEWSWEEK: At your apartment?

CONDIT: Well, no, it wouldn't have been-because I was gone.

ABBE LOWELL: Actually, that would have been two or three weeks before.

CONDIT: Yeah, that's right because I was gone most of April and the first of April I had family in town and so we didn't-I did not see her. It was the first time I'd seen her in probably three weeks. [10]

When did Condit return from Easter-Passover recess? He likely would have returned from California on Monday, perhaps late. He initially answered that he had probably seen Chandra a couple of days before, but his lawyer reminded him he had been in California most of April for the recess from April 7 to April 22 that year.

If he hadn't seen Chandra for weeks as he claims, when did he tell her he was working late, that is, going into the office late and being home Tuesday morning the 23rd? And are we to really believe that she didn't call him Friday or Saturday or Sunday or Monday to tell him her internship had been ended?

Perhaps he wasn't checking his messages? Anne Marie claims they talked every day and that she left him messages. How could he have told Chandra he was working late and not at the same time have found out she wanted his help concerning her abruptly ended internship?

It is possible that Chandra knew he would be coming back to Washington, guessed he wouldn't be going into the office until afternoon, and just dropped by to see if he was home, and Condit was just being helpful to Newsweek in his recollections by wrongly offering that he saw her earlier or told her he would be home, but there is something artificial with this scenario, something that makes her a constituent, a mentored friend, surprising him with a visit to tell him about a lost internship, a job that didn't work out, gratefully accepting his offer of help, and going on with her life back to Modesto.

Instead, this is when a neighbor says she started hearing Chandra in her apartment again. Instead, Chandra e-mails friends that he didn't help her, that he had "promised". There is no way she didn't call him and leave messages when she lost her internship, but he would have investigators believe that he didn't know she lost it. In the zeal to not know what he must not know, he forgot that he should have known.

On Wednesday her co-workers at the BOP had a going away luncheon for her. This would be the last time Sven or anyone else from work were to speak to her. He was on his way off on a long trip, not to return till the next Tuesday, May 1.

Chandra considered her options, e-mailing friends with talk of future plans. Her mother told the Modesto Bee:

She was surprised by the job (ending), but not devastated. She went to see the Holocaust Museum and did some other things. She wasn't down at all. [11]

She was also surprised by something her mother said to her. Susan had learned more details about Chandra's boyfriend from Linda Zamsky; that he "sort of looked like Harrison Ford" and didn't drink alcohol. [12] Susan remembered reading in an article about their local Congressman, Gary Condit, that he didn't drink alcohol either. As the Washington Post reports:

> In late April…her mother called her and asked if the congressman she was dating was Gary Condit.
>
> "How did you know?" Chandra replied, according to Sue.
>
> Mother's intuition, she said.
>
> "She told me that she couldn't say his name," Sue says, "that I would eventually understand." [13]

Susan Levy was able to elicit a surprised "how did you know" from Chandra, but even then Chandra would not confirm that Condit was her boyfriend. Her vow to keep his secret superceded her parents concern and worry about her. Her loyalty to her man remained steadfast to the end.

There was another reason Chandra would need to return to her apartment. Carolyn Condit, the Congressman's wife, was making a rare visit. She was coming to Washington to attend the annual First Lady's Luncheon on May 2, with an invitation to serve on the luncheon's organizing committee.

Anne Marie called Condit and told him she had a few days off and could see him, but Condit told her it was not a good time, his wife was coming to town to see a doctor. In the Larry King Live interview with Anne Marie Smith, Roger Cossack indicates that Anne Marie arrived in Washington April 25 but Carolyn didn't arrive until April 28. Anne Marie tells Cossack:

> Actually he called me when his wife was in town that weekend. He called me, I believe it was Friday night, he called me Saturday, he called me Sunday morning, and then he called me the following week. [14]

It appears that Anne Marie was in town Wednesday and Thursday, offering to see him, but Condit didn't call her until Friday for some reason. During these same days an interesting call was made, according to a D.C. police leak reported by Niles Lathem of the New York Post. A five minute call was made from the Condit's Ceres home to Condit's Adams Morgan condo at a time when Condit said he wasn't home. Who answered it, and what was said? Carolyn arrived in Washington just a couple of days after the call. Had her flight ticket been purchased before the call?

It is odd that Condit didn't pay for Carolyn's luncheon ticket until the following year, when they also payed for the next year's luncheon ticket. [15] Why would they pay for the 2001 luncheon a year later but pay for the 2002 luncheon in advance?

One reasonable explanation is that Carolyn Condit never planned on attending the First Lady's Luncheon, a luncheon held a few days after that phone call, a luncheon held the day after Chandra disappeared. But perhaps not paying was an oversight, an administrative error made by Condit's otherwise able staff. Surely an RSVP wasn't overlooked as well. When did Condit's wife RSVP the Congressional wives that she would be coming to Washington to attend?

The police denied published reports that Chandra confronted Carolyn in the call. Tabloid reports that speculate on who was involved, much less the contents of the call, would seem to be pure fabrication without being able to talk to one of the people in the conversation. Indeed, a conversation is only implied by the length of the call, at five to ten minutes longer than a voice mail would normally be. American Media, publisher of National Enquirer, Star, and Globe, settled a lawsuit with Carolyn Condit over this issue after initiating discovery action on the Condit's phone records. [16]

Chandra called home for the last time on Friday, April 27. "She was looking forward to coming home," her mother said. [17] "She missed being in California," she told People magazine. "She missed the weather, her friends, her car. She was looking forward to coming home and maybe staying home for a while." [18] Her parents sensed no change in her usually upbeat mood when they last spoke. "I'm not happy," she said, "but I guess that's the way it goes." [19]

But Chandra hadn't yet decided to take a train home or fly by that Friday evening for her upcoming USC graduation ceremony in two weeks. She had known about going back to California for her graduation commencement since

December. She had only found out she wouldn't need to come back to her job a week ago. Taking a train couldn't have been an option until she lost her internship. Why had she not already arranged a round trip plane ticket for the May 11 graduation in LA, or had she?

The last time she returned to California, in December for her finals, Condit had supplied her flight tickets. She was so excited about that she e-mailed a friend and told her. She was expecting Condit to marry her, wouldn't she be expecting him to provide another ticket home as he had before?

In the Baltimore Sun, the Levys say:

> Every day, Robert Levy, an oncologist, and his wife, Susan, look for clues by replaying in their minds their last conversation with her. Susan Levy wonders why her daughter had been so fuzzy about her travel plans home. "She wasn't giving us any details or times exactly when she was coming in," she recalls. "It was kind of unlike her."
>
> In another conversation with her mother, Levy had talked about taking Amtrak because, her mother recalls, she liked the idea of looking out the window as the country rolled by. [20]

There was precedent for taking an Amtrak train home. After she took the breakup with her Modesto policeman boyfriend Mark Steele so hard, her mother and her took an Amtrak train trip through the Rockies into New Mexico. The Modesto Bee quotes: "She was disappointed that the relationship didn't work out," Susan Levy said. "But we had a great time on the trip. We really bonded."

She was still undecided on Sunday when she mentioned to her landlord in San Francisco taking a train home from Washington and asked him if he had ever done it. He advised against it.

Her parents were asking her to confirm when she would be arriving as they would be picking up her grandmother as well. But Chandra may have been thinking of taking a train straight to LA to meet them there for the graduation. Checking on prices and schedule at the time, an Amtrak ticket cost $175 for a cross county trip, no matter how close to departure it was purchased.

A ticket for Los Angeles on Tuesday, May 8th, for example, would have had her in Chicago Wednesday morning, then in LA Thursday morning, May 10, the day before her graduation. The DC to LA via Chicago train left about 5pm on Tuesday evening and arrived in LA Thursday morning at 10 am. That is a day and a half. This would have been considerably cheaper and simpler for her to get to her graduation than flying to San Francisco and then later flying to LA with her family, and may have been an additional consideration in thinking about taking a train home.

As her mother sums it up for the LA Times:

> Was she planning to come home by plane or train? Was she coming home that day or another day? If she was planning to tell us when or where, she never got the chance. [21]

The next day, Saturday, April 28, Carolyn Condit arrived in D.C. from California at 7:30 Saturday evening, according to Condit's timeline provided to police. About the same time, Chandra was leaving a phone message for Sven, a phone message that sounded like she wanted to talk to someone. She was inviting him to meet her in Georgetown for lunch.

She had been consulting him about forcing a confrontation with Condit over their relationship. But was there still a relationship now? Sven told Lisa DePaulo of Talk that the message she left him was plaintive. "She sounded different," he said. "The cadence of her voice was different. She had sort of an odd tone."

She then called her landlord in San Francisco a few times and sent him an e-mail, a decidedly depressed e-mail telling him she has lost her job and any reason to stay in D.C. The Washington Post quotes from it:

> It looks like my plans have suddenly changed. I was just informed this week that my job appointment time is up, so I am out of work now.
>
> I am going back to California for my graduation during the week of May 8 and I [sic] moving back there for good. I haven't heard from the other jobs that I applied for yet and I have feeling that it will be at least a few weeks for me to hear back from any of them.
>
> I don't really think it would be worth it for me to stay in D.C. now since I have no job or school to keep me busy here. I would like to vacate the apartment on May 5 or 6 if possible.

> I really hate giving up the apartment but I think I need to be in California for a while to figure out what my next move is. [22]

Although she hadn't talked to Sven yet, she had already decided to move out the next weekend, May 5 or 6, and given that as a firm date to her landlord. Her graduation was May 11 and that would give her plenty of time to either fly or take a train home to figure out what her next move would be.

The landlord returned her calls the next morning but she was still sleeping or not in a mood to talk and he asked her to call him back. He hadn't heard from her by late afternoon so he called again. But something had happened that afternoon, something that changed Chandra's outlook. She now wouldn't know when she could tell her landlord she was leaving until Wednesday. Just the night before she had e-mailed him she was leaving the next weekend. Now she didn't know when she was leaving. What had changed?

Chandra's landlord thought it was odd that she would need three more days to come up with something more definite about a move out date. Her message had changed altogether. She was now not sure if she was moving back to California for good and wanted to stay in Washington. She was planning on returning after receiving her master's degree on May 11, she told her landlord. Was there now the possibility she wasn't moving out after all? What was she expecting to find out by Wednesday?

A message left for her aunt did little to answer the questions. As quoted by the Washington Post:

> Hi, Linda. This is Chandra. My internship is over. I'm planning on packing my bags in the next week or 10 days. Heading home for a while. Don't know what I'm going to do this summer. And I really have some big news or something important to tell. Call me...[23]

Linda told the Associated Press: "She was upbeat and full of life. There was absolutely no indication that she was upset." But she had no idea what Chandra meant by the message.

Big news? Where did she get something important to tell Linda Zamsky on Sunday afternoon? Her FBI application status didn't change on Sunday. A renewal of the relationship with Condit? She hadn't even told Linda the relationship had ended. Important events such as a marriage or a baby? The words she uses to describe not being sure what she's going to do for the summer is not one of a woman thinking of marriage or a baby or anything else that requires preparation.

It is significant that just as she had no firm details about coming home for her parents, she was still three days away from giving her landlord a firm moveout date. Something was still very much up in the air.

The Scream

Chandra had had no qualms about calling Condit's message line on her cellular. When her parents later looked at her phone bill they saw that she called his message line repeatedly. Newsweek's analysis of the calls, though, shows that while she made several calls to his message line they tapered off after April 13. Yet on Sunday and Monday, April 29 and April 30, Chandra was still calling her own answering machine repeatedly checking for messages, according to Fox News which also looked at the phone bill. The New York Post's analysis shows her calling eight or nine times on Monday alone.

Even after the call to her aunt Sunday evening saying she had big news she was still constantly checking for messages on Monday. But she had long stopped calling Condit on her cell phone. Who was she expecting a message from, and where did she get big news to share with her aunt?

One might suspect that she possibly didn't know Sven was out of town and that she was checking for a return call from her invitation on Saturday evening to talk with her over lunch, except for some interesting information from Condit. Frank Murray of the Washington Times reports that Condit told the police he broke off their close friendship on Saturday. This was the day that Carolyn was to arrive in town and Chandra left a plaintive message for Sven, asking to meet in Georgetown for lunch. Rita Cosby of Fox News disclosed it this way:

> When Condit delicately broke things off with Levy with the explanation that she was moving back to California, she was distraught, refusing to take no for an answer and even becoming obsessed with him, the sources said.
>
> Levy called Condit several times on a special line in the 24 hours before she vanished, but he never returned those calls, the sources said. [1]

The Washington Times quoted a Condit lawyer saying that she harassed Condit by phone, calling his pager twenty times Sunday and Monday, and portrayed her as "extremely disappointed and distraught, refusing to take no for an answer".

According to the Washington Post, his San Francisco lawyer, Joe Cotchett, said on the CBS Early Show that she called Condit four or five times as she was preparing to leave for California:

> Let's assume she was calling him to say goodbye, which we suspect was the case. You understand she was returning to California. Also…the congressman has come forward and said they were good friends, as he is with many interns. [2]

As Joshua Micah Marshall writes of these phone calls in Salon:

> The mystery surrounding what, if any, communication took place between Levy and Condit in the final days before her disappearance is riddled with confusion and contradiction…. A flurry of calls Chandra made to her own answering machine is certainly a far cry from calls to Condit's special line. But they do suggest, possibly, a more complicated chain of events…[3]

Amidst this portrayal by Condit to the police and public of Chandra as a distraught intern who was so obsessed with him he had to refuse to return her calls, her parents were somewhat distraught themselves. NBC News reports that Susan Levy tried to tell the police and public "As far as I know…her last phone calls seem to come from Condit". And indeed, after months of Chandra the obsessed, dangerously distraught young woman, Condit suddenly remembered it all differently. There was a phone call Sunday after all, certainly forgettable by the sound of it. Condit describes it to the Merced Sun-Star:

> Condit: I talked to her one time after that on the 29th of April for just approximately a minute on the phone. She called me and I called her back.
>
> Sun-Star: Was she in Washington at the time?
>
> Condit: Yes. She hadn't left yet. Actually I thought she was calling me to tell me her travel plans.
>
> Sun-Star: Then her call was to tell you…
>
> Condit: Well, it was, she was, really, it was pretty uneventful call. She called me and said call me back. I called her and I said are you ready, you got your train reservations? You got your, what are you doing. She said I haven't made any of those as soon as I find out I'll let you know. That was basically it. It was just pretty uneventful. [4]

Chandra had quit calling Condit on her cell phone, but he recalls returning her call on Sunday to ask her if she had bought her train ticket. Where did she call him from, and why after calling him from some other phone did she start checking for his message with her cell phone? Had she been instructed not to leave a trace of contact with him by calling him from an untraceable local line? More importantly, after four months of portraying Chandra in such a way that the police assumed she was a suicidal runaway, was she instead actually dear to Condit's heart? Condit rehabilitates her to Newsweek:

Newsweek: Did you have plans to see her again after that?

Condit: After what?

Newsweek: After that visit on the 24th?

Condit: Oh, you mean before she left?

Newsweek: Before she left or when she was out in California.

Condit: Oh, yeah, we never—there was never a thought that we weren't going to stay in contact or see each other. One way or another. That was a friendship. We were going to maintain the friendship no matter—it was a friendship. [5]

There had never been a basis for her being distraught on Sunday and Monday. She had sounded odd on Saturday in her message left for Sven. She sounded accepting and ready to move on in her message to her landlord that weekend. "There's no reason for me to hang around here any longer", she said. "Can I move out next weekend?

By later Sunday she was upbeat in a message for Linda. Her message Sunday evening was big news. "Call me", she said. What had changed? Whatever was up in the air was about to become derailed.

Even without a car, Chandra got around widely in the D.C. area by Metro to shop. Among receipts she had in her apartment were receipts from a Trader Joe's a half mile down Wisconsin Ave. from the Metro station in Bethesda, and one from a Pendleton clothing shop in Alexandria's Old Town. Whether she was shopping for going home or not is unclear, but she was starting to end her affairs in Washington by cancelling her health club membership Monday evening, the last day of the month. The manager of the Washington Sports Club gym on

Connecticut Avenue NW, Errol Thompson, said she came in about 7:30 p.m. to cancel her mambership.

Jackie Judd of ABC News obtained an interview with the gym manager who had this critical last encounter with Chandra. ABC reports:

> [He] says he even joked with Levy when she came in at about 7:30 p.m. ET on April 30—because she had almost canceled her membership in January.
>
> "I said, 'Are you sure this time?'" he told ABCNEWS. "And we joked. And she said, 'Yeah, I'm definitely going home.'"
>
> The source said Levy canceled her membership, then worked out and left the facility.
>
> The source said he told Levy that since she did not give 30 days' notice of her cancellation, she would have to pay for another month. He then helped her look for a Modesto gym with a reciprocal membership plan—so she could work out near her home during that period.
>
> "I said go to this club for the next 30 days," the source told ABCNEWS. "You've got a free membership there through us. And she Xeroxed it. She said, 'I'll go there.'"
>
> The source said he was confident Levy believed she was going home to California.
>
> "She was looking forward to going home. She was excited about it," the source said. "You could see it in her face, it was very clear."
>
> In fact, they spoke for 30 minutes about which gym she could use in Modesto, he said.
>
> "I know that she was going back home," he said, "Unless she was that well-rehearsed, that she had planned it, and I don't think so."
>
> He said Levys mood "without question" had not changed from the time he met her, in October, until her disappearance.
>
> "She was her normal, jubilant self," he said. "You know, 'healthy body, healthy mind,' is just what she was." [6]

The LA Times reports that the police say that she was there about an hour and left about 8:30 p.m.

The reason she had mentioned cancelling her membership in January was because she had asked her landlord about breaking her lease to move in with her boyfriend. There would be health clubs in the Adams Morgan area closer than this one on Dupont Circle if she had moved. She hadn't moved and hadn't cancelled her membership, so the manager jokingly asked if she was sure this time.

There was some controversy on the internet Chandra sites about whether there was a reciprocal health club facility in the Modesto area where she would have free membership as Errol Thompson told her, or even whether she was actually at the gym.

It's an unfortunate side effect of the confluence of the press and the internet that literally every person named in a high profile crime case is deemed a liar and worse by anomynous posters on the internet, some quite rabid, most just suspicious. This despite the named people pouring their heart out to the police and public for their friend or colleague to help and being asked to take a lie detector test for their trouble.

Then after they have answered every question one could reasonably or even unreasonably think of, they continue to be hounded by reporters or what passes as reporters for tabloids until they are chased into hiding. This only completes the vicious cycle where they are then accused of having something to hide because they tire of journalists and cameramen jumping out of bushes and scaring them half to death, even as they often receive real death threats from anomynous people who may or may not have already been involved in an actual murder.

They usually try to stay anomynous but the press flushes them out, then in the name of objective reporting sometimes inadvertantly manages to attempt to destroy them to boot. This does not lend itself to encouraging people to step forward, which is helpful to the public in understanding what has happened to an innocent person that the public wants to understand rather than wait years for a trial to see if the police found anything out about it.

The press is great about getting the story, but that competition to get something no one else knows drives it to ask the same questions over and over in the hope that someone who has already answered fully with reasonable information will somehow say something different that generates a headline. That drive should be limited to people who have not already answered the questions ad nauseum of legions of headline seeking journalists. At least it is hoped journalists are more discerning about what constitutes a truthful dialogue than anomynous internet posters.

As far as Chandra being there, there was membership cancellation paperwork done at the club, a presumed credit card transaction to pay for her thirty day notice, possibly the Xeroxed list of participating reciprocal clubs in California with the nearest one to her circled as described by the gym manager, and the cancellation receipt found in her apartment. Although no one else has been named by police as having seen her at the gym Monday night, the police interviewed many club members and it certainly would have been an issue worth commenting upon had no one but the manager seen her during the hour he said she was there Monday night.

It would have been ironic and the source of neverending conspiracy had Vince Flammini's gym in Modesto been on the list. The question of what club would have been circled by Errol Thompson for Chandra was answered by a phone call to the Washington Sports Club from www.justiceforchandra.com internet poster propria. She posts:

> i have just spoken with jeff at chandra's health club, and he tells me that members have reciprocity in the form of discounts that apply at midtown athletic club in sacramento, as well as at '24-hour fitness' clubs all over california…perhaps the xerox copy was a listing of those clubs, with the ones closest to her circled. [7]

The 24 Hour Fitness Center in Manteca 17 miles away would qualify as near Modesto, although she might not choose to continue making that trip to work out after her month notice ran out. It would be puzzling if the closest reciprocating gym was the Midtown Athletic Club in Sacramento, but with the 24 Hour Fitness Centers on the list, Manteca would be circled as the club near Modesto. There seems to have been only a reciprocating discount agreement between the chains which perhaps included a free thirty day trial membership as the gym manager told her, "a free membership there through us", or perhaps he overstated it or was mistaken. She had to pay anyway and this was at least a gesture from the Washington Sports Club.

It was 8:30 p.m. Monday evening, April 30. Did Chandra make it home from the gym that evening? Excepting a deception of professional caliber, the gym cancellation paperwork found in her apartment indicates she made it home. The Washington Sports Club on Connecticut Ave. NW was about five blocks from her apartment in the Newport on 21st St. NW. The area was hardly crime free, but Connecticut Ave. is a heavily populated pedestrian thoroughfare where many people do not have cars and walk about the neighborhood. Bill O'Reilly talking to the Levy's lawyer Billy Martin had this conversation on the O'Reilly Factor:

> O'REILLY: ...You know, I walk the neighborhood where Ms. Levy lived. I walked that neighborhood. I went through it. That's not a menacing neighborhood.
>
> MARTIN: It's not.
>
> O'REILLY: And that's a neighborhood if somebody grabbed you, you scream, 18 people would hear you.
>
> MARTIN: That's not a dangerous neighborhood. I used to have a law firm located right near Dupont Circle. I would walk out of my office at midnight to go get a snack or get coffee. There are people on the streets all the time. That's not an unsafe neighborhood, Bill. [8]

On the other hand, eight robberies, two at gunpoint, had taken place in the previous four months in the block of 21st where the Newport is located. A robbery every couple of weeks in the block outside your apartment building isn't exactly Better Homes and Gardens, but only one of the robberies, back in January, was cited by the police as an example of a violent crime in her block. A robber forced a woman to the ground and stole her purse before jumping in a getaway car with a driver. One other successful robbery of a purse at gunpoint was cited by the police as taking place the previous month a couple of blocks away.

Of more serious concern, a murder was to take place not far from where Chandra lived. Isikoff describes what one would hope is an isolated event in Newsweek:

> Just last month prosecutors tried four men for grabbing Vidalina Semino, a 54-year-old hotel waitress, off the street as she walked to her car not far from Chandra's neighborhood. According to police, the men forced Semino into the trunk of their car and then, after stealing her ATM card, shot her and dumped her body in the woods several miles away. [9]

This unfortunate kidnapping, robbery, and murder of Ms. Semino would take place in five days. The Department Of Justice press release of the conviction of the men describes the crime:

> The evidence at the trials indicated that, on May 5, 2000, Downing and his three co-defendants traveled by Metro from Southeast D.C. to the Woodley Park area for the purpose of breaking into a residence there and robbing them at gunpoint. Once in the area, however, they changed their plan and decided to rob someone on the street. Ms. Semino, a 54-year-old immigrant from Peru who worked as a waitress at the Omni-Shoreham Hotel, was walking to her car when she got off work near midnight. The four targeted her, eventually taking her car and putting her in the trunk. After driving throughout the metropolitan area for over ninety minutes, they drove the car to an isolated wooded area near 22nd and T Streets, S.E. They then marched Ms. Semino into the woods where a co-defendant, Robert Moody, shot her twice and killed her. The four fled the area on foot. Downing then used Ms. Semino's bank card twice within the next hour both in D.C. and Oxon Hill, Maryland where he lived. A third co-defendant's (Leon Butler) use of Ms. Semino's VISA credit card led the police to him in November, 2000 when all four were arrested. [10]

The Omni-Shoreham Hotel is at Calvert and Connecticut Ave., familiar territory to Chandra as it is only a couple of blocks from Condit's Adams Morgan condo and on the way to his apartment up Connecticut from the Newport. She would never know about this murder so close to home, though. She was not to see May 5, although her own murder days before would be in eerily similar circumstances. How eerie, and how similar, remain to be seen.

So Chandra brought her gym cancellation paperwork home Monday evening, but in the stillness of Tuesday morning, at 4:37 a.m., a scream for help was heard by a Newport resident and 911 called. A D.C. police officer was dispatched but nothing was found. Chief Ramsey of the D.C. police describes the 911 call to Bob Schieffer and Gloria Borger of CBS Face The Nation:

BORGER: You have her computer. You have her cell phone records.

We've all heard that there was a lot of activity on her computer that morning of her disappearance, sometime between 9:30 and 1:00, that she visited a lot of travel web sites. What can you tell us about that? Did she book a flight somewhere?

RAMSEY: No, we don't have anything that shows that she booked a flight. And we've checked flights, we've checked rail, we've checked all means of methods of transportation. And nothing that we've come up with yet.

But there was quite a bit of activity for about a three-hour period from 9:30 on, which is important for a couple of reasons: One, there was a call that came out early in the morning from an individual in the building of what she thought she heard some kind of scream. Now, we did dispatch someone to the scene, didn't find anything. But we do know that Ms. Levy was very active on her computer more than three hours after that particular call came in, so it doesn't really point to that being something that we need to be…

SCHIEFFER: Wait a minute, let me go back. You're saying that the police were called to her apartment on the day that she disappeared?

RAMSEY: Yes, there are some transcripts. And, of course, part of what we did was check all 911 tapes. And we did that early on in the investigation. And it is apparent that there was a call from a resident in the building about four hours prior to that activity that we talked about on the computer. So that's a vital piece of investigation.

SCHIEFFER: She heard a scream?

RAMSEY: Well, she heard what she thought was a scream. And we dispatched right away, and the officer didn't find anything. But now we know from computer records, and we've known for some time that from 9:30 to 1:00—and this was like 4:30 in the morning, if my memory serves me correct—there was a great deal of activity on her computer.

So, again, something that we're looking at. We're looking at all aspects of this thing. But that computer activity, a significant amount happened afterwards.

BORGER: So you're saying Chandra was in her apartment at the time somebody called 911 reporting to have heard a scream. Does that lead you to believe that that was completely unrelated to Chandra?

RAMSEY: Well, we're certainly looking for every link we can and anything, whether she was in her apartment at that time or wasn't in her apartment or whatever. But from the e-mail message she sent her mother, from the surfing of the web, for lack of a better word to describe the other activity that was taking place, there's nothing that would be suspicious in nature that would lead us to believe that, you know, she had been attacked or there was some problem or whatever. It could just be coincidence, but certainly it is something that our investigators have looked at. [11]

It seems an awfully risky plan to lure somebody out to the front door and beyond at 4:30 in the morning and lure them into a vehicle or overpower them and drag them into a vehicle, unless she knew them well. The Newport deskclerk/security would be a problem. Somebody would have to come in and carry her out, or she would tentatively go out the door probably saying something to the deskclerk and not come back, not to mention the scream. And somebody spent the morning on her computer regardless.

Is this another coincidence that's too much of a coincidence to be a coincidence? Many people want to believe that that scream came from Chandra, because it makes sense, and nothing much else does.

We are all confused. There was a scream at 4:30 am. A 911 call. With an abduction in the early morning hours, Chandra for all intents and purposes didn't exist when she disappeared. No alibi would even be needed.

Chandra disappeared when she didn't disappear, and disappeared again without anyone noticing. And when we look back, we see a 911 call, a scream, an abduction. Is that what was intended?

The only thing standing between us believing she was abducted with a scream in the wee hours are obscure and ambiguous computer logs. Was someone not technically savvy enough to have thought out history logs of internet use, or could there be someone savvier than we think?

On Her Computer

Tuesday morning, May 1, Chandra logged onto the internet at 9:30 a.m. Chandra spent the morning "surfing the web", Washington Police Chief Charles Ramsey told Bob Schieffer of CBS Face The Nation "…from the e-mail message she sent her mother, from the surfing of the web, for lack of a better word to describe the other activity that was taking place, there's nothing that would be suspicious in nature that would lead us to believe that, you know, she had been attacked or there was some problem or whatever. It could just be coincidence, but certainly it is something that our investigators have looked at."

Yet, nothing actually identified Chandra as being on the computer. The password for logging onto the internet is commonly left in the login dialogue box. The e-mail sent to her mother was actually "a very generalized e-mail about Southwest specials flights", Susan Levy told the Today Show. It was a "snippet of information about a sale fare from Southwest Airlines" that had been forwarded from Chandra's computer to her parents in Modesto. [1] Lisa DePaulo describes it in Talk:

> On May 1 the Levys got their last communication from their daughter in the form of an e-mail sent to them at 10:45 a.m. Washington time. Contrary to reports, Chandra did not write about her plans to fly home. The message contained no personal note, just a list of supersaver flights between Modesto and Los Angeles. (The family planned to fly to Chandra's graduation together.) What the Levys didn't know at that point was that Chandra hadn't yet made any plans to get back to California. had no airline ticket, no train ticket, no car. [2]

It could be considered awfully strange to send an e-mail home, forwarded or not, without adding a comment, especially when leaving a message for her aunt a day and half earlier that she had "big news, call me".

She had big news for Linda Zamsky but did not mention it to her mom, not even a "wait till you hear this" alert. Nothing. Condit was a secret that Chandra had inadvertantly confided to Linda. Could the big news have been something she could have only told Linda, at least right away?

The last time Chandra had talked to her parents was Friday evening, more than three days earlier. In that time she talked to Condit and had vacillated between telling her landlord on Saturday of a moveout date on the coming weekend and on Sunday saying she would have a firm moveout date on Wednesday, tomorrow in fact. She had left a call for Sven on Saturday, wanting to talk. She had big news for her aunt on Sunday. Her parents were looking for word from her of when she would arrive to make plans for the family to attend her graduation. Yet all that was sent from her computer on Tuesday morning was an e-mail notification from Southwest of supersaver fares forwarded to her parents without comment. Was it Chandra on the computer who forwarded that e-mail?

The questions were to persist. Two weeks after Ramsey first told Bob Schieffer it was Chandra on the computer, Schieffer had him back on CBS Face The Nation:

> SCHIEFFER: And, Chief, let me ask you this because this is a question that so many people have asked me. Are you satisfied that the computer traffic on her computer that day, how do you know it was her? Could it have been someone else?
>
> RAMSEY: Well, I mean, obviously it could be, but we doubt it because of the nature of the traffic. We've been able to go back not just that date but a couple of months, and what we found is a regular pattern of sites that she visited and things of that nature. So there's no reason for us to believe that there was anyone other than her on the computer that morning. [3]

Is there something in that surfing that tells us what was to happen to Chandra? Or something that someone wanted us to think happened? The surfing was extensive, over three hours visiting a wide range of sites. Washington's ABC affiliate WJLA provided the list:

Chandra Levy Website Addresses

Earlier this week, the Metropolitan Police Department announced it would release a list of websites visited by Chandra Levy on May 1, 2001, in the hopes it may generate additional tips into her disappearance. Some of those websites follow:

http://www.agriculture.house.gov
http://www.altavista.com
http://www.amtrak.com
http://www.baskinrobbins.com
http://www.drudgereport.com
http://www.eonline.com
http://www.gofrance.about.com
http://www.google.com
http://www.hollywoodreporter.com
http://www.hotmail.com
http://www.house.gov
http://www.latimes.com
http://www.lexis-nexis.com
http://www.lycos.com
http://www.microsoft.com
http://www.modbee.com
http://www.mrshowbiz.go.com
http://www.msn.com
http://www.nandotimes.com
http://www.nationalgeographic.com
http://www.nexis.com
http://www.sfgate.com
http://www.southwest.com
http://www.thomas.loc.gov
http://www.uclick.com
http://www.usatoday.com
http://www.vicinity.com
http://www.washingtoncitypaper.com
http://www.washingtonpost.com
http://www.yahoo.com

Additional websites and specific pages visited within those sites will not be released at this time. This information is considered evidentiary and part of the ongoing investigation. [4]

Michael Doyle of the Modesto Bee summed up the sites visited as "three-plus hours the morning of May 1 tapping into more than 30 Internet sites from her laptop computer. The sites covered everything from the House Agriculture Committee, on which Condit serves, to Southwest Airlines, Amtrak and the Hollywood Reporter."

CNN pointed out that ahe "also visited thomas.loc.gov, a site operated by the Library of Congress that contains information about activities in Congress" and "visited sites for her hometown paper, the Modesto Bee in California, as well as the Washington Post, USA Today, the Washington City Paper, the San Francisco Chronicle, Nando Times, the Hollywood Reporter, National Geographic, the Drudge Report and the Los Angeles Times".

CNN continues:

> She viewed sites for Southwest Airlines, Amtrak and gofrance.about.com, which has information about traveling to France.
>
> Other sites on the list included the popular search engines Yahoo, AltaVista and Lycos; Hotmail, an e-mail site; vicinity.com, which gives users maps to specific locations, two entertainment sites, E! Online and Mr. Showbiz; the portal site msn.com; and the site for ice cream chain Baskin-Robbins. [5]

According to the Mercury News, police said she bounced from site to site. "She was all over the place, some for a tenth of a second," Executive Assistant Police Chief Terrance Gainer told the Mercury News. "Clearly, she was tracking Condit."

In my opinion, that is Chandra's entire bookmark list and indeed not much more than a cursory visit to the entire bookmark list was done. It's somewhat unusual to use Lexis-Nexis, Google, AltaVista, Yahoo, and Lycos search engines in one three and a half hour session along with six newspapers and three Hollywood gossip sites, and travel sites and Baskin Robbins, in terms of time. Only a very focused search could be done over that range of material in one session.

It's my experience that different search engines produce different results, and in the past I have gone through a few before I was able to find something, but so rarely I dropped them off my bookmark list. I use Google exclusively, and it had links for AltaVista, Lycos and Yahoo at the time.

She might have had a meta-search site that drops the same search into every site. I tried it a couple of times but it was pretty cumbersome. Throws up a window for every search site. Also there are the techniques to harvest new references like newspaper articles with a bot on an ongoing basis, so that every day you can produce a new list of articles that reference the search.

The point is, whether Chandra used one or not, the concept of searching through all search engines to perform usually repetitive thorough searches is valid, and in fact automated as well as can be done by meta-search sites. It doesn't make a person a computer whiz to search in every search engine. It does make them extremely thorough, and this is yet another incident with multiple explanations. It is consistent with being interested in a job working for Condit. It is also explainable as her being very interested in his actions for some reason. I think that she just clicked through to AltaVista, Lycos, and Yahoo from Google to perform the same search. Thorough, and would have resulted in articles on his lunch at the White House on Monday.

And I didn't even mention the government sites, which are very static and change infrequently, which makes for a quick check but also a very tiresome check to do any more than infrequently, and also National Geographic included in that 30 sites.

That's an average of 7 minutes per site, somewhat reasonable on the face of it, but then there was time involved in handling e-mail, forwarding one to her parents, taking a break once in a while, but still some sites can be clicked through somewhat quickly, but the first screen for Lexis alone dripped in like molasses. How do you look at a newspaper in 5 minutes, just scan the front page looking for a specific type of article? The two things listed by police with specifics, the Baskin-Robbins special and the map of the streets and park around Klingle Mansion, take a little effort to bring up and take a look at.

I'm satisfied that she used Lexis-Nexis for the Congressional World services. It has detailed information on all congressional activities. That would be where she would be able to see scheduled activities of committees that Condit was on.

She would have used a government signon for Lexis-Nexis that she used at the BOP. There are also extensive personal information research capabilities at Nexis, and she may have had access to those services as well in working with criminal related research at the BOP. She did internet searches and scanned newspapers in her job in the information office at the BOP. But the Congressional World service is exactly what she would have wanted for searching on Condit.

Of course, this conjures up that she's on to something and digging into his past, whereupon he has to stop her, but that's a vast conspiracy image. It is so difficult to envision her tracking everything that could be associated with him after telling her landlord there's no reason to stick around anymore, unless he told her something Sunday that got her very interested in his area of responsibility.

That might be bringing her back to work for him in D.C. That would be big news for Zamsky and something she wouldn't want to broach with her parents until necessary. That would placate her for him not helping her with a Federal job, and she would believe it even if he was just telling her something to get her off his back.

She was digging way deeper than what one would do to determine his schedule, and quite frankly you couldn't determine much of anything of his schedule or whereabouts even with an exhaustive web search. For example, he was in a meeting with Cheney. That wouldn't have been anywhere on the web.

To dig that deep, she was researching his past or had been told she would be a legislative aide for him as soon as he could arrange it, and she was digging deeper than ever into all possible issues affecting his office, becoming an expert. The big news she left for Zamsky was not dark and mysterious, indicating a dig into a dark past. It was upbeat and enthusiastic. Maybe she was coming back to D.C. to work for Condit.

And I didn't mention the travel sites specifically. Amtrak, Go France, Southwest, 7 minutes a piece, ok, a tenth of a second on some, but clicked through to leave enough time for things like checking schedules on Amtrak.

In the only trip Chandra made home during her half year in DC, she flew with a ticket from Condit. There is no indication she made any travel plans to go to her graduation, even as she was telling fellow workers at the BOP that she was going.

On the other hand, any travel arrangements at that time would have been a round trip, as she expected to remain employed at her internship at the BOP up until a week before she disappeared.

Even in the week after her internship was terminated, she made no travel arrangements. Her parents wonder why she was so fuzzy about her plans to come home. Susan told the Baltimore Sun, "She wasn't giving us any details or times exactly when she was coming in. It was kind of unlike her". Only in the Saturday e-mail to her landlord, even as Carolyn was arriving at the airport, did she e-mail her landlord and say that there was no longer any reason for her to stay in D.C., and that she must terminate her lease.

But the next day she talked to Condit again, and then called Linda Zamsky to say she had big news. And e-mailed her landlord that her move out date of the next weekend was now uncertain. She would have a definitive moveout to tell him on Wednesday. What would have made it become definitive tomorrow, and did it have anything to do with checking her answering machine repeatedly for a message?

Chandra visited the Amtrak website the morning she disappeared. She would be able to go get on a train and be in California in a day and a half. Was she contemplating making her moveout sooner than the next weekend, or later? What was she waiting for, an answer from Condit as to whether he was still going to give her a flight ticket she would have been expecting to use? Why was it uncertain?

The police came out with a list of websites asking for help from the public. Some sites were not made public, cited as "evidentiary". [6] An incomplete list provides for incomplete or misleading help. I guess we're lucky to have any list at all since it was so hard for them to find out what was on her computer because the hard drive crashed on them.

I didn't try to visit all the websites and time it, but I did go through the list and try to see what Chandra would have done on those sites and try to determine if the list was consistent with what we would expect from Chandra's web surfing. There is no end to the conspiracy to imitate Chandra on her computer Tuesday morning theories, debated at length on the internet.

The most frequent suggestion is that the sites were visited at some other time than Tuesday morning. However, the Internet Service Provider that Chandra dialed into would normally record the 9:30 a.m. login and the 1:00 p.m. logout from that phone line, and e-mail was recorded at multiple ISP's as being sent at 10:45 a.m. from there. These activities cannot be faked elsewhere at a different time.

Also frequently suggested is changing the time on her computer clock. Any timestamp on the computer is irrelevant on its own, but if within the ISP recorded log in and out times, then it is much more legitimized but of course still prone to manipulation. These are three timestamps that are of interest:

a) browser history file. I am looking at my browser history file now. It shows the time that each web page was visited. It shows long URL's for each page including search parameters. It is very comprehensive.

The history time stamps would accurately show the time each page was visited and therefore how long was spent on each page before visiting the next one. It is not reasonably easy to go through the history info and edit it but of course it is data on the computer, and a specialized program could be used to do it. It would need to be browser and version specific, and after a person visited all the pages as quickly as possible, the program could start at a certain point and spread out the times over a longer period.

A remote possibility is a recorded script from another computer that recorded visiting all the sites, then was played on Chandra's computer keystroke for keystroke to simulate it. Given the vagaries of internet response time, it is beyond possibility in my opinion to get an accurate rendition of the first session.

Even assuming a script program that duplicated the time lapses between each keystroke, one missed or late screen would throw it off until the next URL was entered somehow or selected from bookmarks. From my experience of pop up windows, pages with frames, and the necessity of getting focus to enter data, the script would have to capture mouse clicks at extremely precise pixel locations as well as keystrokes, and the computer where the script was created would surely have to be her own at some time when she wasn't home. The script would have to be recorded and replayed that morning.

Naturally, this now brings us to the possibility of accessing the computer remotely to start the script, but of course the computer needs to be online to access it remotely. I have seen everything postulated concerning these possibilities, and one tossed out frequently is that she may have had DSL and her laptop online all the time. You still are logged in to an ISP over a DSL or cable network, and the police say she logged in to the ISP around 9:30 am.

Again, this is CIA level stealth and so unworkable that I've never heard of it being attempted. An internet browser is probably the worst thing in the world in which to have to recreate a previous computer session verbatim. The vagaries of internet page generation and the high degree of mouse activity and precision required makes this probably an impossible task. Certainly not when a person could sit there and do the same thing from a written script.

b) browser cache file timestamps. Browser cache files are computer files with names and timestamps just like any other computer file. The timestamps are easily changed with a tool. However, they would have to be changed to match the history timestamp of the page where they came from, and it is not trivial to go through a cache and match each file with the page it came from. This also would have to be done ahead of time and be done by a program to implement the changes. A tremendous research effort.

The police said, for example, that Chandra only visited some sites for as brief as a tenth of a second, although my history timestamps are accurate only to the second. The precision was probably from the cached file time stamps, which are recorded at millisecond precision. It would be possible forensically to see the files in chronological order and note where the content came from had changed to another page, and see only a tenth second on a page in between two other pages.

It is also possible to change those times stamps, and change them in coordination with changes made to the browser history data. And that is after all the pages were visited as fast as they could be clicked. We're only talking about the time being spread out of page visits between log in and log out. It would take longer to do that than to sit with realistic pauses on each page to recreate a three and a half hour session.

c) e-mail time stamps. E-mails are archived at the e-mail host as they pass through, so the computer time is irrelevant. In addition, Susan Levy received the 10:45 am e-mail at 7:45 Pacific time. The scripting would have to include interaction with the e-mail program and obviously a requirement is that a realistic e-mail from Southwest would have to be bogusly created to a degree that even examining it today would not be able to determine that Southwest didn't generate it.

Some have suggested that some software may have been installed surreptitiously and then deleted itself after performing the websurfing. If files were deleted, they are not cache files that are being looked at to determine what Chandra looked at, for example the map of Rock Creek Park.

Commercially available erase software would overwrite data with nulls (the conceptual equivalent of blanks in binary, but not the same as text blanks) rather than leaving the data there and Windows just marking the space as available. Defragging would also make it likely deleted files would be overwritten. What would be erased? Some of this software we're talking about that would need to be installed before using.

Believe me, it is infinitely easier to sit there for three and a half hours and visit ice cream and Hollywood gossip sites.

So assuming that whether Chandra or someone else, this looks to me like right down her bookmark list. Search on Condit? There's a no brainer. An e-mail for a flight to LA? Okay, forward to parents. No brainer. Lexis-Nexis? Now that's more interesting. They would have a record of login and search history, at least number of them, results retrieved, etc. The person must use the same login as Chandra used at the BOP. Ahhh, I can hear it now. Sven, run, run, the mob is coming after you again…

Then there's the ever popular the computer was sanitized. Far from sanitizing the computer from references to Condit, her activity that morning is totally oriented around Condit. The police described her as stalking him.

The interesting aspect of this is that it is a behavioral analysis, not a technical analysis, to determine if it was Chandra on the computer. The computer recorded what happened regardless of who the person was. It is up to us to judge the behavior of that person. It looks like Chandra to me, at a minimum going through her regularly bookmarked sites to stay up to date as an insider, at most sleuthing and finding something that cost her her freedom.

It would be a typically bad B-movie script to be researching a person such as Joyce Chiang on the internet, another government employee from California who disappeared five blocks from Chandra two years earlier, then go to a closed, isolated mansion in a nearby forest and turn up missing as well. But this whole saga has been too unbelievable to even dream up as a script. It would get tossed.

Klingle Mansion

The San Jose Mercury News published a partial list of the sites visited with comments from D.C. police:

> WEB SITES LEVY VISITED
> This is a partial list of the Internet sites that police say Chandra Levy visited between the hours of 9:30 a.m. and 12:30 p.m. on May 1. The Web sites were provided to the Mercury News. Police say they will release a complete list today.
> Amtrak
> Drudge Report
> House: Agricultural Committee
> Los Angeles Times
> Modesto Bee
> National Geographic
> Rock Creek Park
> Southwest Airlines
> USA Today
> Washington Post [1]

Rock Creek Park is on the partial list of sites provided by San Jose Mercury News. Police said that Chandra looked up a map for Klingle Mansion in Rock Creek Park that morning. Chief Ramsey told the Washington Post she looked at MapQuest maps for locations in Washington and California, including Pierce-Klingle Mansion, the park headquarters of Rock Creek Park.

The Klingle Mansion park administration building is a restored 1823 historic estate home about a mile north of Condit's condo location on Adams Mill Road. Condit's condo is about halfway between Chandra's Newport apartment on Dupont Circle and Klingle Mansion in Rock Creek Park, and Rock Creek Park runs for miles through the District of Columbia, including along Adams Mill Road.

Baskin-Robbins had a "Free Scoop Night" Wednesday special that Chandra might have been looking at to plan to visit the next day. Following is an internet posting from a Washington area skaters's group which had a prelim skate rally on Wednesday night, May 2:

Date: Wed, 02 May 2001 17:00 EDT
From: David
Subject: Fwd: Free Ice Cream

A suggestion for tonights skate:
Today is Free Cone Day at Ben and Jerry's Ice Cream (www.benjerry.com). It's also Free Scoop Night at Baskin Robbins Ice Cream (www. baskinrobbins.com) from 6:00pm-10:00pm. Enjoy!

Date: Wed, 2 May 2001 17:14 EDT
From: Carl

Here's an idea:

Since the free ice cream at B&J's is until 8:00 pm and the free ice cream at B-R is from 6:00–10:00, I'm now planning on doing tonight's skate BACK-WARDS. We can get free ice cream at the beginning of the skate (Ben & Jerry's) in Georgetown and at the end of the skate (Baskin-Robbins), assuming that they'll let us in.

With a detour in the middle, we could get ice cream about 1/3–1/2 of the way through on Connecticut Ave.

There's a Baskin-Robbins at 1410 U Street NW. We can head there from Union Station.

Date: Wed, 2 May 2001 17:16 EDT
From: Julie

The baskin-robbins that used to be on U street is no longer there. But there is one on connecticut just north of calvert.

Date: Wed, 2 May 2001 17:18 EDT
From: Carl

OK, thanks for the tip. We can still stop by the Conn. Ave. location.

------------ [2]

The Baskin-Robbins at Calvert and Connecticut is just down the street from Condit's condo apartment. Chandra told her landlord she would have a definite moveout date on Wednesday, May 2, and ice cream was her and Condit's favorite food to eat together. But Carolyn's luncheon was on May 2, and she didn't fly back to California until the next day. What information was Chandra going to have on Wednesday to tell her landlord about leaving, and where was she planning on getting it?

Greta Van Susteren makes that point with Clint Van Zandt, former FBI profiler, on CNN The Point:

> VAN SUSTEREN: Are you concerned with the fact that when she was looking at her computer she was looking at Baskin-Robbin's and she was looking at Rock Creek Park Mansion on Mapquest. Is that the kind of thing...
>
> VAN ZANDT: I tell you what, one of the questions that I would ask the congressman is did you two ever go for ice cream together? Did she ever talk about it? Some people go to ice cream when they are depressed, others like to share it with someone.
>
> Why would she be looking at Baskin-Robbins ice cream site on that particular day? [3]

MapQuest is mentioned by Ramsey and Greta, but it isn't on the list of websites provided by the police. Also, Rock Creek Park is not on the official website list either, but vicinity.com is on the list. vicinity.com is a pay site that links to MapBlast. MapBlast shows a better map than MapQuest, but still has no landmark reference to Klingle Mansion. However, www.justiceforchandra.com internet poster jabarn writes:

> If you go to vicinity.com, link to Mapblast.com, then link to smartpages.com from there, and type in Rock Creek Park as a "business name" (and not "type") you get the address 3545 Williamsburg Lane. The map is provided by Mapquest.

I don't see any way that Chandra could look up directions to Klingle Mansion via any internet map tool such as Mapquest. I did find that you could link a directory through vicinity.com that would give you the address for Klingle Manion, but you had to enter "Rock Creek Park." What I was pointing out is that the address for Klingle Mansion is also used as the address for Rock Creek Park (since Klingle Mansion houses the administrative offices). I don't think Chandra was looking up directions to Klingle Mansion, although I cannot know for sure.

I also have heard reference, but cannot confirm it, that Chandra visited the Rock Creek Park website. There she could have accessed a very detailed map of the trails.

It is correct that Mapquest does not give detailed maps regarding the trails in Rock Creek Park, only the streets/roads surrounding it or running through it. [4]

It is significant if she was looking up a map for Rock Creek Park rather than directions to Klingle Mansion. The map is the same, the address displayed the same, but the reason for doing so unlikely to be the same.

I attempted to duplicate what Chandra did on her computer concerning Klingle Mansion. The first attempt or so to even find Klingle Mansion did not pan out. It is often referred to as Pierce-Klingle Mansion in official documentation.

I brought up MapQuest, but I couldn't see where landmarks can be typed in, such as "Klingle Mansion" or "Rock Creek Park", so a street address would have to be entered, meaning it has to be looked up. I did a search on the web, but of course Chandra would also be able to look it up in the phone book. The address is:

Rock Creek Park
Washington, DC

Address:

Klingle Mansion
3545 Williamsburg Ln Nw
Washington, DC
20008-1207, US [5]

and I entered the street address, Washington in city, and DC in state and got a map that even at the highest level of Zoom In on MaqQuest literally displays in the middle of nowhere. Though it has a Williamsburg Lane street address, the red star that marks the location is about halfway between Williamsburg Lane and Rock Creek. There are no landmark labels on the map whatsoever. The only way to know what it is a map of is to look at the address displayed above the map.

In general, the map image on the web page would display the address entered above the map, the map probably was in the browser cache, and an image viewer would display exactly what she entered to get that map. If she entered 3545 Williamsburg Ln NW, it could be for street directions to the Mansion/Park Office, or it could be a means to get a map of Rock Creek Park. This would make her just looking up a general map of Rock Creek Park, and the police misled by focusing on Klingle Mansion.

I then took a more powerful map program, Street Atlas, and zoomed in on this address. It shows an extremely detailed view of streets, including how Williamsburg Lane goes up to that address. But the address was labelled Linnean Hill rather than Klingle Mansion or Pierce-Klingle Mansion, yet another name for this building.

Using Street Atlas, I then positioned start on the 1200 block of 21st Street NW, the Newport apartment building, and the end at Klingle Mansion. It's a fairly straight shot up Connecticut Ave. to Klingle Road and into Rock Creek Park to Klingle Mansion. But at 3 miles, it's not an easy walk.

> M Street NW 0.1 W
> New Hampshire Ave. NW 0.4 NE
> Dupont Circle NW 0.1 N
> Connecticut Ave. NW 1.9 NW
> Klingle Road NW 0.4 E
> Porter Street NW 0.1 E
> Williamsburg Lane NW 0.3 N
> ----
> Trip distance 3.0 miles

But when I looked at Klingle Mansion, what did I see? Would you believe Adams Mill Road running into Klingle Road? I set start for the 2600 block of Adams Mill Road NW, Condit's condo. It's half the distance there:

Adams Mill Road NW 1.0 N
Klingle Road NW 0.3 W
Porter Street NW 0.1 E
Williamsburg Lane NW 0.3 N

Trip distance 1.4 miles

So Klingle Road is at the end of Adams Mill, where Condit lives. So much for Chandra doing some sightseeing before leaving town. Maybe after all those visits to Condit's she wondered where Adams Mill went to?

This is not a meeting place in between where Condit and Chandra lived. As you go up Connecticut Ave., well before Rock Creek Park, you pass Calvert St. which is a short distance over to Adams Mill. Condit practically lived on the corner of Adams Mill and Calvert. In other words, Condit's is on the way to Klingle Mansion and half way there from Chandra's.

You can start with these directions from Chandra's to Condit's, and then finish with Condit's to Klingle Mansion. Here are the directions from Chandra's to Condit's:

M Street NW 0.1 W
New Hampshire Ave. NW 0.4 NE
Dupont Circle NW 0.1 N
Connecticut Ave. NW 0.5 NW
Columbia Road NW 0.5 N
Adams Mill Road NW 0.2 NW

Trip distance 1.6 miles

The point is, Klingle Mansion is in a remote forested area close to Condit's apartment at the end of his street. A description of Rock Creek Park from Central Corridor:

At 1700 acres, Rock Creek Park is one of the largest urban parks in the nation. The park runs due north and south from the MD/DC line, between Oregon Avenue and 16th Street, through the Zoological Park, almost to the Potomac River. [6]

The San Francisco Chronicle wrote about Condit a few years before, mentioning that he kept a bicycle stashed in his office in Congress to take off through Rock Creek Park during lulls. An interesting thing is that Klingle Mansion and most of the park functions are closed Mondays and Tuesdays. Klingle Mansion would be closed and secluded that day of Tuesday, May 1. Aptly, Mary Jocoby of the St. Petersburg Times points out that "The park has been a dumping ground in the past for bodies".

Still, Chandra looked it up on her computer for some reason. Or was someone else looking it up for some reason? The method used to obtain the Rock Creek Park map is very interesting. An extremely sophisticated, obscure method linking through as a place of interest. Someone wanting to plant a clue would likely bring up Mapquest and somehow get a map of the park. Oops, it isn't easy. Maybe that's the only way anyone could obtain a map.

But in reality, rather than a green blob that says Rock Creek Park, they would download a detailed trail map to indicate she was going to hike on trails. Or it could simply be that Chandra had some time to kill before leaving. Instead, it wasn't time that got killed. A call was placed on the cell phone, according to police. At 1 pm she logged off her computer. Chandra was never heard from again.

Frantic

The phone calls started. Sven Jones returned from a long weekend out of town trip late Tuesday and got Chandra's message inviting him for lunch in Georgetown. He called back but never heard from her. He told the Washington Times: "I just thought that was odd because she was the type of person who would always call back".

Her parents, having received the cryptic e-mail from Chandra that morning that was a forwarded Southwest supersaver fares message with no comment, called hoping she had some news for them on how and when she would be arriving home. They weren't worried at first. They had last talked to her on Friday, and she seldom called home more than once a week.

Condit told Connie Chung in her ABC News interview with him that he called and left a message that day as well. Chung's questioning to discern this would put a police interrogator to shame:

> CONDIT: Well, she gave me the impression that she was going to take a train to California. So I assumed in the next few days she was going to take a train to California. So I might talk to her after she got to California, I might talk to her when she got back from California. It wasn't clear to me whether or not she was actually going to move to California, come back and try to find another job. Um, but Chandra was interested in working at the FBI. She was interested in working at the CIA, or NI-, NSA. Something like that. She was very interested in those areas. And so...the reason the, the Federal Prison Bureau uh, job was important to her, because she thought that was the stepping stone in getting into the FBI.
>
> CHUNG: Uh, did you speak with her again after April 29th?
>
> CONDIT: Uh, no. April 29th was the last conversation.
>
> CHUNG: So you're saying that you didn't expect to hear from her for about a week?

CONDIT: Well, actually, I tried to call her, because I...

CHUNG: When did you try and call her?

CONDIT: I tried to call her probably the 30th or the 31st, or some time in that week.

CHUNG: Uh, there, there is no 31st. Uh...it's either the 30th or May first.

CONDIT: (Overlap) I mean, the 30th or May first. I did try to...well, maybe it was later in the week, because I had not heard from her.

CHUNG: Uh-huh. And...you were expecting to hear? You, did you, you just said that you weren't expecting to hear from her for a week?

CONDIT: (Overlap) Well, I thought I might...I, I thought I might hear her about her travel plans. She might leave a message and say she was taking a train or she wasn't taking a train. I never heard that.

CHUNG: So did you call her, you're saying, on the 29th?

CONDIT: (Overlap) Yes, I placed a call...

CHUNG: Or the 30th.

CONDIT: I, I placed a call on uh...sometime during the next few days, to try to find out what her travel plans were going to be.

CHUNG: And you called her apartment?

CONDIT: Yes, I left a...yes, left a message.

CHUNG: And uh...did she ever call you back?

CONDIT: No.

CHUNG: Were you concerned?

CONDIT: I was concerned that she had not called me back. But uh...but also just assumed that she had taken a train. And she told me the train was going to take four days.

CHUNG: You can't remember exactly when you called?

CONDIT: On the...?

CHUNG: Yes, when you called again. When you called, was it the 30th? May first? Second, 3rd, 4th?

CONDIT: (Overlap) Well, it…it could've been…it could've been the first. It could've been the second. Somewhere in that time frame. [1]

The next morning, Wednesday May 2, Chandra would have been missed at work at the Bureau of Prisons had she not found her internship abruptly terminated the week before. The following illustrates what happens when one is still working for the government when they disappear, and what happens when it is known that someone has been intimately involved with the woman who disappears.

On Friday, June 13, 2003 LaToya Taylor went out to lunch from her job at the IRS in Washington. She didn't come back. When she didn't show up for work Monday as well, police went into action. They focused on her ex-boyfriend who was contesting paternity over LaToya's nine month old baby. By evening he was being questioned.

Had Chandra still been working at the BOP, an investigation into the disappearance of someone like herself in federal law enforcement would have been launched immediately with much local publicity, similar to the search that would take place for LaToya Taylor as a missing IRS employee two years later. It can be seen how critical it is that a woman not still be a federal employee if she is to be made to disappear quietly.

And as in any missing woman case, anyone in a relationship with the woman would be investigated immediately until they could be cleared as was done with LaToya Taylor's ex-boyfriend. It can also be seen how critical it is to not be known to be in a relationship with a woman if she were to, say, disappear.

Today, Wednesday, was the day that Chandra had told her landlord, Denis Edeline, she could tell him when she would be moving out. Something happened on Sunday that caused her to change her message to her landlord that she would be moving out this weekend to that she could tell him Wednesday of when she would be moving out. Something perhaps she was expecting to find out on Tuesday, perhaps something in a message she was waiting for. We will never know.

But Wednesday had arrived, and Edeline called from San Francisco. There was no answer. Her parents called again as well.

On Thursday Edeline called and e-mailed. He was thinking something was wrong by now because Chandra always returned messages. Chandra's father was starting to get worried now too. The landlord and Chandra's parents are both calling every day. Bob Levy tearfully recalled to the Washington Post: "I kept calling and leaving messages. Her message machine was full". He called Chandra's Newport apartment building manager and asked him to check if Chandra was there, but the manager refused, saying he couldn't because of D.C. laws. Chandra's father recalled to Larry King:

> R. LEVY: She was supposed to fly home, come home, meet us in Sacramento. She was supposed to be in touch with friends in L.A. that she was going to stay with and see. And we, you know, we didn't hear from her.
>
> We called and left a message and we didn't hear from her the 1st or the 2nd, and 3rd and 4th—well, actually, the 4th we started getting more anxious. And the 5th, I think that was Friday, I started calling the police in Washington trying to get them to check in to things. And finally, by Monday—or Sunday, I knew she was missing. [2]

He asked the D.C. police to check her apartment, and they told him they would. "But they never called back," Bob told DePaulo. As Ross Douthat expressed in his take of it in the National Review:

> For instance, everyone already knows about the incompetence of the D.C. police—but it turns out that the cops were even more Keystone-ish than we imagined. On May 5, four days after Chandra vanished, her father called the D.C. police, told them that he hadn't heard from his daughter for days, and asked them to check out her apartment. They promised to do so and then never called back. [3]

Feeling the D.C. police were not taking them seriously, the Levys called their congressman at home in the nearby town of Ceres. They still had no idea which congressman was Chandra's secret boyfriend, Condit wasn't high on their list of suspicion because the congressman boyfriend was supposed to be a divorced Southern Democrat. This critical first contact with Condit is related by the Levys to Larry King:

KING: Let's go over your contacts with Condit. Talk Magazine reports that you called his home on the night of May 5 after getting no help from the D.C. police. Is that true?

S. LEVY: Yes, that's right.

KING: His wife answered the phone, right?

B. LEVY: I did.

KING: You called? OK.

B. LEVY: Yes.

KING: What happened?

B. LEVY: I said I'd like to get in touch with him, and then I believe he later called back, and I talked to him and told him Chandra was missing.

KING: Was that the first he knew he about it?

B. LEVY: Well, I don't know if that's the first he knew...

KING: What did he say?

B. LEVY: He said, "Oh." He didn't act too surprised or shocked. He said, "Well, she's a good friend of mine." And then he mentioned that he would get in touch with his office and try to get help for us and put up the initial reward.

KING: So he was cooperative.

B. LEVY: Yes.

KING: So when you hung up the phone, you had no reason to feel any ill will towards him?

B. LEVY: Not really. There was some suspicion. We were looking around to find out who she might be dating, since she didn't tell us. We were thinking about him and some other congressmen.

KING: Let me back up, were you surprised that he offered a reward immediately?

S. LEVY: I was in shock, not surprised by his offering a reward. It was just the whole initial shock, the reality of my daughter not here for graduation...[4]

Congressman Condit is able to tell the Levys that Chandra is a good friend but not able to tell them that he thought she took a train home? He instead says "Oh" and offers to set up a reward to find her. He wasn't surprised that she was missing. Why is that?

Condit might have been shocked at the news, stunned beyond reasoning, but if so he never recovered sufficiently to attempt to contact Chandra again or tell the Levys that he thought she took a train home. A reward would have to do. Chandra was gone.

The next morning, Sunday morning, the landlord Denis Edeline checked Chandra's emergency contact number on her condo application and called the Levys at 10 a.m. Bob Levy answered, saying "Oh no, God. We've being trying to contact her all week." [5] The Washington Post quotes the landlord: "Dr. Levy sounded so distraught. He said he didn't know where she was either and said he'd called the police."

In an online interview with Where in the World is Chandra Levy Denis Edeline explains what he was thinking:

> I originally talked to the police on May 6th. I called the Levy's Sunday morning of May 6th once I realized that something must be wrong. I thought that maybe Chandra had returned home and just decided to keep the condo longer and just had not gotten any of my phone messages to the DC condo. I called the parents about 10 am Sunday morning. The father was already worried and was thankful that I called. He wanted me to get the manager to go into the condo thinking maybe she was in the condo and something was wrong. I called front desk person numerous times…trying to get them to get the manager to open the apartment and see if Chandra was in it. Manager could not because of DC laws.
>
> When I was concerned about Chandra on May 5 & May 6th…I asked the front desk people in my many calls to the building on those two days…. The main desk person said she never saw her with a male….the evening desk people could hardly remember who she was…I guess she was not friendly or talkative with the desk people. But no male visitor stories. [6]

Dr. Levy called the police again on Sunday and "begged and begged". [7] He finally convinced them to go check on her apartment by telling them she suffered from bad allergies and there could be a medical emergency. And he was a doctor. Pity the poor parent of a Washington intern who hasn't heard from them and hasn't watched enough ER to convince the police to check on their loved one. Even landlords calling doesn't help. Research was unable to determine how many neighbors must complain of a stench before the D.C. police will check on an apartment.

According to the Washington Post, the FBI says 875,000 persons nationally had been reported missing the year before, and the vast majority turned up unharmed. While the many false alarms of missing person reports can be used to justify such lack of urgency in dealing with a reported missing woman in D.C., that wasn't the case in prominent missing person cases of women elsewhere around the country.

Was the call being on the weekend and called in by a father the problem? Laci Peterson, a 27 year old housewife in Chandra's hometown of Modesto, was reported missing on Christmas Eve by her step-father. The Modesto police responded immediately.

So what, small town instead of the big city? Svetlana Aranov, a 44 year old mother of two who dealt rare books from her home, was reported missing by her husband, who is an oncologist like Dr. Levy, on March 3, 2003. Police in the relatively large city of New York didn't have any problem responding to the report of a missing woman either.

A problem with being asked to check on someone in their apartment instead of being summoned by a husband? Perhaps. The irony is that remote relatives have already waited days to call the police, not knowing if the missing woman is on a trip unknown to them or staying with a friend or any number of legitimate reasons to not return a message for a few days.

By the time they feel they must call, it is even more necessary for police to act urgently, and yet they are treated as a nuisance call. Filing a missing persons report as was done by Chandra's father should move it beyond a nuisance. It probably does almost anywhere else besides Washington, D.C.

And when the Washington police do go check on her apartment Sunday night? Lisa DePaulo tells Larry King what happened in this every parent's nightmare:

DEPAULO: Dr. Levy was so upset by Sunday night, that he called and begged and begged. Please go. And finally the cops go, and guess what they do? According to Dr. Levy, they call him back and say OK, we got in the apartment, she's not there. What they didn't mention was what was there. Her purse, her wallet, her half-packed suitcases, her jewelry. I mean, just were not there.

And so the Levys did not actually understand or find out the circumstances of their daughter's not being in the apartment for several more days. [8]

Bob Levy sums it up. "I guess they thought it was enough that they didn't see a body on the floor". [9] What would it take to get the D.C. police interested in where Chandra was? Unfortunately, that question would persist for quite some time.

Monday May 7 Condit returned to Washington. Interestingly, for some reason he tells Connie Chung that he had just been told the night before by Dr. Levy that Chandra was missing instead of on Saturday as the Levys tell it. He then futher tells Chung:

So right after that…right after that, I was in Washington DC on Monday. I contacted law enforcement. I asked the FBI to be involved. I helped set up the re-, rewan-, reward fund. And so we were consistently quickly involved. [10]

Even saying "I contacted law enforcement. I asked the FBI to be involved.", which should be straightforward, raises questions. The Washington Times reports:

The source said the next step apparently was taken by Michael Dayton, Mr. Condit's top aide in Washington.

"It was the congressman's staff that finally got the police interested, when a member of his staff called police on Monday, May 7, and said a constituent was missing. He called both the D.C. police and the FBI," the source said. [11]

Condit saying "I" may be a royal "I" that includes his staff acting on his behalf, which would very well be expected, but a royal "I" that is two days later and a staff aide less than the way he tells it.

Dayton supports him in a revision of history the Washington Times missed. He tells Helen Kennedy of the New York Daily News, "People are making it sound suspicious, but he's the one who called the cops", apparently unaware that it was two days after the Levys asked Condit for his help and spent the weekend begging the D.C. police to check on Chandra's apartment.

In addition, ABC News reports that Condit's office says the congressman asked the FBI to help with the investigation, but the FBI says it got involved at the request of the Washington police. A disturbing pattern was emerging of Condit's statements differing in both substance and intent from nearly every other statement made by anyone and any organization. Surely it would be more disturbing still if his statements were to start differing in substance and intent from even his own prior statements. Yet such a pattern was developing.

Condit's response of offering an award to find Chandra when told she was missing had aroused the Levy's suspicion. They examined their cell phone bills, both Bob Levy's and Chandra's bills. They had been receiving Chandra's monthly cell phone bill and paying it all along. And Chandra had used her father's cell phone when they were visiting back East over Passover because her phone's battery wasn't charged, apparently from making so many calls to her boyfriend.

Now that Chandra was missing they were looking over these cell phone bills for a phone number, a clue, as to who her boyfriend was and who she had been calling. They noticed one number that had been called several times on both bills. When Bob Levy called Condit's office on Monday to see what information they might have on looking for Chandra, he asked about the number. He tells Larry King about it:

KING: When did you start getting suspicious, Bob?

B. LEVY: Well, I knew someone who she was calling when we were back there in April was the person she was seeing. And then I saw the number on cell phone bill and our cell phone bill several times. And finally, I didn't know who it was. And of course, it's unlisted, so I finally called up Condit's office on Monday—you know, when he said to call their office to get more information about what they could do—and someone told me that was his number.

I mentioned that my daughter—I think my daughter was having an affair with the congressman, and this was the phone number, and they told me that was Condit's number.

KING: And you became immediately suspicious then that he was involved in her disappearance.

B. LEVY: Yes. [12]

This is a remarkable conversation. I think my daughter is having an affair with a congressman, do you know whose number this is? And the staffer says oh, that's Gary Condit's number? Well, all in a day's work for a congressional staff.

Bob Levy describes his reaction to Dateline:

Stone Phillips: "You were aware that she was using your cell phone to make calls back to Washington to a boyfriend."

Dr. Levy: "That's right."

Stone Phillips: "When you later looked at the phone bill, after Chandra disappeared, did you recognize the number she called?"

Dr. Levy: "No. We didn't know what number it was. We just saw it on the phone bill several times."

Stone Phillips: "Six days after she disappeared, you called Congressman Condit's office and that telephone number came up."

Dr. Levy: "Yes."

Stone Phillips: "Tell me about that call."

Dr. Levy: "I talked to one of the assistants and I mentioned that I believed my daughter was having an affair with a congressman."

Stone Phillips: "With a congressman."

Dr. Levy: "With a congressman."

Stone Phillips: "You weren't sure which one."

Dr. Levy: "No. I gave him that number and they said that it was Gary Condit's number."

Stone Phillips: "Were you surprised to hear that?"

Dr. Levy: "I was surprised."

Stone Phillips: "Did it click in your mind at that point?"

Dr. Levy: "Yes. Absolutely. That's when I knew that he was the congressman that she was seeing. [13]

and Susan Levy picks up the story in this revealing Dateline interview with Stone Phillips:

Susan Levy wanted some answers. So that night, she says she called the number on the phone bill herself.

Mrs. Levy: "I got this real airy music. It was kind of romantic music, that kind of elevator music. And I thought, gee, this is really strange."

Stone Phillips: "But no voice on it or anything?"

Mrs. Levy: "No voice on the other end. And I said 'This is Mrs. Levy and would you call me back. And I am concerned my daughter is missing.' And I did get a phone call back."

Stone Phillips: "From?"

Mrs. Levy: "From Mr. Gary Condit. 'Mrs. Levy, what can I do for you?' And I said, 'My daughter's missing. I'm very worried about her.'"

Stone Phillips: "Did you ask him what your daughter was doing calling his pager?"

Mrs. Levy. "Yes. I asked point blank, are you having an affair with my daughter?"

Stone Phillips: "And what did he say?"

Mrs. Levy: "He says, 'I'm only professionally involved with your daughter. I regard her highly. I respect her as a personal friend. And I only had a professional relationship. And 'Mr. Congressman, there seems to be a lot of late calls coming in?' 'Oh, well, we work late in the evenings here on Capitol Hill.'"

Stone Phillips: "Did he seem surprised?"

Mrs. Levy: "No."

Stone Phillips: "Or offended that you would ask whether he was having an affair with your daughter?"

Mrs. Levy: "No. He was very matter of fact. Not particularly emotional at all."

The Levys say despite the congressman's denial, they told both the D.C. police and the FBI early on of their belief that Condit was having an affair with their daughter. But for weeks, the Levys didn't tell the public.

Stone Phillips: "Why?"

Dr. Levy: "The police and FBI, the federal prosecutor said that we shouldn't really talk about the case publicly because they didn't want to harm the investigation.

Stone Phillips: "And specifically not to mention that your daughter had been involved with Congressman Condit?"

Dr. Levy: "Yes." [14]

The Newport

With Condit's office calling about a missing constituent, Washington police responded by sending officers again to check Chandra's apartment at the Newport, including Detective Ralph Durant of the district's Metropolitan Police Department. The San Francisco Chronicle quoted him:

> We just know she disappeared. We don't know how and we don't know when. We just know she is gone and we're investigating.
>
> Her bags were packed as if she were getting ready to leave. But she left everything.... We found all her identification, all the things someone would take with them leaving the house. It was all still there. [1]

Unfortunately, "bags packed as if getting ready to leave" would leave a lasting erroneous and misleading understanding for everyone. The San Francisco Chronicle described her bags as "neatly packed". The New York Daily News described her bags as "neatly packed by the door". The Modesto Bee described luggage "packed and waiting inside". The Washington Post described luggage "packed as if for travel". Dateline said the bags were "packed and ready to go". The Associated Press went so far as to say her bags were "packed for her return to the West Coast".

Even Chandra's mother, as she told the Today show, was led to understand it this way:

> Ms. LEVY: Well, we all have, you know, as she was going to go home, everything was packed, her jewelry, everything that belongs to her, jewelry, necklaces, ID cards, travel bags, and her laptop—top computer, everything was in order. And it looked like she was coming home on the airplane or, you know, ready to leave. [2]

This wasn't even close to being correct. With such a fundamental failure of the D.C. police to ascertain the condition of Chandra's apartment and belongings and communicate it to her family and the press, what chance was there that a coherent investigation into her disappearance would be initiated, or of her family to be able to provide information helpful in finding her, or of the press to provide information that would enable the public to be helpful? None, it would turn out. Tragically, this was just a harbinger of things to come.

Perhaps perception was reality for the D.C. police. The Washington Post reports that a police source told them that they initially believed that Chandra may have left the area for a few days "just to get away". Metropolitan Police Cmdr. Peter Newsham is quoted by the Washington Times as saying:

> This is an adult we are talking about. She is a very intelligent woman, and she would have the capabilities and the wherewithal to disappear if she wanted to. That is just as likely as if she came upon something tragic or terrible. [3]

There were also lesser degrees of walking out envisioned by the police. Sgt. Joe Gentile, a police spokesman, told the Washington Post, "She may have run out to run a last-minute errand when she went missing." But the perception of someone ready to leave and, oops, don't need those bags to remind me of my past remained perilously close to the forefront due to the bags neatly packed by the door attribution of her disappearance.

What would someone a bit more observant find if they had entered Chandra's apartment? Here is a description of the apartment by the landlord as reported by the Washington Post:

> She left behind a half-packed apartment in Dupont Circle. There was a suitcase almost completely packed, a few outfits hanging in the closet, a purse with credit cards, ID, a cell phone and $30 in the entryway. Her toiletries and makeup were in the bathroom, some food remained in the refrigerator, a few dirty dishes were left behind and a comforter was left in the small entryway, said the landlord, who spoke on condition of anonymity. [4]

> Her laptop was left open in the hallway nook of the tidy, whitewashed studio she rented, her landlord said. Her laptop computer was open on a makeshift desk. There were dishes in the sink and leftover pasta in the refrigerator. Several outfits hung in the closet. Her suitcase was half-packed, not far from her purse, which contained her credit cards, cell phone and money. Missing were her keys and a check for $54—a birthday gift, never cashed. [5]

Bob Franken of CNN describes further:

The landlord and building manager have said that their first entries into the apartment found a duffel bag type of luggage near the bed still untied and not completely filled as well as the canceled paperwork from her sports club contract and a laptop computer in a small, open alcove—a former broom closet converted with a desk surface and higher shelving. They also said there was the activated answering machine, with messages, and an unpacked bathroom set, including towels, toiletries and cosmetics that were not yet packed. Nothing was disheveled, according to these two eyewitnesses. [6]

WUSA accompanied Levy's own investigators into the apartment and wrote:

But we now know how things looked when police first set foot in Chandra Levy's apartment.

No signs of a struggle, no signs of foul play and no signs of Chandra Levy.

In the hallway, a cell phone and cash were found on a glass counter.

A hand bag left hanging from a cabinet door.

Next to her bed was a large suitcase. Unzipped and full of clothes.

In the kitchen there was very little in the cabinets and refrigerator. [7]

Michael Doyle of the Modesto Bee reports how Levy's private investigators, Dwayne Stanton and Joseph McCann, "peered inside the closet-turned-desk space, where Levy tapped out late-night e-mail messages on her lap-top computer, and they scanned the platform bed stuffed snugly in an alcove".

Detective Durant was quoted by Associated Press, "We found all her identification in there—driver's license, credit cards, check book, jewelry, cell phone—anything that a normal person would take out with them when they go out the street".

Chandra's diary was also found by police in her apartment, and the picture taken of her with Condit and Jennifer Baker in their first visit to his office was on display. The landlord turned over to police an April receipt from Trader Joe's in Bethesda and a page of local synagogues torn out of the phone book. Newsweek also reported her ATM card and two pairs of sneakers were in her apartment.

There is also this curious report by Michael Isikoff in the Newsweek article: "She also had downloaded discount ice-cream coupons that were found in her apartment...." This implies that Chandra had a printer with her laptop, but this is the only item ever mentioned that would indicate that.

That is what was found, but Helen Kennedy of the New York Daily News describes well what was missing:

> Missing were Levy's size 4 gold signet ring, set with two diamond chips and her intertwined initials—a $416 custom-designed gift from her mother—her apartment key and a thin gold bracelet.
>
> Levy's aunt Linda Zamsky said her niece proudly showed off the congressman's gift at Passover in April 2001. Zamsky described it as a "chain bracelet, a very nice piece of jewelry, double clasp. [8]

In addition to her new bracelet from Condit and her cherished signet ring from her mother inscribed with an intertwined 'CL', the police say her keys were missing, but intriguingly, her father says she left behind her regular key chain with pepper spray. [9] Bob Levy had always urged Chandra to carry pepper spray on her key chain, and she did. But not when she disappeared.

Chandra was a very security conscious woman. Her friend Lisa Bracken from Modesto told the Washington Post: "She was always bugging me to buy pepper spray." She added to CNN: "She always carried Mace and was very aware of her surroundings."

Jeff Jardine of the Modesto Bee writes of how security conscious her landlord thought she was:

> Her landlord in Washington, a Bay Area resident and former staff worker for a California congressman, recalled stopping by once to pick up something that he had left in the apartment.
>
> He knocked. She asked who was at the door before she opened it a crack. She then closed the door, while the landlord remained in the hallway. She retrieved the item, opened the door and carefully turned it over. [10]

Julie Danielson, Chandra's former guidance counselor at Davis High School in Modesto, recalled to CNN:

> Chandra took part in the Explorer Program, which was connected with the police academy.

"She was trained in things a person would be trained if they were entering the police academy, so she was street smart, definitely street smart." [11]

Chandra didn't appear to have taken anything more than keys to get back in her apartment. Had she been abducted in her own apartment building, perhaps on her way to do laundry or take out the trash? Chandra lived in apartment 315 of the Newport at 1260 21st St. NW, near Dupont Circle, on the third floor of a ten story building with a 24-hour guard. Residents must be buzzed in the front door by the front desk, and there was a state-of-the-art security system with cameras recording to videotapes.

Laura Lang as resident essayist describes the Newport in the Washington City Paper:

> Had Levy's parents not notified authorities of Chandra's disappearance, few in the Newport might have realized she was missing.
>
> Residents and building employees say they didn't see her around much anyway. The Newport—like many large buildings in D.C.—is a place where it's easy to keep to yourself. Made up of 156 condos, the 10-floor building is home to about 200 people, more than half of whom rent their apartments. Age and ethnicity vary, but to judge from my own morning and evening trips in and out of the building, there's a heavy proportion of young, working singles-men and women in their 20s and 30s who work or go to school and have busy lives.
>
> A condo association meets regularly in the office of the building manager, located on the top floor. There are few other communal activities, even fewer rooms in which to hold them. A pool sits on the roof of the building, where some take quick dips after work or lounge on the weekend. And there's a lobby on the main floor, right next to a check-in desk staffed 24 hours a day, but most people just pass through.
>
> Not even laundry is the social activity that it is in many buildings. The Newport has small laundry rooms located on each floor, rather than one big one-which limits interaction significantly. The building is staffed by friendly, efficient people who often strike up conversations with residents, but it's the sort of place where you could disappear if you wanted to—and maybe even if you didn't want to—and escape notice. [12]

Edeline describes the Newport facilities as well in his online interview:

> "The front door is operated by the desk person. Tenants do not have keys or cards to the front door. They must be 'buzzed' in by the desk person. There is

a back door to the building, anyone can walk out the door, but they must have a key to get back in. Once out the glass back door, you are in a gated patio area and you must have a key to get in and out of the back gate. Otherwise, one would have to climb over the back fence."

Asked about what would happen if the desk person took a break, Edeline said, "there was no break...just bathroom break...but that is a very good question...they had to wait outside the door...or until someone went out....they'd walk in....it was annoying at times....

"Your back door question....there are actually two different sets of stairways to get to the condo (plus the elevators). One of the stairways exits in the mailbox area...which is next to the back door. So...yes, you would not pass the desk person to go to the back door if you were descending the steps. However, I really don't think that anything happened to Chandra in the building. But that is my opinion."

"There is a laundryroom on every floor in the Newport. No key is needed. It is very small...just room for a washer and a dryer....and a space for you to stand...it is just down the hall from the condo....one apartment away."

Asked if there was a garbage chute: "Garbage chute: very small room next to laundry room...very small chute...you can't have a big sack...and believe me....it would be impossible to get a body down that chute....can hardly get a big bag of garbage down it...in my opinion." [13]

The trash chute was across the hallway from her apartment, and the laundry room one apartment away. If she had gone out to do laundry or take out the trash, she hadn't gone far.

The mystery of Chandra's disappearance was baffling, but theories would be springing forth, disappointing ones from the police that Chandra just wanted to get away from it all, wild ones on the internet, and wilder still from the tabloids. National Enquirer posed theirs in "Chandra Mystery Solved", and in my analysis of their article I touch upon points found in other theories floated on the internet.

A Walk in the Park

While it has been pointed out that Condit's apartment is halfway to Klingle Mansion from the Newport, and that it is possible that she was to meet Condit there and then go on to Klingle Mansion, NE has her making the two mile walk directly there. They show pictures of the route, and it has two bridge crossings, one a pedestrian bridge but within the shadows of a railroad trestle, then onto narrower and narrower trails till Klingle Mansion is reached.

I didn't find that prospect realistic at all. It's possible, but the trip couldn't be for romantic purposes, she'd end up way too sweaty. If it was something short and sweet, like picking up a frequent fliers airline ticket, and Condit told her Carolyn was home and they had to meet elsewhere, I can see it, and can see that she might enjoy the walk there and back given that she had the time since she had not been working for a week. But it's a stretch, and the meeting time would have to be mid-afternoon to have time to get there leaving after 1 p.m., and then back at a safe time. To be picked up shortly after 1 p.m. to go there is one thing, to walk there to meet somebody at a place you have to look up on a map just doesn't make sense.

Klingle Mansion

NE describes Klingle Mansion as a storage facility. Instead, it is the Rock Creek Park administration office. It appears NE deliberately downplayed the nature of the building to make it seem spookier, for example, saying that anyone stopping there to get supplies would be gone by 4 p.m., instead of bringing into the story the complexity that the Klingle Mansion is the park office and is closed on Monday's and Tuesday's. This was a Tuesday afternoon. There was no one to get supplies that afternoon at any time, so NE even screwed that up.

The Comforter

Consider this little gem of logic. According to NE, the comforter was found tossed in a heap inside Chandra's front door. Unbelievably, they say it indicates to investigators that Chandra couldn't have left after signing off on the internet, that she washed and dried the comforter in a laundry room a few feet down the hall first and left later in the afternoon. Could anyone be so stupid as to think a person can't wash and dry a comforter while they're on the computer all morning? That they have to sign off the internet before they can put a comforter in a washer down the hall? I am not making this up. They point out the laundry room is a few feet down the hall, and that the comforter tossed in the doorway proves she washed and dried it after signing off the internet at 1 p.m. With logic like that, and what we've seen from the DC police, it's no wonder this crime is unsolved.

Baskin-Robbins

NE points out that the Baskin Robbins ice cream store is 30 feet from the park entrance off the street she would walk from her apartment, Connecticut Ave., and that she also looked it up as well as Klingle Mansion. They suggest she bought a pint of ice cream to take to Klingle Mansion while she waited, and to share with who she was meeting. They do not explicitly suggest that Condit is the one she met there, but otherwise NE refers to him throughout the article and implies it.

I suggest the NE geniuses who came up with this buy a pint of ice cream on an 82 degree day and see how far they get through the park to Klingle Mansion before it melts. On the other hand, Baskin-Robbins is near the intersection of Calvert and Connecticut, and Condit lives near the intersection of Calvert. Baskin-Robbins is a short walk from his apartment down Calvert.

The Web Sites

NE reports that Chandra looked at four media sites that had articles about President Bush's luncheon with members of Congress, and that all the articles she looked at noted that Condit had a seat of honor at the President's table. This suggests that some of the sites she looked at were based on a search for Condit.

NE then goes on to talk about a web site that a DC police insider told them that Chandra visited, a site about breast implant and reduction surgery. They report the police insider said she downloaded dozens of pictures of breasts of different sizes, and that the police didn't know what it meant. It concludes that some investigators believe Chandra didn't think her breasts were nice enough for Condit, and that she was considering breast implant surgery to make him happy.

First, if she did visit that site, then it's apparent that it's one of the "evidentiary" sites the police didn't list, and possibly the reason they didn't list it was that it was too prurient for them to discuss in newspapers. In reality, it could have been significant in helping determine her state of mind, or it could be a totally baseless rumor NE printed. This is the pain of dealing with leaked police information through biased journalists or worse. Still, it's possible this information is from the DC police.

Second, leave it to NE to say that Chandra found out Condit was a breast man and that they made it breast implant surgery rather than breast reduction surgery, much more lurid to get implants to make him happy versus getting breast reduction surgery to make her more mobile for the strenuous physical training of her chosen career as an FBI agent. Further, Flammini reports that Condit was bragging about her breasts, like melons he said, which suggests that he wasn't complaining to her. As for using that or any other excuse or imagined excuse for breaking up with her in the two weeks after she asked him about Jennifer Thomas before she disappeared, anything is possible, but it's hard to imagine how she would take it seriously. There's just no justification for this at all.

The Sanitized Apartment

In a continuation of unexcelled logic, NE writes that since Chandra's apartment had nothing that linked her to the killer, no newspaper clippings, no pictures, notes, love letters, nothing, this has led investigators to believe the killer used Chandra's keys to return to her apartment and remove any evidence.

The killer didn't remove her diary. He didn't remove her laptop computer or clear it of a trail of web surfing. He didn't remove the picture on her desk of her and Condit and Jennifer Baker. What did the killer sanitize? National Enquirer assumes there were other momentos that must have been removed, and that the killer returned and completed the non-traceable disappearance. A mystery solved, uninhibited by logic.

The killer also didn't remove the Newport security videotapes, but neither did the D.C. police. A 911 call on Tuesday, frantic parents and landlord pleading with the Newport manager to check Chandra's apartment, Dr. Levy begging the police to check Chandra's apartment, a congressman's office asking them to check on Chandra's apartment, none of this was enough for the Newport manager to pull the videotapes and make them available to the police or for the police to even ask for them.

They recycled every 10 days, and pulling the tapes when the police deigned to actually look at Chandra's apartment—a call from a congressman's office cuts it, missing person reports from California doesn't cut it for D.C. police apparently—would have still had on them whatever was recorded on May 1, from those early morning hours of a scream and a 911 call to afternoon when Chandra logged off the internet.

But they weren't pulled; privacy law paralysis? police incompetence? management more concerned about a lawsuit than a missing resident? conspiracy? coverup? just a refusal to take a missing woman seriously?

All have been conjectured. All are egregious. The police made the best of their failure to investigate though. They came and retrieved the tapes more than a week later, after they had finally started taking Chandra's disappearance more seriously, a disturbing pattern that would continue for months to come.

The tapes overwritten by then? No problem. Police found nothing useful in the "grainy tapes" of the surveillance cameras anyway. [14] Chief Charles Ramsey of the D.C. police told ABC This Week:

> There is a video system there. The tape quality is very, very poor. They do tape over the different tapes during the day.

> It was a week before we even knew about the missing person, so unfortunately some of the evidence that we would have had, had we known sooner, we won't have available to us. [15]

The security tapes of the Newport are probably the biggest loss due to police inaction. How could the Newport management have let their surveillance tapes be overwritten when a tenant was reported to them as missing, a 911 call made from the Newport, a missing person report filed, and the police came and looked at the apartment? How could the police not retrieve the tapes as part of their investigation.

What investigation, you might ask. Good question.

Investigation

The Levys were mentioning a congressman boyfriend to the D.C. police from their very first call to report her missing on Saturday, May 5. The Washington Times reports: "The Levys were somewhat brushed off by the police. They didn't get very far at first," said a source with access to police and FBI investigators.

Chandra's friends knew about a mystery boyfriend with political connections, such as the "...My man will be coming back here when Congress starts up again. I'm looking forward to seeing him." e-mail. But despite their suspicions, the Levys didn't air them publically. Susan Levy would answer all questions about the political boyfriend being Gary Condit by saying "that as far as she knows, the relationship between her daughter and Condit was strictly professional." [1]

As far as Jennifer Baker knew, her friend's boyfriend was in the FBI, and this made things all the more confusing for the Levys and police investigators. The San Francisco Chronicle talked to her:

> One friend in Washington, D.C, was a fellow graduate student who worked as an intern in Condit's office last fall.
>
> "I find it unbelievable that she has just disappeared," said Jennifer Baker of Sacramento, who spent yesterday e-mailing flyers to friends to post in Washington and other cities.
>
> ...Investigators are trying to reach a mysterious possible boyfriend that she began dating in late December. She never mentioned his existence to her parents and only talked of him in passing to Baker and other D.C. friends.
>
> "She once said she was dating this guy from the FBI, but then she started talking about something else," Baker said. "She never brought him up again (in later phone conversations or e-mail exchanges). I wish I had thought to ask." [2]

But Jennifer found more than Chandra's disappearance unbelievable. Arthur Santana of the Washington Post reports:

Baker said Levy mentioned in late November a new boyfriend who worked with the FBI and last mentioned him in an e-mail in January. Baker said the two never talked in detail about the man. "She didn't tell me much about him," Baker said. "It just didn't seem important at the time."

Police spokesman Sgt. Joe Gentile declined to say whether police were searching for such a man, and Executive Assistant Police Chief Terrance W. Gainer said he was unaware that Levy had a boyfriend. "People need to know that kind of thing," Baker said. "Should they be looking for a certain guy?" [3]

Baker delayed starting a new job with California Assemblywoman Jenny Oropeza for a couple of weeks when Chandra disappeared to organize rallies in Modesto and Sacramento to publicize the search. "We were all pretty traumatized," she told the Modesto Bee.

If the police were confused about a secret boyfriend, they weren't the only ones who thought Chandra had just wandered off. Linda Zamsky told Fox News: "At first when she went missing, I thought maybe she had gone off on her own," Zamsky said of her thoughts when she first heard the 24-year-old had disappeared. "We still think that someone abducted her."

But by Wednesday, May 9, when the Levys would have been heading to Los Angeles for Chandra's graduation at USC, they instead got in contact with a local organization that helps locate missing loved ones, the Carole Sund/Carrington Memorial Reward Foundation. Susan Levy told the Washington Post that she had taken a card from their booth at a local festival a while back, but "Little did I ever know that I would be in a situation of having to call them."

Also by Wednesday the police, responding to Chandra's parents calls asking about Condit, first questioned him. Helen Kennedy of the New York Daily News reports that Condit told the police that Chandra was a friend who had visited his apartment and then "refused to elaborate." Niles Lathem of the New York Post reports how police sources describe the first questioning of Condit on May 9:

He initially said the grad student visited his D.C. apartment four or five times, but denied having an affair with her.

Condit, 53, whose wife lives at their California home, has daughters about the same age as Levy, who disappeared 19 days ago. He was trying to help her get a job in the FBI or Justice Department when she disappeared.

Asked if cops would search Condit's D.C. residence, police spokesman Kervin Johnson said, "For what reason? This is a missing-persons case." [4]

Police sources told the Washington Times that "Mr. Condit answered most questions about Miss Levy, 'but he found a way to avoid answering one question'—whether the two had been intimate."

Whether Jennifer Baker had been offered an unpaid internship as cover for Chandra's relationship with Condit or not, they had walked into Condit's office together, but the New York Daily News reports: "His staff said they thought Condit had met Levy only once or twice in passing when she visited a friend who worked in his office." The Washington Post quotes Michael Dayton on this cover story:

> Mike Dayton, Condit's spokesman in Washington, said Levy first came by the office in early October with Baker, who was an intern in Condit's office. Since then, Dayton estimated, Levy returned to Condit's office six times, usually to ask for things like White House tour tickets, or to ask for schedules of events on Capitol Hill. He said the last visit was about five weeks ago. [5]

That visit five weeks before the May 17 date of this Washington Post quote would seem to be during the April 7 to April 22 Easter-Passover recess for Congress, establishing the last visit to the office when neither Condit or Baker was there. Did she really make that visit? Who did she talk to? Dayton would likely want us to believe she was looking for yet another White House tour ticket. Was Dayton there and saw her? Who was there when she was supposed to have visited with neither Condit nor Jennifer there, who made the entry that she was there, and when?

And although the Levys had never met Gary or Carolyn Condit, Carolyn Condit was telling reporters that the Levys were friends of her husband. Lynne Hostein of KTLA-TV reports that "Condit denies any romantic involvement with Levy. He and his wife describe Chandra as a good friend." Condit was also telling his colleagues that Chandra was just a friend. The Washington Times:

> The Capitol Hill newspaper Roll Call yesterday reported that Mr. Condit is telling his congressional colleagues he did not have a romantic relationship with Miss Levy. The newspaper quoted Rep. Collin C. Peterson, Minnesota Democrat, as saying that Mr. Condit "told me there was no relationship" with the missing woman. [6]

The Washington Times in quoting Chief Ramsey: "It would have been very helpful had we known that earlier on," Chief Ramsey said in an Aug. 7 interview on WTOP radio.

It also would have been helpful to tell the police that Chandra was taking a train home, if indeed she had ever told him that. The police didn't seem to make any special mention of the possibility she had been on a train. There's nothing about a relationship in knowing she was planning on taking a train home, so why withhold this critical information from the Levys and the police until an interview with Connie Chung months later?

Chief Ramsey told Gloria Borger of CBS Face The Nation:

> BORGER: You have her computer. You have her cell phone records. We've all heard that there was a lot of activity on her computer that morning of her disappearance, sometime between 9:30 and 1:00, that she visited a lot of travel web sites. What can you tell us about that? Did she book a flight somewhere?
>
> RAMSEY: No, we don't have anything that shows that she booked a flight. And we've checked flights, we've checked rail, we've checked all means of methods of transportation. And nothing that we've come up with yet. [7]

The Washington Times:

> Police said they could not find where she purchased an airline ticket to return home. "There's no plane ticket, no train ticket, no bus ticket," said a police source familiar with the investigation. "We don't know how she was going to get home." [8]

This doesn't sound like the police were told she was taking a train home. Would the police have investigated more aggressively had Condit told them what he told reporters in interviews three months later?

The Washington Times reports that it is a common practice among police agencies to not immediately pursue competent adults who go missing, absent signs of foul play. Instead, the police told Susan Levy "it looks like there may not be a crime committed here." Just the very idea of telling her that should be a crime.

Chief Gainer told WUSA of their thinking:

"There are several conventional theories," Gainer said. "One is that she committed suicide. The other is that something criminal has happened to her. Another may be that she wanted to go off on her own and assume a new identity. And I suppose that the last possibility is that she has been injured or incapacitated in some way and that she does not know who she is. So we continue to explore each one of those."

"Our minds are open to any of the possibilities and a review of her financial records, her telephone records, computer records, friends, and neighbors and family have not given us particular information as to where she is at," Gainer added. [9]

However, there was no sign of violence, so to them there was no crime. And without a crime...Gainer told the Sacramento Bee: "We don't have a crime. Without a crime, you don't have a suspect." One symptom of that attitude was that "Levy was an adult and could have just decided to go off on an unannounced trip." [10] A thought more ominous to a serious investigation of a missing woman was that Chandra had staged her own disappearance.

Presumably, the reasoning is that a person has a right to "disappear" if they want. When a person is missing but has left behind every worldly possession except the key to their home, then this alleged reasoning flies in the face of reality.

1. The person could not work or reside legally anywhere without identification.

2. A legal change to another identification would also require current identification.

3. There is no reasonable basis to presume that it is infringing upon a person's privacy to "not be found" if they don't want to be by assumimg they've taken up the lifestyle of an illegal alien.

In short, a missing woman under these circumstances should be presumed missing against their will unless there is a reasonable indication the woman doesn't want to be found. The signifigance? J. N. Sbranti of the Modesto Bee captured a quote from Stanislaus County Sheriff Les Weidman immediately after Chandra was reported missing that epitomizes the signifigance:

"We don't want there to be a loss of momentum" in pursuing the case, Weidman said. He said that is why his office is urging Washington police to make this investigation a priority this weekend. "Time is critical, and we understand that." [11]

And to help Washington police make investigating Chandra's disappearance a priority, he sent a detective, Mario Cisneros, to Washington to help. And like a rare bad McCloud episode, Cisneros found he wasn't in Kansas anymore, or New Mexico, or California, or anywhere else that treats a missing women with urgency. Michael Doyle of the Modesto Bee reports this sad state of affairs:

> East Coast detectives are bearing down on the disappearance of Chandra Ann Levy of Modesto, and West Coast officers have been advised to butt out.
>
> While the FBI and a 31-year veteran of the Washington Metropolitan Police Department are tracking leads, they've advised the Stanislaus County Sheriff's Department not to get involved in the Levy case.
>
> "We're treating this as a critical missing persons case," Washington police Detective Ralph Durant said Monday. "That means she disappeared under suspicious circumstances."
>
> ...Durant, a big, pony-tailed man who has handled some high-profile cases, made it clear Monday that his department doesn't "really need" the hands-on help of Central Valley law enforcement officials. Durant said that while he welcomed outside information, he couldn't use the Stanislaus County Sheriff's Department homicide detective who traveled to Washington over the weekend to offer aid.
>
> Washington detectives instead asked the sheriff's office to provide all of its notes and documents. These include transcripts of interviews done since Friday with Levy's parents and friends, copies of cellular phone records received from the Levy family and notes on possible sources.
>
> "They told us that if they need any help, they'll give us a call," Sheriff's Department spokesman Kelly Huston said.
>
> Sheriff's Detective Mario Cisneros, who arrived in the capital Saturday, was simply told to return home.
>
> Washington police also asked the Sheriff's Department to stop gathering information on Levy.
>
> The repudiation of local help surprised sheriff's officials, who according to Huston, had decided to send Cisneros to Washington because "we had a difficult time initially establishing a relationship with D.C. Metro."

Face-to-face talks did not yield a more welcoming response.

"I don't think we have any better relationship now than we did when we talked to them on the phone last week," Huston said. "(Cisneros) tried to establish a rapport with the agency there, and he really had no luck in doing that."

Huston termed the lack of cooperation between the two departments highly unusual. He said the lead investigating department typically welcomes assistance by a victim's hometown detectives.

"There are things we think we can do here in Modesto and we're surprised they do not want to take advantage of this resource," Huston said. "In cases like this, there's a lot of work to be done in the hometown." [12]

Helen Kennedy of the New York Daily News reports further:

"We are going to interview anyone who knew her," said Washington police spokesman Sgt. Joe Gentile, who refused to elaborate.

Cops in Levy's hometown of Modesto, Calif., said something was odd about the case because Washington police had told them to stop investigating.

"There's obviously a lot of clues to be uncovered here in California—who she talked to, who she may have dated—but they've chosen to decline our help," said Stanislaus County sheriff's spokesman Kelly Huston.

"They've basically said they don't want us to do any interviews. That's got us very perplexed," he said. [13]

The D.C. police may have stopped the Modesto police from investigating, but they couldn't stop the Levys from being suspicious about Chandra leaving her apartment without any identification. Amazingly, she had told them that her secret boyfriend instructed her not to carry identification when meeting him, something more along the lines of an order to a secret agent than a girlfriend. But Condit was on the House Intelligence Committee and he was married, and he did demand secrecy from his other mistress, Anne Marie Smith, but still, it is truly a bizarre demand if and when he indeed did make it.

What if he didn't? It would be extraordinary for her to tell her parents that her secret boyfriend didn't want her to be identified, even if it was true. How does one respond to that? For that and other reasons, the Levys were accused of making this up themselves to cast suspicion on Condit because her identification was left in her apartment. But that seems even more odd for the Levys to dream up. How shall we get the police to look at Condit? I know, he wouldn't let her take her wallet with her when she met him. Who has an imagination like that? Certainly seems to be more spymaster material than that of distraught parents.

Stranger still is that for the most part one would expect her not to be carrying her identification on Tuesday afternoon. Police determined that she left her purse at home when she went to the gym. She went to the gym in the evenings, and had worked out the previous evening, but she may have been on her way there later. Most people don't carry their wallet when they go for a run or walk. While many people drive everywhere they go and need their driver's license, Chandra didn't have a car in D.C. and took the Metro train whereever she went beyond walking distance.

However, the Washington Times reports that police no longer credit a report from Linda Zamsky that Condit told Chandra not to carry identification when meeting him. The timing of this coincides with this statement from Condit to Newsweek:

> CONDIT: ...The one that brings to mind is the one about this elaborate scheme of how you get around and that I would ask someone not to carry identification is just totally absurd. The police—they know that Chandra every time she went somewhere, she has a bag or a backpack. They know that to be the case, so it's just totally absurd that they would suggest that I would ask someone to not carry identification. For the life of me I can't even think what reason that would be for. [14]

In fact, with what she was wearing when found, it would be odd if she did have identification with her. But how would the police know that every time Chandra went somewhere, she carried a bag or backpack? And why did they tell the Washington Times they no longer believe Linda Zamsky when Condit denied the no-id rule to Newsweek four months after Chandra disappeared?

One reason for having identification Tuesday afternoon would have been to cash her $54 birthday gift check from her godparents two weeks earlier. It was not found in her apartment, but her ATM card was, so she couldn't have been depositing it using an ATM machine. It's possible she had the check and was going to deposit it with a teller but never got the chance.

It was Tuesday and she would need to deposit it for it to clear when she would presumedly close her bank account Friday or Saturday before leaving. She had had the check for two weeks and it would have provided some spending money on a train trip home. Others have said they think it just got eaten up in a washer, forgotten tucked away in a magazine that she threw away, or otherwise lost.

She probably put it in her purse at her godmother's. Why would she take it out to be able to lose it? Given that the godparents live in the area, she could have intended to cash the check at a branch of their bank. Was there a branch of their bank in the DuPont Circle area?

Did she have a bank account while she was in DC? When was her last deposit? Had she closed her bank account or talked to them about closing it? Was her ATM card from that bank or was she using a nationwide ATM network to withdraw money and writing checks from a bank back home?

She had only been told her internship had ended a week before. Had she received her last paycheck from the Bureau of Prisons? If not, when was it sent out? Was she waiting on it?

Was she still receiving mail at the Newport? Had she filed a mail forwarding form at the Post Office with an effective date?

None of these questions have been addressed publically by the police or the Levys. The answers should be made available to the Levys if not the public.

Also a puzzle is the comforter beside the door. Many think that it was in her entranceway because she dropped it when she answered the door and was attacked and presumably kidnapped, this despite that she wouldn't even open the door for her landlord.

The suggestion is that it must have been someone she knew very well to open the door, but that suggestion assumes that in addition to that someone she knew well somehow getting into the building, that she had the comforter wrapped around her when she answered the door, a strange thought, and that she and it got separated as she was pulled out the door. Easier said than done.

Actually, she was quite adept at working on her laptop sitting on the floor. That sounds uncomfortable, but a picture of Chandra sitting on the floor with her laptop at home shows that she looks very comfortable doing it, actually bending forward with it on the floor rather than on her lap.

She could have just sat there on the comforter in the hallway within cord range of the plugins in the nook where the laptop was set when she wasn't using it. Then the comforter would always be laying there when she sat down with her laptop.

The comforter was beside the door, but the bags weren't. Chandra had told her landlord on Saturday that she was moving out the next weekend, on Sunday she was no longer sure. Was she thinking of moving out sooner and had packed most of her clothes already, or were they really just never unpacked?

Anne Marie was told not to open Condit's closet in late March when she visited him. Chandra's neighbors didn't hear her stirring around her apartment until the last week before she disappeared. That's when Gary Condit came back from California and a five to ten minute call was made to his condo when he said he wasn't there. Were those clothes packed from his closet when she found out Carolyn was on her way to Washington?

It could be possible that the partially packed bags in her apartment were from clearing her stuff out of Condit's apartment on Thursday or Friday, just before she called her landlord on Saturday and told him there was no longer any reason to stay in Washington.

But the day had arrived that was the reason she was headed home, her graduation at USC, and she wasn't there. Instead of attending her graduation, Robert and Susan Levy offered a $15,000 reward for information on her disappearance. Congressman Gary Condit contributed an additional $10,000 from campaign funds to the reward with the written statement: "Chandra is a great person and a good friend. We hope she is found safe and sound." [15]

He wasn't talking to reporters, he wasn't even going to be talking to his other mistress who hadn't disappeared, Anne Marie. Anne Marie filed this affadavit:

> On or about May 9, 2001, Mr. Condit called me and said, "I may be in trou-
> ble. I may have to disappear for a while. Don't call me for a few days, I'll call

you. Or, if you do call me, don't identify yourself and leave a very short message. Don't tell anyone about this phone call and don't talk to anybody about me if you hear my name. Everything is OK with you and me."

Mr. Condit called only sporadically after that. [16]

Anne Marie told Rita Cosby of Fox News:

"I said, 'Well, are you in trouble? Is it your job? Is it your family?' And he said, 'No, none of that, but I think I may be in some trouble.'"[17]

Jodi Hernandez of KOVR asked Condit about these startling statements:

J: A couple of women have come forward. One in particular, Ann Marie Smith, has gone public, done numerous interviews. She stated in one of the interviews that you, you called her and told her that you were in trouble and that you may have to disappear for awhile.

C: That never occurred. You have to question Anne Marie Smiths' motives. Her motives is to sell a story to a tabloid, that's what she did. And for you to embrace that as just regular news story is a little questionable to me.

J: I'm trying to set the record straight here. You're saying that that in fact did not?

C: Did not occur.

J: You did not?

C: I did not have that conversation with her. [18]

"I may be in trouble". "I may have to disappear". It turns out the Levys aren't the only ones with a vivid imagination. Pretty strong stuff, and it so happens very prescient of Anne Marie if this conversation did not occur. Condit would disappear, to the cave country of Luray.

Stonewalling

The D.C. police, apparently deciding a week was long enough to see if a body showed up, made a return visit to Chandra's apartment on Monday May 14 for "any possible forensic evidence". [1] They retrieved Chandra's diary, laptop computer, cell phone records and the Newport security videotapes.

The 10 day recycling period of the security tapes was just expiring from the time the Levys first reported Chandra missing to the D.C. police on Saturday May 5. It had long expired from when she disappeared on Tuesday May 1. The failure, even refusal, of the Newport manager to help the parents and landlord and save the tapes for the police to deal with Chandra's disappearance in the days following a scream and a 911 call would haunt any efforts to determine what happened to Chandra. Was there something on those tapes that somebody didn't want to be seen?

With the D.C. police rebuffing help from the Modesto police, ordering them to turn over anything they had and cease investigating while telling Dr. and Mrs. Levy nothing, the Levys were outraged. The Washington Post quotes Jennifer Baker:

> "They are fuming at the lack of cooperation, and they want some answers," Jennifer Baker said of Chandra Ann Levy's parents, Susan and Robert Levy. "They have no idea what's going on with the investigation." [2]

They flew in to Washington on Tuesday May 15, telling the Modesto Bee:

> "I'm going to get some answers, and I hope they are doing their job. If they are not, we're going to find out, and we're going to get somebody to do the job," Susan Levy said. "We just want to get this case solved and to bring our daughter home alive." [3]

Susan Levy told MSNBC that she encourages Condit to "share what he does know" about Chandra's disappearance and would not rule out that he had something to do with it. This set the press off in a tizzy and before the day was out she told the Modesto Bee:

> Reporters ask leading and "tricky" questions and sometimes the media misrepresents what she says. "I haven't accused the congressman of anything. Everybody is thinking I'm making accusations, but I haven't."

> "I didn't say my daughter was having a relationship. I don't know anything yet that is to be publicly said." [4]

Condit wasn't talking, but his staff was. Michael Lynch, Condit's California chief of staff, volunteered that at about the time of Chandra's disappearance, Condit's wife Carolyn was staying in Washington with him to attend a congressional spouses' luncheon, and that as far as he knew she had never met Chandra. [5] Michael Dayton, Condit's Washington chief of staff, helped distribute posters and said "I just wish there was more we could do." [6]

Unbelievably, no poster was on display at the Washington Sports Club where Chandra was last seen. Michael Doyle and J.N. Sbranti of the Modesto Bee report on one neighborhood activist who couldn't believe it:

> A 31-year-old public relations specialist who lives across the street from Levy's 10-story condominium building said Monday that she's been disappointed in the lack of neighborhood publicity about Levy's disappearance.

> Susan, who asked that her last name not be used, said the Police Department's missing posters were themselves missing from some obvious locations—including the Connecticut Avenue gym where Levy was last seen.

> The woman said she asked the gym's receptionist over the weekend where the posters were; the gym manager had the posters but hadn't put them up yet.

> "I said, 'I can't believe you don't have one up,'" Susan said. "That's ridiculous."

> The poster still wasn't up at the Washington Sports Club gym Monday morning. Gym officials referred all questions to their New York headquarters, which could not be reached for comment.

> On her own, Susan distributed posters throughout the Dupont Circle neighborhood where Levy moved during the fall. [7]

Helen Kennedy reports in the New York Daily News that friends described Chandra as "a careful person who was afraid to walk the streets alone and preferred policy to parties". She kept her relationship "a deep, dark secret" according to Sven Jones, her friend at the Bureau of Prisons who she confided in most.

Ironically, the Washington police brought in the FBI to help find Chandra and the mystery boyfriend who she had told Jennifer Baker worked in the FBI. The FBI and police said the FBI assisting in a joint investigation was not unusual, that the District of Columbia is under the jurisdiction of the federal government, and that they provide assistance with forensic evidence in district cases.

Whether they considered it unusual that a missing woman had a boyfriend in the political world that she kept so secret it worried her friends was not addressed publically, but they were provided the e-mails from the friends in California that Chandra kept in touch with.

These friends provided e-mails that indicated her boyfriend was affiliated with Congress and "took care of her plane ticket" for a trip to California for school. Michael Doyle followed up on that in the Modesto Bee by noting:

> In discussing how her apparent boyfriend paid for her air travel, Chandra Levy did not specify whether public or private funds were used for purchasing the airline ticket. It is a violation of congressional rules to use public funding for private purposes. It also establishes a potential public-interest connection to what might otherwise be deemed an essentially private matter. [8]

He later reported:

> "Chandra was a very practical young lady, and she didn't need frivolous things, (but) she was going back for her testing in November (or) December," Zamsky recalled. "So he supposedly bought her airline tickets for one of those trips or both of those trips back."

> Condit's campaign treasury did not report paying for cross-country air travel during November or December, though his House office account did report paying for Condit to fly from San Francisco to Washington on Dec. 14.

> But besides campaign and House office funds, House members also enjoy access to frequent-flier miles accumulated in the course of congressional travel.

House members can give the frequent-flier miles to whomever they want, without any need to make a public report. Condit's trips home to his district amount to more than 100,000 frequent-flier miles a year.

One former Condit employee, speaking on condition of anonymity, told The Bee that it was her understanding that the congressman gave his friends frequent-flier miles accumulated in the course of his congressional travel. [9]

Although Doyle allowed for the possibilty that Chandra had legally been given frequent-flier miles to use in her round trip between Washington and Sacramento for her finals in December, he pointed out that Condit's office account had paid for Condit to fly from San Francisco to Washington on December 14.

December 14, 2000 was a Thursday. Condit likely was already home for Christmas, but if he wasn't yet, he surely was not flying from San Francisco to Washington on a Thursday. But Chandra was.

Chandra had written in her e-mail to a friend as reported by the Modesto Bee:

"My short trip to California wasn't much fun, I was sick when I was in Sacramento, and I only got to go home for one night before I flew back to D.C.," Levy wrote. "The nice thing is that the man I'm seeing took care of my plane ticket for me!" [10]

She was only home one night for that trip back to take her finals in Sacramento. What night was that? Her dad had taken a video of her that night and joked as narrator that "Chandra told us all about her adventures in D.C., the Bureau of Prisons, and her congressman friend". [11] Larry King saw that video and remarked to the Levys in an interview:

Did you know that she was having an affair? There was a phone conversation. Dr. Levy, you are heard on videotape—I think on December 13—talking about your congressman friend. [12]

Chandra was home for one night on December 13, returning to Washington on December 14, the same Thursday that Condit's office account paid for him to fly back to Washington from San Francisco. Condit frequently flied from Washington to San Francisco on Thursdays, not the other way around.

Was it Condit that flew back on Thursday, or illegal use of Congressional funds to fly Chandra back? Michael Doyle handed a gift wrapped ethics violation to Congress, the FBI, and the D.C. police to investigate. What did they do with it?

Nothing. It was ignored. Instead, fellow members of Congress had been led to believe Condit flew back religiously to Modesto to tend to a sick wife. A former Blue Dog Democrat, a group of conservative Democrats that Condit co-founded, was quoted by Timothy Burger of the New York Daily News:

> "It makes you hurt to see this going on," said ex-Rep. Bill Brewster of Oklahoma, who called some of the stories linking Condit to the missing woman "a real stretch."
>
> Married at 19 and a father of two, Condit has spent years nursing his chronically ill wife.
>
> "She's had a real battle," said Brewster, who also was a Blue Dog. "I know Gary's taken her to hospitals in a lot of different places." [13]

Granted, he was nicknamed "Mr. Blow Dry" by some in Congress for his always perfect hair and smoothness, but his constituents in San Joaquin Valley didn't believe Condit had anything improper to do with Chandra either. Typical were comments such as this in the Modesto Bee:

> "Nothing in this world would make me believe he had an affair. He's a big family man," said Jacque MacDonald of Merced.
>
> She got to know Condit, 53, a decade ago after her daughter, Debra Whitlock, was murdered in Modesto. The congressman posted a reward to help catch the killer.
>
> "I admire, trust and respect Gary, and I'll support him to the end," MacDonald said. [14]

But the Levys flew in and did tell the police they suspected he was the mystery politician who was their missing daughter's boyfriend and, as DePaulo pointed out on Crossfire, "in a missing person case, by definition, you have to focus on the people closest to the person." And as Paul Katz pointed out to Larry King:

> Well, Larry, I guess that the thing that has been nudging and bothering me is that the police department had the knowledge of the affair with Mr. Condit

and my niece Chandra from the 15th of May…and they had this information, and yet, you know, one gets the feeling that it was suppressed, for whatever reason, for such a long period of time and that's been very frustrating. [15]

Indeed, Niles Lathem was reporting in the New York Post that Condit "continued stonewalling authorities". Those authorities, the D.C. police and FBI, were trying to figure out why Chandra's luggage was found packed in her apartment but not able to find where she had made travel arrangements.

The packed luggage was overstated and in actuality she was not as imminently on her way out the door as they believed from the first blush look at her apartment by Washington detectives, but still no travel reservations could be found to have been made. Why was there such a delay in Chandra purchasing a ticket to get home? In a continuing parents' nightmare with "privacy" laws, even the privacy of a young woman whose search was being covered on national television, Amtrak would not tell the Levys whether their daughter had made reservations, but the FBI told them she hadn't. They also could not get phone records from Verizon nearly three weeks after she had disappeared, even though they received the monthly bills.

Washington police Chief Gainer told 9 Eyewitness News that they had about 40 open missing persons cases they were investigating. "Most of the people are either found or come back on their own," he told them. He expounded further to the Washington Post:

> "The easy thing to think is that she packed up and ran away, but there's no evidence to support that," he said. "But we still can't exclude that. But my police instinct is that she didn't walk away, because the things to support that aren't there."

> "When you're looking for a missing person, you start with concentric circles, and the theory is that the center of that circle is her home," Gainer said. "What we are doing is going out like a ripple in the water and spreading out the search area, from the epicenter, to further away." [16]

They executed on that theory, dragging the Potomac and Anacostia rivers and searching wooded areas near Dupont Circle with cadaver dogs trained to sniff for bodies. The search included "an area around the South Capitol Street Bridge on the Anacostia and a portion of the Potomac around Reagan National Airport", police spokeman Gentile said, but the use of cadaver dogs was just standard procedure and didn't assume Chandra was dead. [17]

The police also obtained a court warrant for a search of Chandra's apartment "so that anything removed from the premises could be used later as evidence in any court proceeding", spokesman Joe Gentile told the Associated Press. They sent their mobile crime unit to search for blood and fiber but found nothing amiss. Her cell phone and laptop were sent to the FBI lab for them to retrieve information about calls and e-mails. They also obtained search warrants for her e-mail and credit card accounts to get information and determine if she was still accessing them.

Petula Dvorak and Allan Lengel of the Washington Post wrote this insight into the thinking of Executive Assistant Police Chief Gainer and searching for a missing woman:

> Gainer said that investigators are operating on the crime solvers' maxim that people such as Levy, if they've met with foul play, are most often victims of someone they know. But without forensic clues, they have to treat Levy as a "critical missing person" rather than a homicide.
>
> "There just has to be some physical piece of evidence that would make us change the case," Gainer said. "Give me some blood in this thing, give me some body fluids, give me some remains."
>
> The most logical and statistically sound course of investigation is to look at people closest to the missing person, said James A. Fox, criminal justice professor at Northeastern University in Boston.
>
> "First, you don't eliminate anyone as a suspect," said Fox, who helps maintain homicide statistics for the Bureau of Justice Statistics. "Sometimes those with the closest relationship have the greatest motive for murder."
>
> Statistics show that people such as Levy—white women 20 to 29—are most often killed by someone they know. According to Fox's figures, collected from 1976 to 1999, 31 percent of female homicide victims in this age group were killed by their husbands. Seventeen percent were killed by boyfriends, 31 percent by co-workers, neighbors or friends and 4 percent by other relatives. Only 13 percent of the women died at the hands of a stranger. [18]

Only 13 percent of women in Chandra's category died at the hands of a stranger in the previous two decades according to Bureau of Justice Statistics, but when the police attempted to obtain a search warrant for Condit's apartment, someone they were told was her boyfriend, Washington police say they were "hampered" by Justice Department rules about approaching a member of Congress in any investigation. The Washington Times goes on to clarify:

> But a well-placed federal official said those rules never applied to D.C. police and simply require a U.S. attorney to inform higher-ups when an investigation focuses on a member of Congress. [19]

That U.S Attorney, who would have to inform higher-ups that an investigation was focusing on a member of Congress, instead told the D.C. police they didn't have probable cause for a search warrant. No one in Washington wanted to touch this. Then again, that is how bureaucrats survive, even if a citizen didn't.

The police, not being allowed to look at Condit's apartment by the politically appointed U.S. Attorney, talked to residents of Condit's condo building, a four-story building called The Lynshire, asking if people had seen her in trying to establish if Chandra was a frequent visitor there. She wasn't well known there.

But interestingly, the police searched a "jogging path in Rock Creek Park, where Chandra regularly walked". [20] How would police know that Chandra regularly walked on a jogging path in Rock Creek Park, a park that runs for miles through the District and alongside Condit's street, Adams Mill?

There were no friends in Washington to tell the police this except Sven Jones, and he didn't tell them this. Jennifer Baker was her closest friend who had returned to California, and she didn't tell them this. So who told the police that Chandra regularly walked in Rock Creek Park, and why?

Also strangely, Andrea Mitchell of NBC News reports that friends say Chandra was seen with Condit socially, but again no known friends of Chandra said this. More curiously, Bob Franken told Greta Van Susteren that the next day after Chandra was last seen at the gym "friends went to her apartment and found her identification card, credit cards and packed suitcases". Someone was feeding these high powered reporters a lot of information about friends that didn't exist. Who were they, and why?

One friend who did exist, Jennifer Baker, remained puzzled as the police continued to investigate a missing persons case. Jennifer told the Los Angeles Times: "It seems to be more than that. With this sort of thing, I say leave no stone unturned!"

It seemed to be more than a missing person to everyone except those who didn't want it investigated, it seems.

Luray

The U.S. Attorney didn't think there was probable cause for the D.C. police to search Condit's apartment, but Joleen Argentini McKay did. On Wednesday May 16 when Condit's picture made the national news concerning the disappearance of Chandra Levy, Joleen went to the FBI in San Francisco to tell them what she knew about Congressman Gary Condit. She also called the D.C. police to tell them what she knew and encouraged them to search his apartment. Who was Joleen McKay, and what did she know that the U.S. Attorney didn't want to know? Kevin Fagan of the San Francisco Chronicle chronicles it best:

> A Mill Valley woman and a high-ranking member of U.S. Rep. Gary Condit's staff have been drawn into the swirling controversy surrounding missing intern Chandra Levy.
>
> The woman, Joleen Argentini McKay, walked into the FBI's San Francisco office in May and voluntarily admitted that she had had romantic relationships with the congressman and his chief of staff, Mike Dayton, according to sources close to the case.
>
> McKay told agents that she had been involved with Dayton in the early 1990s, and after the relationship ended, the chief of staff introduced her to his boss, Condit, and got her a job on his staff.
>
> McKay, who has since married, said she had had a relationship with the congressman in the mid-1990s. In 1994 she was hired by Condit to work as a staff assistant in his Washington office. Almost immediately, McKay was promoted to legislative assistant. But she quit before the year was over.
>
> When she was interviewed in May, she told investigators that Condit had sworn his love for her and vowed to leave his wife. The congressman made similar promises to Levy, according to her aunt Linda Zamsky.
>
> McKay said she had given him a Tag Heuer watch, and then he abruptly dumped her, the source said. [1]

According to USA Today, Joleen McKay also was given rules of secrecy to follow over their three year relationship. Joleen is also from Modesto, like Chandra, and dated Michael Dayton. After meeting Condit for dinner with Dayton, Tom Squitieri and Kevin Johnson of USA Today pick up the story:

> In January 1994, Condit persuaded McKay not to take a new job in Los Angeles and, instead, to come to Washington and work on his staff. He provided an airline ticket for her travel to Washington. McKay says she stayed in Condit's apartment for most of the eight months she lived in Washington.
>
> She was a staff assistant from Jan. 1 through July 31, 1994,...then a legislative assistant from August 1 to August 31..., congressional records show. She ended the affair in August and left Washington. She says Condit called her later in the year after she moved to San Francisco, and their relationship resumed until she ended it in 1996. McKay, who is now married, was single then. [2]

Much like Chandra, she spent most of her time in Condit's apartment in Washington, was provided airfare to California, and was promised Condit would leave his wife and marry her while at the same time obeying strict rules of secrecy. January 1994 is also about the same time that OC Thomas says his daughter, an 18 year old black teenager, started having a secret relationship with Condit in Modesto, and in fact, a light colored man got her pregnant around that time as she had a mixed race child in September, 1994. Also noteworthy is that both OC Thomas and Joleen McKay said that the respective affairs with Condit ended about the same time two years later in 1996, in Jennifer Thomas' case, due to strange sexual demands, she told her father.

Did OC Thomas know something about Condit's affair with Joleen McKay and transform it in his mind to his own daughter's situation when Susan Levy poured her troubles out to him in her flower garden that day in March? Or could Condit have been running two secret mistresses in 1994 even as he was rumored to be switching Republican to help Newt Gingrich with his family values Contract With America? He was capable of it. He had two secret mistresses seven years later, at least until one of them disappeared.

Condit gave his new staff assistant mistress the nickname of Peanut, according to Vince Flammini, who was Condit's driver in California then. [3] He should know. He sat out in front of her house in San Francisco at least 25 times, he told Geraldo. She gave Condit an expensive Tag Heuer watch and Flammini also told

Geraldo Condit was upset because he didn't wear watches. How upset is unknown, but they had it out right after that. Flammini told the New York Post: "He was angry because they had it out...He said, 'Darn it, she kept my best jacket,'" Flammini said.

Condit's chief of staff Dayton ought to know something about it. He dated her. He introduced her to Condit. He worked in the office with her. He told the New York Post:

> "I dated Joleen for a year," Dayton said, adding that he doubted she had an affair with Condit.
>
> "I am disappointed in her, especially if it's true," he said of the affair claim. "Obviously, she worked for us and knew Mr. Condit's a married man." [4]

Condit, in answer to Connie Chung's questions, said:

CONDIT: It was a gift.

CHUNG: From?

CONDIT: It was a gift.

CHUNG: A woman in the office who worked in your office?

CONDIT: Years ago.

CHUNG: And did you have a relationship with her?

CONDIT: I did not. [5]

Amazing. Another woman with such a vivid imagination she went to the FBI as soon as she saw Condit's name involved with a missing woman. Other Condit staffers, obviously Dayton not being one of them, also hallucinated this for Michael Doyle:

> "There were lots of manifestations that this was a relationship that went beyond the purely professional, like arguments and her running out of the office, crying," said one former Condit staffer, speaking on condition of anonymity.
>
> This one-time congressional staffer vividly recalled following the tearful woman outside after she had rushed from Condit's Capitol Hill office.

Independently, another former Condit staffer likewise recalled seeing the woman running from the office in tears. The woman was "nearly hyperventilating" in emotional distress, according to the staffer who recalled following her and spending about half an hour on a humid day trying to get the woman to calm down.

"I asked her flat out and said, 'Are you having an affair with Gary?' "the former staffer said, recalling the discussion the two had on an outdoor bench. "And she said, 'Oh, my god. Oh, my god'…and then she said, 'Yes, it's him.'"

The two staffers would subsequently talk, but carefully. The woman confided that she was upset because she wanted Condit to leave his wife, according to her confidante, but Condit showed no inclination to do so. The woman also described "lots of rules" she had to follow to keep the relationship secret, including a "secret telephone number she had to call" to get in touch with Condit.

"She was constantly paranoid," the former staffer said. "She didn't want Gary knowing that anyone else knew." [6]

We can assume Dayton would be disappointed.

By Thursday morning, May 17, police had been urged to search Condit's apartment by a former top Condit aide who lived with him there but stopped from searching by the U.S. Attorney. They had to content themselves with searching in the alley and dumpster behind the Lynshire apartment building.

Had Condit become aware of Joleen McKay calling the FBI and the D.C. police, or the request for a search warrant, or the searching going on behind his apartment that morning?

Or were other pressures mounting for the silent congressman? Amy Keller and Damon Chappie of Roll Call report that the Federal Election Commission notified him that they had been investigating him:

> In a May 17 letter to Olson, John Gibson, assistant staff director for the FEC's reports analysis division, instructed the campaign to respond to inquiries for additional information on prior reports by June 6…. According to FEC records, Condit's campaign committee has been under scrutiny by the FEC's reports analysis division over the past several months. [7]

For some reason, Condit left the House floor after making the first vote of the day, a routine procedural vote at 10:26 that morning. He would miss the remaining three votes of the day, 11:26 pm, 12:32 pm, and 2:09 pm, the first votes he missed all year.

A statement was issued on his behalf, but he was unseen, not to reappear until the next day. As quoted in the San Francisco Chronicle, the statement read:

> "It is not appropriate for any of us to make any further public comments about the facts of this case or to speculate about a matter that is under police investigation," Condit, 53, a six-term congressman, said in a prepared statement.

> "All of us should focus our attention on getting her home," he said. [8]

Anne Marie Smith flew in to Washington that afternoon and turned on the tv. In the days prior to that, the world still didn't know about Condit and Chandra Levy. They were searching for a mystery boyfriend. But first Joleen McKay and now Anne Marie Smith were seeing his picture splashed up on the tv screen with Chandra. Anne Marie tells Larry King her reaction:

> KING: OK, when you hear about Chandra Levy—which is in all the newspapers—she is missing, and she was a friend and worked for, knew the congressman. Did you phone him, talk to him about it?

> SMITH: I did. Well, he phoned me initially and asked me to not call him. He said he was in trouble, he may have to disappear for a while.

> KING: Really?

> SMITH: And said not to call him for a few days. So then, a weak later, I had a trip to D.C., and it was—I called him, I waited for like a week, and then finally called him. And I was very concerned about him. I didn't know any of this, we hadn't heard about any of it on the West Coast yet. And I called him and said, you know, I'm going to be in D.C., let's get together, let's have dinner, and he called me back and he said, "I can't. I can't see you, there is a situation, and it is…"

> KING: So you didn't know the Chandra story?

> SMITH: I didn't know it yet at this time. And so, I got into D.C. and I went into my hotel room and I turned on the news and I saw it, and I was just shocked beyond belief. And I called him, and I said: "What am I supposed to believe?" [9]

DEPAULO: Anne Marie, I'm curious. Did he tell you, one of my constituents is missing?

SMITH: No, he never mentioned a word of it, and it wasn't until I went to D.C. on the 17th of May and I turned on the television and I heard the news that I realized what was going on. And at that point in time, I called him and left him a message. And I was like, you know, you need to explain this to me. [10]

And Condit did return her call, at midnight, from a darkened payphone in Luray, Virginia, home of Luray Caverns, a scene so difficult to fathom that it is easier for the press to ignore it than to print articles worthy of a tabloid. Condit didn't tell her where he was, only that he was not in the area and couldn't meet her. She tells Larry King, Lisa DePaulo, and Cynthia Alksne about the call:

SMITH: Well, he called me back, and that was the phone call from Luray, Virginia.

DEPAULO: Right.

SMITH: And he called me, and he once again, you know, made me feel good about everything. He's like: Everything's OK with you and me. You know, I just want to assure you that there's nothing wrong with our relationship, but he said, I'm just dealing with this situation. And basically, he wanted to sit down and explain it to me, but he also said that you wouldn't believe what they're trying to do to me. And I don't know who these people were that he was referring to.

DEPAULO: Did he tell you right away that he was involved with Chandra?

SMITH: No, I asked him, and you know, I was pretty straightforward with him. And he said no. And he said, I can't believe you're asking me these types of questions. And if—if, you know, if you feel like I had anything to do with any of this, then you've been dealing with the wrong man.

ALKSNE: Anne Marie, did you ever travel in with him in the areas surrounding Washington, or did you ever have any—you mention this one phone call from Luray, Virginia, did you ever go to Luray, Virginia with him or do you know what he was doing in Luray, Virginia?

SMITH: I have no idea what he was doing. It was about midnight when he called me from Luray.

ALKSNE: And this was on May…

SMITH: May 16, May 17.

ALKSNE: So this was after you learned that Chandra had disappeared, he was in Luray, Virginia.

SMITH: Right.

ALKSNE: Did he tell you what he was doing there?

SMITH: No, he didn't. He said that he was not in the area and he was not able to see me. [11]

Rita Cosby reported briefly that Anne Marie got the caller id number on her cell phone to know that he called from a McDonalds in Luray, Va., chronicled in the Ether Zone:

"...as has been verified by Ms. Smith's caller ID, through phone records leaked by one in the Washington D.C. police department, and as reported by Fox News' Rita Cosby—a McDonald's fast-food restaurant, 709 E Main St., Luray, VA 22835..." [12]

The first mentions of Luray trickled out on the internet. All searches of the web and especially news sites came up empty for Luray. A Google search of news-groups found this though:

"Fox's Rita Cosby reported last night that the authorities traced Gary Condit's call to Anne Marie Smith from Luray, Virginia (a known "dumping ground" for bodies in the DC area") in front of a McDonalds." [13]

I tried to find out if Fox reported this. A wonderful lady named hawkeye posted that she saw the Fox newscast reporting a phone call that Condit made from a payphone at midnight from Luray, Va. two weeks after Chandra disappeared, and I insisted that information that explosive would have made headlines, yet there was no mention of it other than in the Star, despite Anne Marie Smith confirming it on Larry King Live in early August.

Rita Cosby had reported it on air on Fox one afternoon, and the story was suppressed and never mentioned again anywhere. Hawkeye had seen that news report, yet without any publication of it I implored her, how could you actually have seen that? Not one reporter and editor in the nation will even print it? It is apparently beyond belief. Even the Star only had one front cover story on it, aping the writeups on Luray already posted on internet Chandra boards by myself and others.

It was so remarkable that it was either a major story that should be headlines or it was a rumor. It's so unbelievable people think it's a hoax. How could a congressman being questioned about one missing mistress call another mistress from a darkened McDonalds payphone at midnight outside some caverns? naaaaah....

It never made it to print, and until Anne Marie filed an affadavit mentioning it the Larry King Live interview was the only source of Luray. The press has treated it as a UFO sighting, scared to take Anne Marie Smith's word over the silence of Gary Condit, who claims that Anne Marie is a publicity seeking profiteer of Chandra's death.

And our vaunted news organizations talk to each other about whether they should cover a sex scandal, completely ignoring Luray and whether they should cover a murder. Why was this not an eyebrow raising, head snapping, say what lead to a story? I know reporters want fame and glory. What is it about this story that reporters were waiting on?

They reported on neckties tied to Condit's bedposts, based on Anne Marie's say so. Why is bondage sex alright to report based on one person's story but a congressman being investigated concerning a missing intern outside some caverns at midnight not alright to report, based on the same person's say so? What's the difference? Neither one proves a thing, but the sex was reported and the midnight call wasn't. Sex sells, caverns don't? Only our free press will be able to tell you.

Anne Marie filed the addadavit in California in a request for a grand jury hearing:

> 8. On May 17th, Mr. Condit called me from Luray, VA, phone # ###-###-####, on my cell phone, saying, "There is no way I can talk with you." "Everything is OK between us." I asked him if he was guilty [of Levy's disappearance]. Mr. Condit's response was to become extremely angry, asking me "how [I] could ask [him] that." However, Mr. Condit never said "no." [14]

And finally the word Luray made it into a news report, Bob Dart reporting for Cox News Service:

However, in her sworn statement, Smith said it was a relationship.

On May 17, Smith said, Condit called her from Luray, Va., and she asked him "if he was guilty" involving Levy's disappearance.

Condit's "response was to become extremely angry, asking me 'how I could ask him that'," Smith said. "However, Mr. Condit never said 'no'." [15]

Many internet posters on Chandra boards thought that Condit said "I've got to disappear" from Luray, but he had said that a week earlier when he tried to shut their relationship down and break off calls between them temporarily. When he left the House floor mid-morning and went to Luray Thursday May 17, he didn't expect he would have to deal with her from there. He had asked her not to call the previous Friday, making it clear he had to go undergound, so to speak, to disappear himself, and having an auditable call to her would break silence.

Instead, she was very firm in her message about getting an explanation from him, and he had to respond to keep her quiet. This was an important callback at midnight to keep his girlfriend's loyalty. It was all about reassurance even as he stood there outside of a closed McDonalds at midnight in Luray. It is incongruous, but important. It's not "I need to disappear" from Luray, it's "I assure you nothing's wrong with our relationship, you wouldn't believe what they're doing to me, but I'm dealing with it and we're ok".

He has to keep Anne Marie on board to keep her from talking. He must keep her reassured. He must respond to her message to explain himself, yet not let her know where he is, because the alternative is to lose her loyalty and some control, enough to keep her from talking if she's alarmed at him having another girlfriend she didn't know about, a girlfriend who just happened to disappear.

She of course should have associated the disappeared girlfriend with the hair she found in his bathroom in March and her suspicion that Condit was seeing someone else, and should have called the police, but instead she tried to stay out of it, until her roommates revealed the truth of her relationship with Condit, albeit to a tabloid for money.

Out of that, however, she was able to tell the police that Condit occasionally drove her around in a five year old red Ford Fiesta. The police didn't even know that Condit had a car until Anne Marie told them. Dayton kept it for him. Did

Condit drive his car to Luray that night? Why was the car kept a secret from the police?

The McDonalds closed at 11 pm, while the Amoco station next to it closed at 9 pm. He would have been very conspicuous if he had called while McDonalds was open, as the payphone is in the path of the front door, along the newsstands. He waited until McDonalds closed, the crew left, and all was dark and quiet to make his call to Anne Marie. I think the phone call from a darkened McDonalds pay phone facing a closed Amoco station parking lot says it all. This was a furtive mission. Condit is not a secret agent, but he plays one.

Condit made an appearance the next day in Washington, so he drove back from Luray sometime after midnight. It's three hours from Luray to Rock Creek Park and downtown Washington in early morning traffic, taking the route to Washington the locals would. I had taken a shot at driving to Washington from Luray the way the locals wouldn't, over the mountains and through a national forest in the summer of 2001, well before Chandra was found in Rock Creek Park.

I took a drive into the mountains, through the George Washington National Forest of West Virginia and into Virginia and onto Skyline Drive of the Shenandoah National Park, and then into the Shenandoah River valley in between harboring the town of Luray.

I live just off US 33 in Columbus, Ohio, and found myself at US 33 again, this time in Elkton, Virginia. Interstate 64 had been cut through the mountains to enable a quick journey there. Had I followed US 33 over hill and dale, through every town on the way, large and small, I would have arrived days later. Even not that long ago, a trip to the coast required passing through Cumberland Gap, where West Virginia, Maryland, and Pennsylvania converge well northwest of Washington, DC. For the first time for me, I was able to drive east through the Appalachians as easily as in any other direction.

What I saw when I arrived in the Interstate 81 corridor on the other side of the mountains of Shenandoah National Park from DC was not encouraging for someone seeking the whereabouts of Chandra Levy, whose Congressman boyfriend had made a midnight phone call from Luray, VA outside Luray Caverns two weeks after she disappeared. The signs appeared with frightening regularity.

Weyers Cave. Grand Cavern. Shenandoah Caverns. Skyline Caverns. Endless Caverns.

US 66 from DC to I-81 forms a rapid access path to the gateways to these many caverns. The gateway to Luray, Endless, Skyline, and Shenandoah Caverns is the little town of New Market. There are shops, fast foods like McDonalds, and of course pay phones, all at the exit from I-81. To venture further to the caverns is to follow VA state route 211 as it twists and turns through the village, and onward up a mountain on a modern four lane road. At 1600 feet the mountain crests and the road descends into the Shenandoah South Fork river valley, and Page County. It is another 7 miles to Luray.

Luray, and the official entrance to Luray Caverns, is on one of those business loops off of route 211. It is not a quick stop off of a busy road, nor a handy place to make a phone call. The length of Luray is traversed by Main Street, populated by the entirety of a small town and all that entails, interspersed with frequent stop lights. No, one does not end up in Luray by happenstance.

Congressman Gary Condit ended up here at midnight, May 17, to make a phone call to his other mistress, Anne Marie Smith. Anne Marie's cellular caller id showed that the call came from the McDonalds on Main St. in Luray. I looked for that McDonalds.

I saw it, started to pull in, and was stunned to see a Bobcat partially blocking the entrance. It was too eerie for words. The sidewalk and street curb in front of McDonalds had just been poured with concrete and was protected by orange cones, with a Bobcat tractor blocking off a portion of the entrance that had just been poured. I missed the entrance all together and pulled into the Amoco station next door. I needed to get gas anyway.

As I pumped my gas, I looked around and saw a drive up pay phone with an Amoco logo at the edge of the parking lot next to McDonalds. I walked over and then completely around McDonalds. There was no other drive up phone. The drive up phone is an Amoco phone.

I checked it out, but the dial tone was dead. Even putting money into it didn't bring it to life, and the coin return failed to yield my money. The phone had been sabatoged, it seems. It was labelled:

East Amoco
717 E. Main St.
Luray

The Amoco station manager said it had been working the day before, and that it wasn't owned by the station but was operated by another company. He put in a call to the management company to let them know about it. This phone would not have returned a caller id for McDonalds, anyway.

I walked back over to McDonalds and looked at their pay phone. It is on the wall between the front door and the outdoor playground, next to the Washington Post and local newsstand boxes. It is labelled:

McDonalds #4448
709 E. Main St.
Luray

There was a dial tone on this phone. I dialed home, and a recording told me to put in a dollar to connect. I did, and later when I got home my caller id said "Virginia call". It does this for some types of calls that are not fully participating in the caller id signalling, for whatever reason, but is from a fixed location versus a cellular call.

It is difficult to picture Condit standing there at midnight, leaning on a news box, and reassuring Anne Marie that all was well between them after she had left him a message earlier in the day when she arrived in DC urgently requesting an explanation for what she saw on the news about Condit and Chandra Levy. McDonalds closes at 11 pm, and the Amoco station closed at 9 pm. It would be dark and quiet in that little town at midnight. But why was he there?

The previous day the Levys had arrived and were interviewed for three hours by the DC police and FBI. Condit himself had made a public statement proclaiming Chandra Levy as "a great person and good friend". But the next morning, earlier on the day of this midnight call, USA Today later reported that the police searched the alley and dumpster behind Condit's condo. At mid-morning, after making a 10:30 am vote on the floor of the House of Representatives, aides "escorted" Condit off the floor, according to one news account. He missed three more votes that day, the first votes he missed all year, and ended up making a phone call from Luray, VA at midnight. Why would he go there after the police searched behind his condo?

There is another way to Luray from DC, the direct route of 211 branching off US 66 and going through Shenandoah National Park to Luray, rather than following US 66 to I-81 and down to New Market, then back to Luray over a mountain and across the river. It would seem to be the route to take, in fact, until I took it.

Driving to DC from Luray takes you into Shenandoah National Park after passing Jellystone Park campground. The mountain that is crossed makes the 1600 foot pass to enter Luray from New Market seem like a molehill. It is for bicyclists and people driving a red convertible with the top down on a Sunday morning, like myself, but would not be a pleasant trip at night, to say the least. The twists and turns are rugged. It is not narrow, being a well paved four lane highway, but would be treacherous driving at night. After driving for a long time to cross this mountain, I was still 74 miles from DC. I turned around and went back.

Condit had successfully given everyone, including the police, the impression he didn't have a car. However, Foxnews has reported that Smith's lawyer, Jim Robinson, said that Anne Marie told police that Condit used to drive her around in a red Ford Fiesta, about 5 years old. If it had not been for Smith telling them that, they would have not known about the car. They did search it for forensic evidence.

Condit didn't have to have an aide drive him to Luray that day, but maybe one or more were with him. Maybe they decided to retreat from the press and stay at some place like Mimslyn's Fine Food and Lodging across from the park like entrance to Luray Caverns to get away from the police digging into his personal life and the press covering the Levys on Larry King Live that night. Maybe, and maybe he didn't want a record of calling Anne Marie and went down the road and found a pay phone at McDonalds to call from.

But unless he and his aides are able to produce a record for that trip, or a recollection from staff somewhere and the bogus names used to sign in, we have to conclude that Condit drove the red Ford Fiesta to Luray that day after walking off the floor of the House of Representatives, spooked by the Levy's interview with the police and subsequent search behind his condo. What did Luray hold for him, solace and privacy from the prying police and press? And why Luray? We have seen that it is not easy to get here, and Main Street in Luray is hardly a secluded cabin on the Shenandoah River.

While caverns sound ominous, the commercial ones are like any tourist business, with entrances and employees collecting admission. The area is obviously rife with caves and national forests, but it is often difficult to find a place to hide something in an unfamiliar area without being noticed. Skyline Caverns are 20 miles from Luray on another road, with farms and woods in between. Endless Caverns are even farther away.

The Luray area is an area with ancient cabins set off from the road and along the river after passing through the dense Shenandoah National Park. It's remote, but not so remote that anyone is noticed. The caverns bring in many strangers to the area. I drove the back roads and along the river, and saw very little but old cabins.

We can only hope that Chandra is alive in one of those old cabins by the Shenandoah River.

Obsessed

Things quieted down. The police gave up searching the woods near Dupont Circle and Adams Mill with dogs. Reporters almost gave up getting Condit to say something about it to them. Congress tsk'ed tsk'ed about their colleague's bad luck with some intern disappearing. And then...

Had Chandra obeyed her spymaster without one slip, Condit's disavowal of knowing anything more about her than meeting his constituent as she visited one of his office interns and sought advice on getting a job with the FBI would have been the end of it. "A good friend", put up a reward, and life goes on. Reporters get tired and go away. Police get distracted by other murders and go away. Parents have their 15 minutes and virtually go away. Life goes on. The rules of secrecy abetting the prime directive, plausible deniability, keeps his world from prying eyes, and life goes on. For most.

Chandra almost didn't slip. Just a month before she disappeared she explained to her visiting family her calls as to a friend in government. "A boyfriend," her brother asked, grinning. No, just a friend, she replied.

But she slipped once. Over a Thanksgiving visit to her aunt Linda Zamsky a half year earlier, she accidentally said his name when describing how his office answered when she called her boyfriend. "You didn't hear that?", she quickly said to Linda. Linda shook her head no. But she had. Chandra never said his name again but Linda had heard.

As a month passed with Chandra missing, the police saying nothing to Chandra's family, Condit saying nothing, Chandra not reappearing, it was time to remember that slip. It was time to let Condit know that his secret wasn't safe, that the significant other of a disappeared woman needs to be investigated, needs to be cleared. But first the police have to know he was an intimate. And the police would only say they had "heard all the rumors, hearsay, second-party information. At this time, there's nothing to substantiate those rumors." [1] It was time to substantiate them if the police wouldn't. And they wouldn't.

The Washington Post's Allan Lengel opened a portal into that secret world:

> U.S. Rep. Gary A. Condit told D.C. police that Chandra Levy has spent the night at his Adams Morgan apartment, according to law enforcement sources, who also said the missing intern told a close relative that she was romantically involved with the congressman.
>
> …the Levy relative said, "Chandra has told me things that seem to contradict what the spokesmen for Congressman Condit have been saying."
>
> The relative, who spoke to The Washington Post on condition of anonymity, said that she spent last Thanksgiving and Passover in April with Levy, 24, and that the intern told her about her romantic life in Washington. The relative declined to provide more detail. [2]

The relative who remained unnamed was Linda Zamsky, and if the police wouldn't listen to her, maybe the Washington Post would. The Levys confirmed they knew of what the relative was saying, and NBC added:

> The Levys also suggested that pressure was being placed on potential witnesses to keep quiet, though they would not elaborate on which witnesses or what sort of pressure.
>
> "A lot of people are afraid of coming out to say anything because they're afraid of things happening to them," Robert Levy said. "I think a lot of people know something and they're not saying anything." [3]

That pressure they couldn't talk about were anomynous threats being phoned to acquaintances in Modesto, Chandra's friend Jennifer Baker, OC Thomas, the Ceres minister who was the Levys friend and gardener, and his daughter Jennifer. Chandra's uncle, Dr. Paul Katz, tells Larry King:

> If I could say something here. Throughout this whole thing, there has been a humor, if you will, of intimidation. It started first with, you know, with actually some of the prior women that Mr. Condit had an affair with, an intimidation, even of Chandra, that she should conduct herself in a certain manner or she would lose this relationship she had. An intimidation of both the Thomas—apparently from some source, we don't know who, we can't necessarily link it to Mr. Condit—and an intimidation of Jennifer Baker also. That hasn't been mentioned. Jennifer Baker sat in the home of my sister and with Bob,

and told us clearly in no uncertain terms that had there not been a public view to her, that her response in public would have been different. She was his intern, confided in how she was intimidated. By Mr. Condit's, one of Mr. Condit's aides, was intimidated personally and felt that her future, her job would be at risk if she was to really reveal how she personally felt about what was going on there. And you know, she can say whatever she'll say in public, but we know what she said to us in private. [4]

Jeff Jardine of the Modesto Bee talked to OC Thomas:

Thomas said his daughter became agitated one day in May while watching a television report detailing a $10,000 reward posted by Condit in Levy's disappearance. When she heard that Condit had expressed concern for the missing woman, Thomas recalled, his daughter jumped up and exclaimed, "That's a lie."

Thomas told The Post that his daughter told him that Condit had warned her after the breakup not to tell anyone about the relationship.

Levy said that after her daughter disappeared, she asked Thomas specific questions about the relationship between Condit and Thomas' daughter, which he provided. The Levys notified the FBI.

Thomas said his daughter does not want to talk with the FBI and has left the area out of fear. He asked The Bee not to disclose her name or whereabouts.

Thomas said he received an anonymous telephone call about three weeks ago. The caller said, "Shut up and listen," then warned Thomas against talking to anyone about Condit.

The caller, he said, knew things about Thomas' family, and Thomas called the experience "very intimidating."

Thomas said he has urged his daughter to cooperate with authorities, and said he believes she would be safer by coming out publicly with her story.

"I'm just trying to do the right thing for the Levys, and I wanted to answer all the questions the FBI had," Thomas told The Post. "I don't want to drag my family into this. But I want to tell the truth about everything I know." [5]

Tom Squitieri and Kevin Johnson of USA Today revealed a similar threat to Joleen McKay, the former aide and girlfriend who went to the FBI and called the Washington police as soon as she saw Condit on tv linked to a missing woman:

Joleen Argentini McKay also told USA TODAY that she called Dayton, a high school friend, four times to urge him to convince Condit to cooperate fully with authorities, reminding Dayton of what she says was the pain Condit caused her. Dayton declined to comment on Wednesday.

McKay says Dayton acknowledged her pain but urged her not to talk to police about her relationship with Condit. She says Dayton told her to "leave it in the past or it will ruin you." As for talking to authorities, she says he told her, "You don't want to do that." [6]

Meanwhile, the other mistress who hadn't disappeared, Anne Marie, when finding out about Chandra became afraid and called some friends, saying "I'm not the type of person to disappear. If anything happens to me or—excuse me—to commit suicide—if anything happens to me, that's not the cause." [7]

The Star published the story for which they paid Anne Marie's roommmate $2500, that of an unnamed Anne Marie who had told her roommate she had been in a relationship with Condit for the last year. The FBI had learned of her about the same time the Star did, and contacted Anne Marie to question her about Condit. She called Condit to let him know, having already talked to them, but was letting him know. He became very angry and told her not to talk to anybody, and that she didn't need to talk to even the FBI.

Soon after that his lawyer sent a statement, written up as an affadavit, to her lawyer, Jim Robinson, for her to sign. It essentially was for her to deny that they had had an affair, perjured testimony, and was a ploy to taint everything she said once she was a perjurer. He tried both to coax her and scare her into signing it, saying that by saying there was no affair the police had nothing to talk to them about, that she would be letting him down if she didn't sign it, and that it would never go to trial, just what wouldn't go to trial being left unsaid.

Condit's lawyer, Joseph Cotchett, denied on Good Morning America that Chandra stayed overnight at Condit's, but added, "If she spent the night, she spent it on a couch somewhere. If she did, she had to spend it on a couch because Congressman Condit's wife was in Washington the entire week she was missing."

Condit issued another statement to be handed out by the barrier that surrounded him, calling speculation he had a relationship with Chandra "sheer and utter nonsense". [8] So how does he explain that Chandra had told a relative she was romantically involved with him? Easy. Infatuation. ABC News:

Sources close to Condit told ABCNEWS that Chandra Levy may have been infatuated with the 53-year-old married congressman, or even that the two may have been "involved," but they insisted that whatever relationship there might be between the two has nothing to do with the young woman's disappearance. [9]

While the New York Post and Fox News also reported that "friends" of Condit, reporter speak for Condit's lawyer, I don't even think Lynch would touch this one, were saying that Chandra was infatuated with Condit, Andrea Mitchell of NBC News raised the ante:

Tuesday, NBC News correspondent Andrea Mitchell reported that a relative had told investigators that Chandra Levy had become "infatuated" with Condit last November and that Condit tried to end the relationship this spring. NBC News aired part of a home video in which Robert Levy can be heard referring to his daughter's "congressman friend." [10].

How intriguingly ambiguous. Relative of who? Condit's relative was the "friends" who were saying Chandra was infatuated with Condit? Or Chandra had a relative who said she was infatuated and that he tried to end the relationship?

Is it possible to picture Linda Zamsky or Susan Levy describing Chandra as "infatuated" with Condit? Or saying that he tried to end the relationship? They didn't have any idea what happened. Now is it possible to picture them saying this at the same time "friends" of Condit were saying the same thing? An anomynous consensus between the Levys and Condits had sprung up overnight that Chandra was "infatuated" as soon as the Washington Post divulged from Linda Zamsky that Condit's secret was no longer secret?

I don't think so. The nuts and sluts game was on. Chandra was a little bit nutty, a little bit slutty. That's how you deal with girlfriends who talk before they disappear. Infatuated. Obsessed. Suicidal. Who knows what she was capable of? The hapless Washington police would try to guess.

They wanted to requestion Condit a second time, six weeks after the first questioning, but he had been stalling them for ten days. Assistant Chief Gainer told the New York Daily News: "We need to know more about his relationship with Miss Levy and what he might know about her mindset."

Condit just didn't seem to have the time for them. Busy congressman, you know. Who would have guessed this is the same guy that had time for two mistresses until Chandra disappeared? Well, he couldn't put it off any longer, and since Joe Cotchett couldn't keep the police away after volunteering that Carolyn Condit was in town when Chandra disappeared and got her involved, he changed lawyers. Abbe Lowell, described by Niles Lathem in the New York Post as a "top-gun criminal defense lawyer", would protect him from unwarranted questioning.

Rita Cosby of Fox News reports that Condit told the police he "broke off his close friendship" with Chandra two days before she disappeared. She goes on:

> When Condit delicately broke things off with Levy with the explanation that she was moving back to California, she was distraught, refusing to take no for an answer and even becoming obsessed with him, the sources said.

> Levy called Condit several times on a special line in the 24 hours before she vanished, but he never returned those calls, the sources said. [11]

Helen Kennedy of the New York Daily News reports that Abbe Lowell told Condit's spokesman that Condit said none of this. "Either the police sources or the reporter were smoking something that was probably illegal," Michael Lynch said.

But Niles Lathem of the New York Post reports from police sources what Rita Cosby had and more:

> Rep. Gary Condit has admitted to cops he broke off all contact with Chandra Levy two days before the intern vanished, sending the dark-haired, hazel-eyed beauty into an emotional tailspin, police sources said yesterday.

> In a second interview with Washington police on Saturday, the California Democrat said the 24-year-old intern became extremely distraught when he broke the news to her on April 29 that he was ending their "close friendship," the sources said.

> She refused to take no for an answer, he said.

> Condit said Chandra made several calls to his paging service the next day, April 30, but he didn't return them.

> He said she was becoming too infatuated with him, and he tried to distance himself by telling her to go home—that there was nothing more he could do for her career.

Chandra, who also was upset because her internship was suddenly cut short when she told a personnel official she had officially graduated from college in December, had asked for Condit's help in getting a job with the FBI.

When cops pressed the congressman about the relationship, his lawyer, Abbe Lowell, stepped in and told him not to answer. [12]

"Condit said Chandra made several calls to his paging service the next day, April 30, but he didn't return them."

This police leak from the June 23 requestioning of Condit reported by Rita Cosby and Niles Lathem was a source of great controversy. Condit said Chandra made several calls to his paging service the day before she disappeared and he didn't return them, the police revealed.

Was Chandra distraught, bombarding Condit with messages when he told her to go home? Was she obsessed, crazy, suicidal, likely to do something for revenge, like disappear? Condit portrayed details that convinced the police of this.

And if she did call Condit repeatedly on Monday, did it have anything to do with the optimistic big news Chandra had for her aunt the evening before that was yet to be revealed publically by Linda Zamsky? How could a distraught Chandra be reconciled with the usual happy self that checked out of the gym Monday night saying she was looking forward to going home?

But more importantly, did the calls even take place? Condit said they did. He's the one that checks his messages. He ought to know. Does Chandra's phone records confirm this?

The phone in Chandra's apartment was in the landlord Denis Edeline's name and she was to reimburse him for any long distance calls, but she never did make any long distance calls on it. Condit's message line was a 202 area code number, local to her Dupont Circle apartment, and Gainer told reporters that "Phone companies do not keep records of local calls made on standard phones." [13] If Chandra made local calls from her apartment, there would be no record.

Chandra's cell phone billing address was her home in Modesto, and Chandra's parents paid the bills when they came in. Complicating the call records analysis is that in the previous month of April the Levys had visited Chandra the week of

Passover of Saturday April 7 till Chandra's birthday on Saturday April 14. The battery on Chandra's own cell phone wasn't charged and she used her dad's cell phone to make some calls during that week. Because of that, calls on Dr. Levy's own cell phone bill also needed to be examined.

The cell phone records looked at initially by the Levys were what they had on hand when Chandra failed to return their calls in the first few days of May. Those bills were from the previous month's billing and of course would not include calls from April 30 just a few days before. They did contain the calls Chandra made on her dad's phone while the Levys were visiting in Washington over Passover, so Condit's 202 area code message line phone number appeared on both Dr. Levy's and Chandra's cell phone bills.

The Levys still had not received Chandra's phone bill from Verizon three weeks after seeking who Chandra had called before disappearing, but by June 14 Cmdr. Jack Barrett of the Washington Police, in charge of the investigation, told MSNBC that they had obtained Chandra's bank, phone, and e-mail records with a grand jury subpeona, which is required for personal data. MSNBC reports:

> The records obtained by subpoena "have been very helpful," Barrett said, in creating a timeline of events for "each and every hour of those last eight or nine days" before Levy was last seen April 30. [14]

By June 17 Niles Lathem of the New York Post was able to report that Chandra made several calls to Condit the last two days before she disappeared. ABC News reported based on the Post article that Chandra "called Condit's answering service 'several times' on April 29 and 30.".

John Lehmann of the New York Post followed up a few weeks later by saying that Chandra "reportedly phoned his pager number eight or nine times in the 24 hours before she vanished". Reportedly? The New York Post had been reporting it.

Kenneth Bazinet of the New York Daily News reports that Time's Washington correspondent Viveca Novak reported that the Levys found about 20 calls to Condit's pager line and called him, and they spoke "briefly and awkwardly". But Novak says the Levys found these numbers while going through Chandra's phone records in late May. The call she describes was the call Susan Levy made on May 7 to see what number Chandra had been dialing and leaving a message.

As we know, Condit called back and said he had a professional relationship with Chandra. The 20 calls was obviously on a bill that Susan Levy was looking at when Chandra disappeared, from mid-April and earlier, so any references from reporters to the 20 calls the Levys found has nothing to do with the days right before Chandra's disappearance. It is important to know who she had been calling, and the Levys found out, but actually included the period of time when they themselves had been visiting with her in Washington for her birthday, not when she disappeared two weeks later.

Dale Solly of WJLA reports a hybrid of the other reports the same day, June 18, that Chandra's cell phone records "show a number of calls to Condit's pager the day before she vanished". He goes on to say that the Levys called the number and Condit called back.

If true, this would accurately be stated that a number the Levys had called earlier and found to be Condit's had appeared on Chandra's bill several times the day before she disappeared. They had called the number weeks earlier when Chandra disappeared based on earlier bills and only found what numbers she had called when they finally received her phone bill, an important distinction if the Levys actually found those numbers on their bill for April 29 and 30.

The Washington Post quoted Condit's lawyer at the time, Joe Cotchett, suggesting an explanation for "four or five" calls "in the days" before Chandra disappeared:

> But Cotchett quoted unnamed authorities as telling him that Chandra Levy phoned Condit four or five times in the days before she was last seen. She was preparing to leave for California to attend her graduate school commencement.
>
> "Let's assume she was calling him to say goodbye, which we suspect was the case," Cotchett said on the Early Show. "You understand she was returning to California. Also...the congressman has come forward and said they were good friends, as he is with many interns." [15]

Several calls in the two days before she disappeared, even eight or nine the day before, or four or five over a few days? Interestingly, Cotchett wouldn't survive as

Condit's lawyer long enough to appear with him three days later for his second questioning, where with Abbe Lowell Condit instead described Chandra "[calling him] several times on a special line in the 24 hours before she vanished, but he never returned those calls" [16] He had stalled the D.C. police ten days to change lawyers and take a different story in.

Just to make things interesting, the police, who had just said they received subpeonaed Chandra's phone records and presumedly would know what they were talking about, said "there were not numerous calls to him immediately before her disappearance". Jim Keary of the Washington Times quotes Gainer:

> "There has been a lot of published communication that has caused some con-
> fusion for everybody that frantic calls were made before her disappearance.
> That was not the case," Chief Gainer said. [17]

So who was Niles Lathem's source for several calls to Condit's message line the two days before Chandra disappeared, the police, Condit's people, or the Levys? Only Condit was to tell the police this in his requestioning a few days later. The police said it wasn't true, the Levys talking of bills a month old.

But Niles Lathem followed the police disavowal a day later by reporting "Phone records have shown that she made several calls to Condit on her cell phone the week before she disappeared." What different set of phone records was the New York Post and the Washington police looking at, and why was Condit insisting the calls, which could only be construed as frantic, took place?

Rita Cosby of Fox News weighed in a month later by obtaining the Levys phone records. She reports that Chandra was "constantly calling her answering machine for messages" and left a two minute call for her aunt, which we know was Sunday evening. Inexplicably, the report adds that the last person she called was her friend from the BOP, Sven Jones, when the message was left Saturday evening.

What to make of this? With no mention of a call to Condit's message line, there must of not been any. Surely it would be important to report. So what phone records was the New York Post looking at? What phone records was Condit's lawyer referring to? And with the last person called as Sven, even after mentioning the call to Linda Zamsky, did Chandra call him again on Monday or

Tuesday and not leave a message? The police said she placed one call Tuesday without identifying who she called.

Michael Isikoff of Newsweek attempted to clarify with reporting based on "sources with access to Levy's cell-phone records [who] reviewed them for NEWSWEEK". He reports a hybrid, that call record history indicates that Chandra would routinely call Condit's message line and then within an hour start calling her answering machine at her apartment to check if he had returned her message. Isikoff adds that the calls to Condit "tail off" in mid-April, specifically mentioning a call she made Friday April 13 when she was with her parents and, unbelievably, yet another date for a call to Sven, early afternoon of Sunday April 29.

He reports there are no calls to any number for Condit in the last week. Isikoff quotes law enforcement sources as saying records show there was also no calls to Condit from her home phone, even though Chief Gainer had said "Phone companies do not keep records of local calls made on standard phones."

Did the phone company in the Washington area keep records of local calls after all? That would require more than a six week retention of all local calls dialed to be able and go back and look at calls made on May 1 from when they subpeonaed records. Considering that local calls aren't being billed for, that would be unusual, although phone companies have been wanting to bill for local calls so perhaps have the system in place. It certainly would be required for Isikoff's law enforcement sources to be able to tell him that.

The information that Chandra called Sven Sunday afternoon is interesting. It would possibly explain Fox News saying that she called him last if she called him right after leaving a message for her aunt. One problem with that is not only was the message left for Sven on Saturday evening about 7:30 when Carolyn Condit was arriving at the airport, but she sounded funny to Sven, as if she needed to talk to somebody. When Chandra left a message of big news for her aunt the next day on Sunday she was back to her normal, upbeat self.

Still, calling Sven again about the big news after leaving a message for Linda makes sense. Had Chandra called Sven on Saturday evening from her apartment phone and left a message but tried again on Sunday from her cell phone without leaving a message? That would explain a last call to Sven on Sunday without multiple calls from her cell phone to Sven, but it doesn't identify the call placed on her phone Tuesday. The reporting by Rita Cosby and Michael Isikoff implies there was no call made on Tuesday. Where did Chief Monroe get his information that a call had been placed on her phone that day?

Also odd about Isikoff's sources with access to the Levy's records is that Chandra was using her dad's cell phone when she was with them, including Friday April 13. The calls were on his phone bill and was the number they called to see who it was because it was unlisted. If it was her dad's phone bill the sources were looking at, the calls to Condit would "tail off" mid-April because he returned to California from their trip that weekend and would have brought his phone with him.

But Isikoff also mentions a call to Sven on April 29, indicating the sources were looking at Chandra's phone bill as well. It may also be possible she used both her phone and her dad's phone on the same day during the trip.

Joshua Micah Marshall of Salon wrote an analysis attempting a synthesis of Rita Cosby's and Michael Isikoff's reports with this impactful summation:

> A flurry of calls Chandra made to her own answering machine is certainly a far cry from calls to Condit's special line. But they do suggest, possibly, a more complicated chain of events that may give some clue as to why two news organizations are standing behind such contradictory versions of events. They also follow a pattern detailed in Isikoff's story, which reports that after contacting Condit's special line "Levy would start calling her home message machine, sometimes up to six times in a row, apparently to see if Condit had returned the call." So there may be some truth to both reports, though, like so many developments in this story, it all simply raises more questions than it resolves. [18]

Chandra ceasing calling Condit from her phone from mid-April onward corresponds with when she told her mother that Condit had "explained it all, knows all about it" about Jennifer Thomas which OC Thomas had warned her mother about. It would be much better if the calls tailed off because they were looking at her father's cell phone bill, much less ominous. But the next week, after that mid-April cessation of calls to Condit, Chandra suddenly, surprisingly, abruptly, had her internship terminated. And a week later she disappeared. As Susan Levy said, "What can I say? Kind of strange to me. Real strange." [19]

And along with their requestioning of Condit the police must have said something like, oh, by the way Congressman Condit, it's been nearly two months since Chandra disappeared, and we know how busy you are, but where were you when Chandra disappeared? Because Condit provided a timeline alibi. Columbo would be proud.

Alibi

Timothy Burger and Helen Kennedy of the New York Daily News reported it, the release from Condit's office of an alibi timeline to ABC News:

> Rep. Gary Condit has compiled a detailed account of his movements in the days surrounding the May 1 disappearance of Chandra Levy—showing he was either working or with his wife when the intern vanished.
>
> A source close to Condit gave ABC News a comprehensive time line of the congressman's many activities, covering the six-day period from April 28 to May 3.
>
> But, adding to the general confusion surrounding the case, Condit's office promptly disavowed the time line once it was published on ABC's Web site.
>
> "It's not accurate. It's not complete. It's just bits and pieces," his chief of staff, Mike Lynch, told the Daily News. [1]

The New York Times added that the schedule given to ABC included "omissions." Michael Doyle of the Modesto Bee was told: "It went out when it wasn't ready to go."

"Bits and pieces with omissions that went out when it wasn't ready to go". In other words, "oops, Condit didn't want you to see that. If it was exposed to the light of day, then people who ask questions would be able to see just what lies he was getting away with for an alibi." Can't have that now, can we?

How had this timeline been exposed to the light of day, what "bits and pieces" in it were not ready for its antiseptic glare, and why?

Just before Chandra logged off the internet for the last time and disappeared, Condit went into a private meeting with Vice President Dick Cheney in Cheney's office he keeps in the House of Representatives to discuss the California energy crisis, that crisis of a deregulation experiment that was bringing down Condit's ally, Governor Gray Davis.

Cheney's press secretary, Juleanna Glover Weisss, said the meeting happened between 12:30 p.m. and 12:50 p.m., "at Condit's request." [2] The Newport is just ten blocks from the Capitol, and Chandra logged off ten minutes after Condit left the meeting. What a coincidence. The D.C. police say Condit is not a suspect. Surely Condit has an alibi to not be a suspect? We will see.

The next day, Wednesday May 2, Condit met with an ABC News reporter, Rebecca Cooper, where Salon's Jake Tapper reports "they discussed the efforts the White House was making to reach out to him, as a conservative "Blue Dog" Democrat, especially on energy policy." She met him at the Rayburn Building, where Condit had his office, at 3 in the afternoon, waited for him to finish voting, then took a cab with him to the Tryst, a restaurant close to Condit's apartment. She interviewed him and left about 6 pm, going back to ABC and writing up a memo summary for her reporter colleagues.

It was familiar territory. Cooper was married now but used to date Condit according to colleagues, reports Niles Lathem. Interestingly, Lathem goes on to report:

> She is an attractive, well-liked and hard-working off-air reporter at ABC News whose lengthy association with Condit so concerned her network bosses that they barred her from working on the Levy story when she offered to land the elusive Condit for an interview. [3]

She was not in a position to seek Condit out for an interview, but the day after Chandra disappeared, three days before the Levys would call him and tell him Chandra was missing, he sought out an ex-girlfriend reporter to talk to her about the Republicans reaching out to him, for a meeting he had requested, that took place just as Chandra was logging off for the last time.

Michael Isikoff of Newsweek cites "sources familiar with the meeting", vague enough to be from Condit or the Republicans, as saying that Cheney and two aides met with Condit "at the suggestion of Republican leaders". Weiss the press secretary described it to CNN as a typical meeting.

A 12:30 pm lunchtime meeting with Cheney without lunch sounds like Cheney was accomodating a last minute request from a critical Congressional vote, Condit, for a meeting with him, possibly made by Condit during the previous day, Monday, when Condit was at a White House lunch. Was Isikoff's source a representative of one of those Republican leaders or of Condit? How long in advance was the meeting requested? Is there a Republican leader who says he sought an urgent meeting between Condit and Cheney? Was there another member of Congress from California who Cheney also met with for the same urgent reason, or were they just "reaching out" to Condit?

Did Condit usually meet with Republican leaders such as the Vice President and aides without any of his own staff as he did for that meeting? Was Cheney aware who the Republican leaders were who requested it? If Republican leaders requested it, wouldn't he need to know the specific agenda to address to Condit? Or did he, in fact, come to listen to Condit, because there was no Republican leaders asking for a meeting?

But what does it matter anyway if Condit's meeting with Cheney ended before Chandra disappeared? The fact is, no one would have known just when Condit was out of that meeting if Rebecca Cooper hadn't learned of the existence of a timeline and asked Lynch for it, curious as to how her meeting with Condit had been portrayed in it.

She was puzzled as she looked at the entries for May 1 and May 2:

Tuesday, May 1

Condit rides with staff to the office in the morning. At 12:30 p.m. ET, he meets with Vice President Cheney. He returns at 3:30 p.m. for meetings and phone conversations with constituents. At 5 p.m., Condit has a doctor's appointment. At 6:30 p.m., he votes on the House floor. From 6:30 to 7:30 p.m., he meets with a reporter at the Tryst restaurant in Adams Morgan. Later, he and the wife stay home and eat dinner.

Wednesday, May 2

Condit rides into work with staff and attends Agriculture Committee and Select Intelligence Committee meetings. At 11:30 a.m., Condit casts votes on the House floor. At noon, he participates in a meeting with the California congressional delegation. From 12:30 p.m. to 2 p.m., he participated in a bipartisan meeting at the White House. At 2:30 p.m., he returns to the Intelligence Committee. Later, he casts votes on the House floor, meets with congressional leaders and heads home for dinner with his wife at 5:30 p.m. After dinner, they go shopping at an "Off The Wall" store. [4]

The critical time of Chandra's disappearance was well alibied for the police. A meeting with the Vice President at 12:30 pm, returning at 3:30 pm. Meetings, phone calls, a visit to the doctor, votes, another meeting with a reporter at the Tryst. A busy day indeed to account for his time, dominated by an afternoon with the Vice President when Chandra disappeared. That is what returning at 3:30 pm means, doesn't it? After all, if he wasn't with the Vice President, where could he be?

But, puzzingly, her meeting with Condit on Wednesday afternoon wasn't there. Instead, it said he met with congressional leaders when he was at the Tryst with her from 3 pm to 6 pm. He did have a meeting with an unnamed reporter at the Tryst the previous evening, the day Chandra disappeared. Why would he tell the police he met with some other reporter at the Tryst but not her?

ABC contacted Michael Lynch and Abbe Lowell and asked. Lowell said it was a draft and contained mistakes. Lynch said he had been chastised by the lawyers for handing it out to ABC, and no more would go out, including no corrected version that ABC was asking for. Getting no answer from Condit's people, ABC also contacted the Washington police and explained the discrepancy to them.

A month later, the police had yet to get back to a surprised Rebecca Cooper, or even question her as the unnamed reporter in the timeline that she was able to identify herself as. Jake Tapper of Salon followed up with the Washington police on the erroneous timeline:

> "First of all, I don't know if we know about that," said Sgt. Joseph Gentile, public information officer for the D.C. Police Department, when asked about the mess-up in Condit's schedule. "Second of all, why are you asking about Condit's state of mind? We're looking for Miss Levy, we want to know about Miss Levy's state of mind. Third of all, we don't identify the people we talk to." [5]

The police wouldn't be asking Cheney or his staff about his meeting with Condit either. But the damage had been done. By ABC News posting Condit's timeline on its website, even including making a helpful correction by moving the meeting at the Tryst to Wednesday afternoon since Condit wouldn't provide a corrected one, the wording in the timeline that implied that Condit was with the Vice President for three hours while Chandra disappeared had been exposed.

So if a carefully parsed phrase that indicated Condit was with Cheney for three hours couldn't stay, they would say how long the meeting was. Duncan Campbell of the Guardian quoted the Condit "camp" as saying that Condit met with Cheney "just 30 minutes before Ms. Levy logged off her computer" and that the meeting lasted 45 minutes. "This would put Mr Condit away from Ms Levy's apartment at the time the police believe she went missing."

15 minutes past Chandra's log off puts Condit away from her apartment when the police think she disappeared? Not only was the Condit source lying, it was only 20 minutes, not 45, but what kind of instantaneous disappearance did Condit have in mind that clears him if he was in a meeting 15 minutes after she logged off? What does he know that makes him think that's an alibi?

The three hours with Cheney was replaced with, according to Isikoff, returning to his office after a 20 to 25 minute meeting "taking phone calls" and meeting with staff members. "He may also have gone to the House gym and worked out," Isikoff reports.

"Taking phone calls"? "May have gone to the gym"? English translation. He wasn't in his office and no one knows where he was. Taking phone calls means there's no record of dialing a number to know who he was talking to which would have confirmed he was there. What did he do, play Frasier to Dayton's Roz saying "caller on line 3" and him answering with "I'm listening"?

Investigators told Michael Isikoff: "He was in his office [that afternoon]," said one law-enforcement official. "We've spoken to his staff and we're comfortable with their responses. His time is accounted for."

Was there even one constituent who reported talking to Condit Tuesday afternoon? Any staff besides Dayton? Dayton appeared with other staffers on Larry King Live but it was only Dayton who said:

> On May 1, I was with him probably every day that week. We went over, we met with the vice president that day, I was with him then, I picked him up, and we went to the meeting together, the vice president was gracious, and it

was the first time I got to meet the vice president. Then we went back to the office. So I was with him, you know, the whole day. [6]

Except that Condit may have gone to the gym, the corrected timeline now says. Any congressmen that lifted weights with him that afternoon, or just a solitary unmemorable workout? Could Condit leave the Rayburn Building where his office was without anyone noticing? Consider this excerpt from Time's Matthew Cooper as a horde of reporters chased Condit around the building:

> Indeed, the "Ag" committee has rarely been so packed with TV cameras going live—although the media horde trailing Condit somehow missed him leaving a late-night committee session last week to meet with the FBI and Washington police for a fourth interview. [7]

It doesn't matter much anyway if he doesn't have a car, and he noted prominently in his timeline that he doesn't have one, reports the New York Daily News. ABC News reports that his staff says he doesn't have a car. Makes it hard to be involved with a missing girl or make a call at midnight from Luray if you don't have a car, doesn't it?

In fact, the police wouldn't have known that Condit drove a red Ford Fiesta if Anne Marie Smith hadn't told them. Michael Isikoff of Newsweek reports the car was owned by a Condit aide. Where was the Ford Tuesday afternoon? How did Condit obtain it when he used it? Was the car registered with the Capitol Police and have a tag? Was it parked in a Congressional parking lot?

He got to a doctor's appointment somehow around 5 pm, according to his timeline. No doctor was reported to have seen Condit. The modern miracle of medical record privacy probably makes this a difficult area to investigate, probably not even possible to determine without a subpoena if he saw a doctor, when he made the appointment, or whether something happened to him that required a doctor Tuesday afternoon. Had he been deadlifting 110 pounds and hurt his back?

And subpeonaing a member of Congress can take awhile. When subpeonaed for some information later, Condit told Mark Sherman of the Associated Press that "he was considering whether to comply". Separation of powers and other weighty constitutional issues to be studied carefully first, we can presume. Just too much trouble. So ok, he went to a doctor.

Tabloids alleged it was a chiropractor Condit said he saw. Couldn't be that obvious, because the slang definition of a chiropractor appointment is:

> to Have a Chiropractor Appointment v. To purposely not be somewhere when you're supposed to be, especially school, to ditch. [8]

Naaaah. Couldn't be.

So no verifiable alibi for the whole afternoon when Chandra disappeared. He didn't vote until 6:30 pm. That is five and a half hours from when Condit left the meeting with Cheney until he voted, with only Dayton vowing to have been with him, except when Condit "may have gone to the gym". Five and a half hours is extreme, but given that Dayton told Joleen McKay that talking about the past "will ruin you", essentially unalibied.

The meeting with the reporter at the Tryst that didn't take place from 6:30 pm to 7:30 pm, one of the "bits and pieces not ready to go" in the first timeline, was replaced with a staff member driving him home at 7 pm.

That's odd. Odd, you say? Didn't people see Dayton driving Condit to and from work all summer as reporters chased him around? Sure, but before Chandra disappeared, Dayton usually didn't drive Condit home at night. Dayton often didn't drive himself. He tells Larry King:

> Well, OK, I live in Alexandria, Virginia. I mean, it's been treated like it's 100 miles away. I ride my bike from my house to the office. [9]

Condit also rode a bike or took a cab, as Dayton tells Thomas Frank of Newsday:

> Dayton, the Condit aide, said Condit no longer rides his bike to work or takes a taxi because the media throng outside his Washington apartment "makes it hard to get a cab." Aides pick him up each morning and bring him home each night. [10]

For example, the day after Chandra disappeared, Condit took a cab to the Tryst restaurant near his apartment with ABC News reporter Rebecca Cooper.

And no staff member gave him a ride home all week in his first timeline. But when the timeline was corrected, a staff member was driving Condit home.

Why did Dayton drive Condit home the day Chandra disappeared, when it appears it was not his normal procedure?

What was different about Tuesday for Condit to be driven home, other than his mistress disappearing? Did Dayton actually drive him home that day, and if so, why only that day?

Questions for us, but obviously not enough questions to make Condit a suspect to the Washington police. Niles Lathem of the New York Post reports:

> A shift in the search for missing intern Chandra Levy from Capitol Hill to Dumpsters near her apartment is expected to take the heat off her "good friend" Rep. Gary Condit—at least for now, police say. New information, based in part on careful analysis of Levy's cell-phone records and e-mails from her laptop computer, has led police to believe she was in her downtown Washington apartment for most of the afternoon on May 1—a little less than 24 hours after she was seen canceling her membership at a health club. [11]

How the police think that sending an e-mail at 10:45 in the morning and signing off the internet at 1 pm leads them to believe that Chandra was in her apartment for most of the afternoon is anyone's guess. Cell phone records? Independent reviewers of her cell phone bill reported no calls at all that day, much less in the afternoon.

Yet the heat was off. Condit had provided an alibi. Close enough for government work.

The Watch

The police were mollified. Chandra had been distraught, even obsessed, with the congressman. Who knows what she could have done? Maybe she just went away.

But what Condit thought should have went away, didn't. After seeing Condit in the news linked to a missing woman, after the FBI came to talk to her, and after being told by Condit not to talk to them, Anne Marie was scared. She told friends she wasn't going on any long trips and wasn't suicidal, so if she disappeared, that wasn't the cause. But at some point, she decided that only going public would make her feel safe from disappearing with her secrets.

She went public with what Helen Kennedy calls a "blockbuster interview" with Rita Cosby of Fox News. Kennedy of the New York Daily News quotes:

> Smith, a United Airlines flight attendant, said she went public because she fears for her life.
>
> "I was concerned about my safety," she told Fox News in a blockbuster interview. "This person doesn't want this relationship exposed. By my telling the story, setting it straight, telling the truth—I'll be much safer." [1]

Jim Robinson, a lawyer friend from her home town of Seattle, agreed to represent her pro bono. Anne Marie started being followed and getting strange calls and had to move out of her San Francisco apartment after she wouldn't sign this affadavit sent to Robinson by an investigator for Condit's lawyer:

> I, ANN MARIE SMITH, declare:
>
> 1. I am Ann Marie Smith, a flight attendant based in the San Francisco Bay area.
>
> 2. I regularly fly to the Washington, D.C., area as part of my job.

3. During the course of my employment I have become acquainted with Gary A. Condit, a U.S. congressman who is a frequent flier from San Francisco to Washington, D.C.

4. In addition to Congressman Condit, I also have become acquainted with other elected officials and their numerous staff members who travel weekly to the nation's capital.

5. I do not and have not had a relationship with Congressman Condit other than being acquainted with him. I do not and have not had a romantic relationship with Congressman Condit.

I declare under penalty of perjury under the laws of the United States of America that the foregoing is true and correct.

Ann Marie Smith [2]

After talking to the FBI and D.C. police for hours, investigators learned among other things from her that Condit drove a car, a red Ford, kept by an aide. They located it as a car kept by Dayton and searched it for clues to Chandra's disappearance, but found nothing.

Possibly emboldened by Anne Marie, and against the advice of the Levy's lawyer, Billy Martin, as well as against the request of the police, Linda Zamsky, the "unnamed relative" of the last few weeks, also went public with her charges against Condit. She released a 15 page statement detailing what Chandra had told her about her relationship with Condit, information that Zamsky had provided police and the FBI from the beginning.

Hervey Pean of Cox News Service quotes from it:

Levy had "described, in detail, some of their bedroom encounters," the aunt, Linda Zamsky, said in the statement.

"The Levy family is frustrated and outraged that Congressman Gary Condit and his associates have mischaracterized Chandra Levy's relationship with the congressman," Zamsky said in the statement. "From my many conversations with her, it was clear, without a doubt, that they were involved in an intimate relationship."

"Chandra's family feels strongly that everyone, including Rep. Condit, who was close to Chandra must cooperate fully with the investigation so that she can be found," Zamsky's statement read. "We believe that Rep. Condit's lack of candor is hindering efforts to find Chandra. We call on him to do what he would want others to do if one of his children were missing—give a complete account of his relationship with Chandra, what he knows about her whereabouts on the days leading up to her disappearance and any information he may have that can help investigators." [3]

Linda Zamsky knew Chandra wasn't distraught and obsessed, she had received an upbeat message of "big news" from Chandra just before she disappeared. And yet, behind the scenes, Chandra was being victimized yet again, forcing the Levys after two months to confront not only Condit's misportrayal of Chandra but the resulting police inaction as well.

The Levys would receive some criticism for it. How could they talk about their daughter's immoral behavior, nay, not just talk about it, but insist that Condit talk about it?

How shortsighted the criticism. The point wasn't yes, Chandra may be missing, but she was in love when she disappeared, and we insist you admit to the affair rather than deny it, the point was, as Allan Lengel of the Washington Post writes:

> Police searching for a missing person generally focus on those who were closest to the individual, attempting to establish frame of mind, habits and behavior before the disappearance.

> In cases involving women who vanish, police pay particular attention to the person or persons with whom they were last known to be having a sexual relationship. [4]

The police responded to these public exposures from Anne Marie Smith and Linda Zamsky, as the Washington Post reports:

> District police are still hoping for a fuller account from Rep. Gary A. Condit, who has had two interviews with investigators but has not clarified the nature of his relationship with missing intern Chandra Levy, a senior police official said yesterday.

> "We need more clarity in his relationship with Chandra and anything else he and others can add to her state of mind and lifestyle," said Terrance W. Gainer, the executive assistant police chief and the second highest-ranking officer in the department.

"It is not scheduled right now, but we would like another one with him," Gainer said, referring to a third interview. "Clearly we have an interest in doing that." [5]

Condit all of a sudden found time to meet with the police, that night even, when Zamsky revealed details of his relationship with Chandra that must have shaken him to the roots. As Petula Dvorak of the Washington Post reports:

The congressman was interviewed by police for a third time Friday night, and two sources familiar with the 90-minute meeting said Condit—who is married and has two grown children—reversed a denial that his aides had maintained since soon after the intern went missing after April 30. [6]

Newsweek reports that Condit told investigators in the interview following Zamsky's public statement that he "had a long-term sexual relationship with Chandra Levy". Michael Isikoff of Newsweek also added that Condit told the police there was no break in their relationship and that he had a final, routine phone call with her on Sunday, April 29.

He would later describe this publically as a one minute call to return her message, a routine call where he asked her if she had got her train ticket yet. Talk of a distraught Chandra who he told to go home and wouldn't return her calls had disappeared, just as she had.

The difference? Once he was linked romantically with Chandra, as he should have been from day one, any indications of emotional problems point to him. Once linked, his story changes. Which story to believe? The Levys wanted a lie detector test.

Inexplicably, reporters asked police if these revelations would give the police an excuse to search Condit's apartment. Just what the reporters who asked this think the police might find in Condit's apartment is puzzling.

Blood? Condit might have bludgeoned Chandra in his apartment and disposed of her as trash, while his wife was visiting?

True, Carolyn Condit was at the Washington Hilton Tuesday afternoon when Chandra disappeared, helping prepare for the First Lady's Luncheon to be held the next day for congressional wives. But why reporters would think that

Condit might invite Chandra to his apartment for a delightful afternoon before his wife returned, much less leave traces of blood in his apartment in the process, is difficult to fathom. More likely traces of perfume would lead to traces of blood, and it wouldn't be Chandra's.

Still, given the unexpected revelations, Condit was in full damage control mode. The police could search his apartment if they "thought it was helpful." [7] A late night search was arranged for Tuesday, July 10.

But a funny thing happened on the way to his apartment to meet the police. A man, well let's let him tell it, to Paula Zahn on Fox News The Edge:

ZAHN: Welcome, sir. Good to have you with us.

UNIDENTIFIED MALE: Good to be here, Paula.

ZAHN: If you would, can you take us back to the day that you spotted Gary Condit near the trash can we're seeing on the air here?

UNIDENTIFIED MALE: Certainly.

ZAHN: What did you see?

UNIDENTIFIED MALE: I was in a car driving behind a black Volkswagen. The black Volkswagen pulled over to the side of the road right at the corner. I couldn't tell whether or not it was going to turn right or if it was trying to park. And at that moment, a passenger got out, it was a man. He turned and looked at me, and I recognized him immediately from the media coverage as Gary Condit.

ZAHN: Now did he seem startled that you were looking him in the eye?

UNIDENTIFIED MALE: Well, I don't think startled. He definitely was not happy. He looked at me and then just took a few steps. He didn't look back. Took a few steps over to the garbage can, reached his hand in. And then after he put his hand in the garbage can, looked back at me with a scowling look on his face and got back into the car.

ZAHN: But at no point did he say anything to you?

UNIDENTIFIED MALE: He did not....

ZAHN: How close would you say you actually got to the congressman?

UNIDENTIFIED MALE: I would say about 15 feet away.

ZAHN: And were you able to make out who was driving the car? Can you describe him for us or her for us this evening?

UNIDENTIFIED MALE: I—all I could see through the window of the car, the rear window was it looked like short hair. It looked like a man driving but I couldn't—I didn't get a good look at him. I was surprised enough to see the congressman in that neighborhood in Alexandria.

ZAHN: And when the congressman got back in the car and you're trying to figure out what you just witnessed, what went through your mind, because you had been following this story pretty closely, right?

UNIDENTIFIED MALE: I had. I just immediately thought: I wonder what he threw away, you know. I wonder—he didn't just toss whatever it was into the garbage can like a wrapper or something. He reached his arm in, and I thought, that was interesting. So I immediately ran over to the garbage can to see if there was anything unusual in it.

ZAHN: And what did you find?

UNIDENTIFIED MALE: I found a cardboard box for a watch. It was actually torn into little pieces about four-inch square pieces and the watch—the manuals, warranty information, all of that for a watch.

ZAHN: And when you made this discovery, what went through your mind? What were you thinking?

UNIDENTIFIED MALE: I just—I thought it was—that was an interesting thing to have in a public garbage can on a street corner. I didn't know that that was exactly what the congressman had thrown away, but it was definitely unusual. I didn't really think very much of it until the next morning when I heard on the media report that his apartment had been searched the night before and talked to a police friend of mine who encouraged me to call, said something like that could be a big deal....

ZAHN: All right, and one last question for you. Once you reported this to local police, is it your understanding they in turn called the D.C. police?

UNIDENTIFIED MALE: I reported it to the D.C. police. I work in the District and so I reported to them. And then they—I talked directly with them, and they were the ones who actually went to the trash can and retrieved the box.

ZAHN: And did they give you any kind of reaction to your discovery? Did they say that this was relevant to the investigation, interesting, important?

UNIDENTIFIED MALE: They told me that, actually, it doesn't—it seemed to have anything to do with the disappearance of Chandra Levy, which is where they're focusing most of their attention, that it might come into play in other investigations, and you know, I might be contacted in the future about those.

ZAHN: And you expect to be contacted. I know the U.S. attorney's office called to thank you for your cooperation. Do you expect to be questioned by them?

UNIDENTIFIED MALE: They said they might contact me with—you know, in a few months, two or three months they might get back to me. But they're also working on finding Chandra. That's definitely first in their minds right now…. [8]

With the police coming to search his apartment, Condit tore a cardboard box for a watch into the the side and bottom pieces to flatten it and threw it away in a trash can in a park, along with the manual and warranty card that had been in the box. Except he didn't toss it as one normally would. He reached into the trash can and placed it in the trash can so suspiciously that a man driving into the park to walk his dog thought he'd better check what it was once he recognized the man as Condit.

When he checked, he saw something unusual. He didn't know that Condit had placed the torn down watch box and manual in the trash can, he just noticed that was an unusual thing to be in the trash can when he looked. And he did notice it just laying there in the trash in view, as he notes. Then he went home.

It wasn't until he saw on the news the next morning that Condit's apartment had been searched overnight that he thought he'd better tell someone, and then it was only to call a policeman friend, who advised him to call the police. So even though this happened a few hours before the police searched Condit's apartment, they did not know about it as they searched. D.C. police came and found the watch box still in the trash can the next morning.

Tom Squitieri of USA Today reports what they found:

Authorities have indicated that among other things, they want to ask Condit why he allegedly discarded a watchcase in a trash can in Alexandria, Va., just hours before police searched his apartment July 10. The case was traced to a Tag Heuer watch given to Condit by a 29-year-old San Francisco woman who was on his staff during the mid-1990s. [9]

It was the box, manual, and warranty card for an over $400 Tag Heuer watch that Joleen McKay had given Condit in 1996 just before they broke up. Several news reports such as USA Today's above referred to it as a watch case rather than a watch box, which was confusing because Tag Heuer watches come in a nice zippered leather case inside the box. This was the cardboard box, torn down, in which a leather case enclosed watch would be sold along with the manual and warranty card. The Tag Heuer watch and leather case was not with the box and manual in the trash can.

Joleen was the former Condit girlfriend who went to the FBI as soon as she saw Chandra in the news linked to Condit. She also called Dayton a few times to encourage him to get Condit to cooperate with the police. She apparently didn't believe the "good friend" statement Condit issued, as OC Thomas says his daughter Jennifer didn't either. They know him so well.

So he was throwing away a gift box from a girlfriend given to him five years earlier. What's the big deal?

Many people were rightfully concerned about obstruction of justice. The New York Daily News reports that "One investigator was quoted as saying the watch case may have no bearing on the Levy case, but its disposal 'shows a pattern of deceit.'" What else might he have thrown away before they searched his apartment?

Well, that's the silliness of a voluntary search of his apartment two and half months after Chandra disappeared. One would have to expect that he would throw out anything he didn't want the police to see before a scheduled search. If there ever was cause to search, such as Joleen McKay calling the D.C. police and urging them to search his apartment, which is what she did as soon as it hit the news, then that is the time to search. But if there wasn't probable cause then, there certainly wasn't two and a half months later after he cleaned out his apartment.

The police were counting on the infallibility of detecting blood, no matter how minute, if it had ever been there. True, but the concept of a bloodily murdered Chandra in his apartment, accidental or otherwise, and then somehow disposing of her in his dumpster or sneaking her body out of his apartment building is, to put it tactfully, not probable.

Instead, this was a public relations exercise. Condit had admitted to an affair. A public search of his apartment, a lie detector test, and everyone could go on about their business. Condit could be cleared and resume his public life. The press could focus on other questions and life would go on.

But it just wouldn't go away that easily. The watch that had come in the watch box was given to him by a former staffer, hardly a reason to be afraid to throw it away in his own trash either at home or at the Rayburn Building, where the staffer and he had worked and where he would say that he had it. How could a cardboard watch box with a manual and warranty card arouse suspicion, even if it was found to be a gift from a staffer from five years ago?

Vince Flammini remembers when she gave it to him. He tells Geraldo Rivera:

RIVERA: She's the one that got him the watch?

Mr. FLAMMINI: She's the one that got him the watch, and I remember when he got—when she got it for him. He was upset because he don't wear watches. [10]

Condit knew Joleen had called Dayton a few times. He didn't know the police and FBI had talked to her. He could be trying to erase any evidence that they had ever been close should the police ask him. Still, the real question is, why did he have a five year old watch box with manual and warranty card, either at home or in his office?

How big a Congressional office and apartment would a representative need to keep such things as empty cardboard watch boxes sitting for five years after they get it? Wherever the box was, it must have held the watch until recently. Otherwise, why would someone keep an empty watch box for five years?

It had been posted on the internet that the reason people hold on to Tag Heuer watchboxes, other than their being status symbols, is that the box enhances the value of the watch as a collector's item, as well as its re-sale value. It's a way of authenticating it. The post said that there are hundreds being offered for sale on the net, and many of the ads refer to the "original presentation box."

It might make a difference in sale price, and also makes it suitable for re-giving as a gift, depending on whether the watch had been worn more than a few times. But by whom? Condit was upset to even get it as a gift. Yet he had the watch box it came in five years later. Where was the watch?

Why haven't the police released the serial number? Perhaps the watch box, warranty card, and the store where Joleen bought it don't have the serial number and the police have no Tag Heuer serial number to look for. There was no announcement of an alert to pawnshops as there was for Chandra's ring when Chandra was found. Wouldn't an announcement like that be critical to finding the watch?

Or do the police know where the watch is? You would think that if Condit had the watch, there would be some comment along the lines that he threw out the box but kept the watch. Strange.

Someone else must have the watch, and it would appear they got it not that long before Chandra disappeared, otherwise Condit held onto an empty watch box in his tiny Congressional office or apartment after giving the watch to someone months or years earlier. To whom, and why didn't he give the box, manual, and warranty card with it?

Condit did something else strange besides throw a watch box in an Alexandria, Virginia park trash can just before police searched his apartment. For some reason, he explains that he threw it away in a french fries box. Judy Bachrach of Vanity Fair tells Larry King:

> KING: What about mystery of dumping the watch in Alexandria, Virginia—nowhere near where he lives?
>
> BACHRACH: Well, he dumped…
>
> KING: The watch box.
>
> BACHRACH: …the watch box, I was told by a very good friend of his, in a package of McDonald's french fries. He had gone out to buy a hamburger and

french fries for his wife Carolyn and he then drove with an aide to Virginia, and dumped that watchbox inside a package of McDonald's french fries and then threw it in trash. [11]

A week later, his daughter Cadee told Larry King:

KING: What did you make of the missing watch box?

CONDIT: Well.

KING: I mean how do you piece together that story? It is a strange story.

CONDIT: It is a strange story, and the only thing I can say with the watch box is there were French fries involved.

KING: There were?

CONDIT: Yes.

KING: Well, I don't know anybody who drives that far to drop off French fries in a box.

CONDIT: Knowing at the same time that Mike Dayton, they had been to his house, it wasn't like they drove out of town just to throw something away. They were in that town.

KING: He was with Mike, and Mike was out with Gary. In other words, he didn't take a box from a room, and say "let's drive seven miles."

CONDIT: No, and he didn't take anything from his apartment either. This is from his office. He never took anything from his apartment. [12]

Half a year later, it changed to Five Guys restaurant and the reference to being in a french fries box was dropped, but the concept of going for fast food remained the same, as Condit tells Larry King:

KING: We'll be taking calls for Gary Condit. And it must be—I think the thing that may have hurt you the most in all this was why you took a gift of a watch to another city to throw it away. What happened?

(LAUGHTER)

GARY CONDIT: Oh, that watch box thing.

KING: What happened?...

GARY CONDIT: Well, actually, you know, the watch box had nothing to do with Chandra. I mean, I cleaned out my desk and the tabloids were going through all my trash. As they may go through your trash from time to time. So I threw it in a trash can. I didn't drive somewhere particular to throw it away. I just—the first trash can that came along, I threw it in a trash can with some garbage. And we stopped, as a matter of fact, my wife was in Washington, we stopped at Five Guys restaurant, we got some food to take home. Me and another gentleman and we were taking it home and I said pull over, I'm going to throw this trash away. And I threw it away, and Larry—

KING: Your wife was with you?

GARY CONDIT: No, she wasn't with me. Another gentleman was with me. As soon as I threw it in the garbage can, it wasn't a dumpster or anything. It was just a garbage can on the street. There was a guy who ran up beside my car and dove in the garbage can. I could see his legs hanging out. Now, he was with the tabloids. That watch box story came from the tabloids.

KING: Did the watch have any meaning?

GARY CONDIT: None.

KING: It was a gift from a friend—a girlfriend?

GARY CONDIT: It just—it had no meaning. It was just in my desk. In congress when you move from office to office, one of the things that goes with you from every office you move into, as you move around offices is your desk. So, you know, I never cleaned my desk out, But what I did, Larry, was I cleaned my desk out simply because I knew people were going through—you know—they wanted photographs of my family. I cleared all the family photos out, all the letters that I had from—you know—both presidents, from Bush—President Bush, President Clinton, Al Gore. All those people I had in my desk, I took everything out, put them in a file under lock and key. Because I just didn't want the tabloids to end up with those letter. So—and I saw them going through my garbage at my—where I live in Washington, D.C. I mean, I actually saw them talk to the garbage men about going through my garbage. So that's what that was about, it had nothing to do with anything. [13]

It is puzzling what putting the box in a french fries holder was supposed to be about, especially since he didn't do it. The man who looked in the trash can just saw the torn down watch box and manual laying in the trash, not buried or hidden within other trash. And it appears that Condit has changed to Five Guys from McDonalds to explain driving to Alexandria for some fast food. There are two Five Guys restaurants in Alexandria.

But it was more complicated than that. Condit didn't just drive out for some fast food for him and his wife with an aide. The New York Post and the Washington Post report that Dayton was the aide that was driving Condit when he was seen in the Alexandria park. Dayton lived in Alexandria, on Upland Place just off Route 7, or King St., the main east-west drag through Alexandria.

The major park in Alexandria is Chinquapin Park at 3210 King St. King St. runs to I-395, and there is a Five Guys there. Chinquapin Park is about a mile from Dayton's Alexandria home towards I-395 and a Five Guys restaurant.

If you were taking Condit from Alexandria to Adams Morgan to, say, get his apartment searched, you would take I-395 up. And a mile up Route 7 from Dayton's house you stop at the park and throw away something. There would be no food involved yet. That would be when you get to I-395 and stop at Five Guys on the way north.

Now it is entirely possible that the empty box was in Condit's office for five years, and that he chose to clean out his office when his apartment was to be searched, and took the box with him all the way to Dayton's house, then stopped at a Five Guys restaurant to get a burger and fries, and on his way home stopped at a park to throw it away.

I think instead it's a whopper.

It's more probable that they got the watch box from Dayton's house to throw it away. There would have been more room there to store it, and Dayton used to date Joleen. But either way, the only conclusion one can draw is that Condit did not expect to see the watch again.

Garance Franke-Ruta writes in Washington City Paper:

> While 13 TV-news cameras train their sights on Democratic California Rep. Gary Condit's condo building on the night of July 10, waiting for the congressman to come home so the police can search his apartment, 15 of Condit's neighbors gather on the stoop of 2611 Adams Mill Road, clutching cigarettes and red plastic cups filled with beer.
>
> When the haggard but smiling congressman finally arrives home, around 8:40 p.m., Troy, who lives on the second floor, bounds up the steps to open the

door, walks him down the hall toward the elevator, and then returns to shoo reporters away. [14]

The haggard but smiling congressman finally arrived home, minus a watch box. Mission accomplished.

Police entered his apartment to search for "blood, hair, telltale signs of a struggle" at 11:30 pm. [15] ABC News reported later that no forensic evidence turned up to help find Chandra.

The next day police tried to put Condit's role in Chandra's disappearance to rest. They asked Condit to take an FBI-administered polygraph. Helen Kennedy of the New York Daily News quotes Chief Ramsey: "It's in the best interests of everyone concerned to answer the questions," Ramsey said. "He wants to put this to rest as much as we do."

But Condit was trying to limit what he would answer. Ramsey told Kennedy: "If we can't have an interview in which we can ask the questions we want to ask, there's no point in doing it," said Police Chief Charles Ramsey.

Apparently there wasn't. Condit's lawyer Abbe Lowell announced that Condit had passed a privately administered polygraph. Bob Dart of Cox News Service reports:

> His attorney announced that Condit had taken and passed a lie detector test answering the "only questions that matter." He said these were whether Condit knows where Levy is, whether he ever harmed her or had anyone else harm her, and whether he has anything to do with her disappearance. [16]

The D.C. police expressed their surprise and disappointment. From the Washington Post:

> "My impression was that we were going to continue that dialogue. I took him at his word," Executive Assistant Police Chief Terrance W. Gainer said of the negotiations with Lowell. "I just didn't expect it quite this way." [17]

CNN reports more of what the police had to say:

> "I'm not happy with how they did it. I don't know how an examiner could possibly give an exam like that without knowing all the facts in the case,"

Ramsey said. "They didn't ask us; in fact, they misled us into believing it was somehow going to be a cooperative effort. That didn't happen."

"We were told that the congressman was busy, attending sessions, things of that nature," he said. "Obviously that wasn't true, so we would just like everybody to be up front and honest and if you're going to do a private exam, just say so." [18]

Condit had paid an ex-FBI polygraph consultant, Barry Colvert, $1,031 to ask him three questions. Colvert passed him. In contrast, consider what a real lie detector test entails. Elizabeth Smart's father was asked to take one, and like most people except silent Modesto men Gary Condit and Scott Peterson, he of course agreed. Elizabeth's uncle, Tom Smart, describes what her father went through to Nancy Grace on Larry King Live:

GRACE: A lot of focus has been placed on your brother, Edward Smart. We all know he's taken a polygraph. What was his response to that?

SMART: He said it was four hours of hell. And he's willing to go do a polygraph. He didn't know that—he didn't volunteer that. But somehow a polygraph—something got out and I said, "Ed what about a polygraph?" And he just went, yes I've been through four hours of hell—and whatever.

The entire family is willing to take polygraphs. We'll do whatever you want. I don't know who has and who hasn't. But the family's—the family will do anything. Just...

GRACE: I'm trying to imagine my own dad strapped to a polygraph for four hours trying to answer questions, the whole time, wondering where the heck his daughter is, you know, taken in the middle of the night. Did he pass the polygraph?

SMART: Yes. I was told that he passed the polygraph. When you do a polygraph, and I know because I've done one just recently—I should never say that...[19]

Four hours of hell. That's what the police would have needed to stress Condit to see if he was telling the truth. Not three pre-arranged questions, four hours of hell, if it was worth doing, which by arranging for a private one seems to be the case.

The police wanted to polygraph Condit when they knew he had pitched the watch box just before his apartment was searched but he didn't know that they knew. They reluctantly revealed this information after he arranged for Barry Colvert to ask him three general questions shortly after his apartment was searched. When Condit's lawyer announced this and that they would not take the police test, the police could no longer use this as a question that would have tested Condit's truthfulness and established a baseline to compare to other detailed questions about May 1.

Helen Kennedy reports:

> Ramsey said he also has questions about the congressman's alibi.
>
> "It could just be a mistake, but it could be something more than that," Ramsey said. "If we're going to have a polygraph examination, those are the kinds of issues that we need to kind of lock down." [20]

The irony is that if Condit had lied as expected if he were asked about throwing away evidence, they would have a non-trivial lie to compare to his answers about Chandra. Answers about not knowing anything about Chandra's disappearance could have been determined to be truthful with a high degree of assurance because they would have a known lie to compare to it.

Of course, he may have even told the truth about that as well. No one will ever know. Condit chose not to go through that particular hell.

For some reason, everyone else but Condit did.

Exposed

OC Thomas had been questioned by the FBI shortly after Chandra disappeared, when Susan Levy asked him specific questions about the relationship he had told her about between his daughter Jennifer and their congressman, Gary Condit. She then called the FBI, who approached OC to talk to him.

Special Agent Todd Irinaga conducted the interview and also wanted to talk to Jennifer, but OC told them she was afraid. She refused to talk to the FBI for weeks despite him trying to convince her that she would be safer by telling her story. Jennifer was still at home with her parents and her now six year old son, but the FBI didn't press her about talking for two months.

At the same time, as Linda Zamsky told the FBI and Washington Post what she knew about Chandra and Condit, she told of the role that OC Thomas and Susan Levy talking in the Levys' garden and calling Chandra may have played in her disappearance. The Levys were at a minimum disturbed at her sudden disappearance after warning her about Condit. The Washington Post followed up by approaching OC to interview him. Allan Lengel and Petula Dvorak of the Washington Post describe it:

> Thomas, 54, was approached by the FBI in May, after Levy's parents told investigators that Thomas had told them in mid-April that his daughter had had a relationship with Condit. In six lengthy interviews, Thomas, a part-time gardener at the Levys' California home, told the Post that his daughter had broken off the relationship with Condit and that Condit had warned her at the time not to tell anyone of the affair. [1]

> Thomas said he did not think about his story until Levy disappeared and her family encouraged him to come forward. When the FBI approached Thomas, the minister described an affair that he said had taken place in the mid-1990s, after his daughter met Condit at a political rally on a college campus. Agents tried to meet with the daughter, who is now 26, but Thomas told them she was in hiding. [2]

OC was also interviewed by Jeff Jardine of his hometown newspaper, the Modesto Bee, and told them the same story, a fairly detailed history of his daughter's relationship and breakup with Condit. But as he was being interviewed by reporters, he told them and the Levys, even calling Paul Katz and Linda Zamsky in Maryland, that he had just received an anomynous threatening phone call, a "very intimidating" experience he told them, since they knew things about his family. "Shut up and listen,", he was told. "Don't talk to anyone about Condit". [3]

It was too late. Word was out to the press, and they were staking out his apartment complex. A few days before July 12, after weeks of interviews with the Washington Post and Modesto Bee, as well as an interview with the FBI, he agreed to go public to help find Chandra. They published his story on July 12.

But in trying to get Jennifer's confirmation for the story, she would have none of it. "I don't want to talk about that," she told the Washington Post when she answered the phone, and she told them she didn't want her picture in the paper.

OC said his daughter was scared. Anne Marie Smith understood why. She told Helen Kennedy of the New York Daily News:

> "She's very scared and I totally understand where she's coming from," Smith said after being grilled for 12 hours over two days by investigators probing Condit.
>
> "I don't need to be afraid anymore—they reassured me. I feel much better. But now I'm worried about [Thomas]." [4]

The story came out, and this note was posted on the Thomas' door:

> My name is Jennifer Thomas. This letter is to anyone with an interest in me or my father. We are not interested in an interview, we do not want to be on TV for any reason. I will tell you that I never knew Mrs. Levy's daughter. I never met that congressman who's involved in all this.
>
> I don't even have an interest in politics as it is. Mrs. Levy's daughter and I were never friends in school or anywhere else, I don't even know if we went to the same school or something together. I don't know this family personally. I never met Mrs. Levy until she showed up at my father's house looking for me. I don't even know how both me and my father got mixed up in this, we don't know anything so stop calling us and showing up at our door. Jennifer Thomas. [5]

OC Thomas wasn't around to see the note though. He had told his downstairs neighbor, Betty Hoffman, three days earlier that the FBI suggested he leave town to avoid the media, and she hadn't seen him since. She also said that Jennifer Thomas had a mixed-race son, who Jennifer told her was Mexican. She said of OC's story, to Timothy Burger and Helen Kennedy of the New York Daily News:

> "I would never have thought it," said Hoffman, 47, of her neighbor's reported liaison with Condit. "She don't seem like the type. Very, very, very quiet. Very, very, very shy."

> But Hoffman said Rev. Thomas wouldn't lie. [6]

Vince Flammini didn't believe it for a second, and he was Condit's driver in Modesto in 1994. He told Jeff Jardine of the Modesto Bee:

> "That's a bull—story," Flammini said. "I worked for him all through that time. I was his driver. I've never seen that girl in my life."

> Flammini also disputed that Condit took Thomas to his home in Ceres, as her father contends.

> "Gary would never do that," said Flammini, who earlier confirmed Condit's relationship with Smith, the flight attendant. "There's no way I ever took girls to Gary's house. I don't know how it could have gotten by me." [7]

OC Thomas, his wife, and Jennifer lived in a Ceres apartment complex about a mile down Richard Way from Condit's Acorn Lane home, but did they live there in 1993? That would be within walking distance for the college freshman who her father said was helping with Condit's campaign, and Flammini wouldn't necessarily need to be involved. But if Jennifer told her father she went to Condit's house and didn't, was any part of her story true?

Jeff Jardine of the Modesto Bee reports on what others thought of OC Thomas:

> Others affiliated with his church, the Prayer Mission Church of God in Christ in Modesto, said they do not believe he would fabricate a story such as the one he has told regarding his daughter and Condit.

> "I just can't see him doing that," said Ester Ard, wife of the church's pastor. "He's a very caring person. There's nothing he won't do for a person."

Thomas was described as compassionate, honest and upstanding. He served as a pastor at another church until heart trouble forced him to retire. Thomas does volunteer maintenance at Prayer Mission Church.

Pamela Niblett, who occasionally attends the church, described Thomas and his wife as giving.

"They're good people," said Niblett, 34, of Modesto.

Thomas' daughter does not attend the church, Ard said. [8]

The pastor's wife of OC Thomas' church doesn't mention another daughter, a twin daughter. On Wednesday July 11, when reporters were getting the story for the next day's release of this story, neighbor Betty Hoffman thought Jennifer was home:

Thomas told the Post his daughter is afraid to talk with the FBI and has gone into hiding, but Hoffman said Jennifer Thomas works at a local fast food restaurant and was home Wednesday. [9]

The next day reporters learn that Jennifer has a twin sister, Janet:

Meanwhile, the FBI tried to find Jennifer Thomas, the California woman whose father claims she went into hiding for fear a previous relationship with Condit would be discovered. [10]

A neighbor in the complex said Jennifer Thomas has a twin sister named Janet. The neighbor, Betty Hoffman, said media who went to the apartment Wednesday night probably spoke with Janet and not Jennifer, who is believed to still be out of the area. [11]

Her twin sister, Janet, has refused to talk to the media. [12]

Did Jennifer and her little boy leave with her dad three days earlier to avoid reporters? CNN reports the note signed by Jennifer Thomas was found on the door on Thursday. The previous evening reporters had been banging on their door and Betty Hoffman said Jennifer was home. The next day a note is up signed by Jennifer Thomas but the neighbor says they were probably talking to Jennifer's twin sister, Janet.

Did Jennifer write the note before she left? Did Janet write it and sign it Jennifer? Does Jennifer even have a twin sister Janet? Jeff Jardine and Michael Mooney wrote this in the Modesto Bee:

> The Stanislaus County Library has received numerous requests from the media to take photographs of Levy from Davis High School yearbooks. So the library staff simply listed on the cover of each book where her photos could be found inside.
>
> Likewise, there have been requests to take pictures of a photo of Jennifer Thomas, and there is a Jennifer Thomas in the 1993 Modesto High School yearbook. [13]

And that 1993 Modesto High School picture of Jennifer Thomas was displayed in news articles, labeled as an undated high school photo. The problem is that it is a 1993 junior picture of a Jennifer Thomas who went to Modesto High School, and there is no Janet Thomas picture along with it.

For Jennifer Thomas to be going to the California State Stanislaus campus in nearby Turlock in 1994 as her father described she would have to have been a 1993 high school graduate, requiring a senior picture in the 1993 yearbook. And where was her twin sister?

Was this the wrong Jennifer Thomas displayed in the newspapers? Maybe Jennifer got her wish and her picture wasn't in the paper. On the other hand, they currently lived in Ceres. Did the 1993 yearbook in the Ceres High School library have senior pictures of Jennifer and Janet Thomas?

If not, what does it mean for the Thomas' to have moved from Modesto to Ceres close to Condit's house after going through something which made OC Thomas cry telling Susan Levy about it? Susan told the Modesto Bee: "I had him in my living room and he was full of tears," she said. "...I've never seen a man broken up like that."

Also not mentioned in OC's story as reported by the Washington Post and Modesto Bee is any reference to Jennifer having a child during the relationship. The New York Post reported finding a birth certificate with father's name as "withheld" and noted it was during the alleged two year relationship, but no quotes from OC or Susan Levy concerning it.

The New York Daily News referred to the possibility of Condit "siring the son of a minister's daughter in Modesto, Calif." because the minister "told the FBI she was seeing Condit when her son was born in 1994."

In fact, what he did tell the Washington Post is the opposite of any long term link to Condit such as a child:

> He said he advised her to end the liaison immediately. She did so, and the father and daughter never spoke of it again, he said. "I didn't really think much about it since then, until Mrs. Levy asked me about him," Thomas said. [14]

For OC to have been shocked for Jennifer to tell him she was seeing Condit and wanted advice with the problems she was having with him, he would have to have known or thought someone else was the father of his grandchild.

Was the name of the father withheld from her parents as well as on the birth certificate? What father would demand such secrecy? Why was the child not mentioned by the Levys or the Washington Post? Was this to protect the child?

Susan Levy did not specifically say that she mentioned the child when she called Chandra to warn her about Condit, nor is it clear what if anything OC told her, the FBI, and the Washington Post about Jennifer's child in his story. But whatever he told them, when OC returned to Modesto he stood by it. He told the Washington Post:

> "Why would she lie about that? Why would I lie about that? I have nothing to profit from this," Thomas said. Of his daughter, he said: "She's so angry with me, she doesn't even want to talk to me. She's scared. She's a very quiet and shy person to begin with, so she doesn't want all this attention." [15]

He would answer his own question a few days later. The FBI now wanted to talk to Jennifer, and OC "backed off" his story, according to the FBI. [16] OC Thomas told Allan Lengel and Petula Dvorak of the Washington Post why he told Susan Levy the story in the garden:

> "I just figured I would try to comfort her a bit," Thomas said. "I just dug a hole I could not get out of. I can't really explain something like that."
>
> Thomas said that every time he shared his story—with the Levys, the FBI and The Post—he was "hoping it would go away." Instead, the media descended on the apartment complex after his story was published, straining relations with his relatives. "They were hurt," he said of his family, adding that he and his wife have spent many days crying.

Thomas said he met the Levys—the session took place at the FBI offices in Modesto—and told them that he had fabricated the story and apologized. He said federal authorities had mentioned obstruction of justice charges but also said this was unlikely if his current version holds true. [17]

The FBI concurred:

"After what we believe to be a thorough investigation of allegations previously made by O.C. Thomas regarding Congressman Gary Condit, we believe these allegations to be unfounded," Chris Murray, spokesman for the FBI in Washington, said yesterday. [18]

That's a mighty interesting story, wouldn't you say? Imagine making up a story out of thin air and then retelling that story so consistently and with no obvious validation errors over two months to Susan Levy twice, the FBI, the Modesto Bee, and the Washington Post six times that they all found it credible.

Odd that he could just make up details like his daughter being a campus rally volunteer for Condit when he met her, having a two year affair, and his daughter having to break off the affair out of fear because of strange sexual demands from Condit.

What strange details to sit and make up as you cry and warn Chandra's mother. Odd that a minister would make all this up and sit and listen to her mother call Chandra and hear her be told to mind her own business. How comforting is that?

Isn't later making up his daughter yelling at the tv "that's a lie" and the telephoned threat where he was told to "shut up and listen" and then given a warning he found "very intimidating" to be an extremely imaginative embellishment, to say the least?

Some investigators thought he was backing off his story to protect his daughter. Paul Katz believes his story is true. He tells Larry King:

KING: Do you know Reverend Thomas?

KATZ: Yes, I met him.

KING: And do you believe him?

KATZ: Yes, I believe him.

KING: And why, then, is the daughter—or was the daughter denying it?

KATZ: I think that clearly the daughter was frightened and, therefore, was not willing to come forward. He sat there in Susan's den and poured his heart out to the Susan, Bob, and I. And the sequence, so far as I see it, in the way that it happened is that he revealed to Susan and the situation between his daughter and the congressman, Susan immediately called Chandra on the phone.

Chandra's response was: I'm big enough to take care of myself. Don't worry about it. And a week later, she called Susan back. Tells Susan, I talked to him about it. It's nothing to worry about. A week after that. Chandra disappears....

The other part about this whole thing is that you know, when—when the reverend called and spoke to Linda and myself, he told us about how he was physically—well he was threatened, verbally over the phone.

KING: By whom? Did he tell you who?

KATZ: Just some male voice. Didn't mention any names, just a male voice. And he was clearly frightened. And, you know, just these events. There's clearly something submerged still to be discovered about all of this. [19]

Susan Levy believes his story is true. She tells Newsweek:

What did you make of Otis Thomas, your gardener, who said his daughter had also been involved with Condit and who took back his story?

MRS. LEVY: Even though he apologized to me because he lied to me, my intuitive gut feeling was that he wasn't [lying]. I can't see how someone could have brought up a story like that in the first place if it wasn't [true].

When did you and Mr. Thomas have this conversation about his daughter's alleged involvement with Condit?

MRS. LEVY: Early April, end of March. We were talking about daughters in general, and it just kind of came out about his daughter. I didn't tell him anything about whom [Chandra] was seeing because I did not know. But I used a mother's intuitive thing to put two and two together and that's how I knew, and I asked my daughter about it directly afterward on the phone. And told her to be careful, because I didn't want her to get hurt. [Later] she told me she had talked to her friend and she said, "Everything's OK. He knows everything," and then a little bit later my daughter no longer has her job and a few days later she disappears. What can I say? Kind of strange to me. Real strange.

You think that conversation was pivotal?

MRS. LEVY: I have no idea. I know the relationship was supposed to be very secret. And something happens and it gets out, and all of a sudden my daughter's missing. I feel responsible in a way. Maybe if I hadn't raised that story, things would be different. I don't know. It makes me wonder. [20]

Consider that the story of the staffer Joleen McKay who gave Condit the watch whose box he threw away in a public park trashcan just before his apartment was searched and the details of this girl's father's story all took place in 1994, a long time ago with all the details of a true story to blurt out to a worried mother as he prunes her roses.

The coincidence of Susan Levy telling a gardener that she's worried about her daughter dating an unnamed Congressman and the gardener's 18 year old daughter also having a relationship with a congressman who later turns out to be the same man defies imagination.

Yet OC Thomas answered questions that made believers of Chandra's father, mother, and uncle, suspended disbelief for six interviews from hard core Washington Post reporters, not naive to the political implications of this, and kept the FBI intrigued for months.

Just out of curiosity, how would Jennifer entering a witness protection program have been handled any differently?

Rock Creek Park

The wind was calm in Ft. Lauderdale. Condit's perfect storm had sucked in Chandra Levy, Anne Marie Smith, Jennifer Thomas, Joleen McKay, and a cast of thousands, but Condit's other brother Darrell didn't care. The storm hadn't reached him, and he had his own problems. The police were looking for him. They had been for the last six years.

Easy enough. He wasn't Darrell Condit. He was Stanley Johnnie Buchanan, the identity of one of his many cellmates in jails spread out over five states, for drugs and whatever it took to get the money to buy them—armed robbery, car theft, battery. He had violated parole for a 1996 run in with the law, this time for driving with his license suspended, possession of marijuana, and driving under the influence. A $50,000 warrant for his arrest had been issued in Key West.

The Levys wanted the D.C. police to question him about where he was May 1, but the D.C. police didn't even know where he was now. Brian Blomquist of the New York Post:

> D.C. police spokesman Joe Gentile said he wouldn't know where to send FBI agents to talk to Darrell.
>
> "We don't know where in the hell he is," Gentile told The Post.
>
> Gentile said D.C. detectives remain more interested in interviewing all of Levy's neighbors, as well as people at her D.C. health club. [1]

Were the Levys grasping at blowing straws to sic the police on Condit's fugitive brother? While a fugitive from Florida, Darrell was also wanted for drug charges in Stanislaus County, home of Modesto, only a year and half earlier. Serious drug charges, four years prison worth. He was a fugitive from Modesto as well.

He had fled back to Florida and been arrested in Ft. Lauderdale in October for possession of cocaine, possession of drug paraphernalia, and resisting arrest without violence, and arrested again as recently as February for possession of marijuana. For some reason, no matter who arrested him, no matter how many times, he was released.

Did he owe his congressman brother more than anyone dared think, or would a distinguished congressman even be talking to a brother who was a fugitive from his own district?

All of a sudden Darrell, who thrived on being known as Stanley Buchanan, was in the news. American Media, publisher of National Enquirer, Star, and Globe, had their offices located in the area. Could their ace reporters find Darrell in their backyard before anyone else? The editor of the Star claimed to have on Geraldo, citing reports of local construction workers who said that Darrell worked most of April, then disappeared and returned in early May, walking with a cane.

This is standard American Media fare, someone surely did tell them this, and they published it, but confirming details of the company, dates, corroborating details that could have been provided, weren't.

No newspaper touched it. Wouldn't it have been interesting journalism to rebuke the claim by seeing the day labor pay records for early May for Darrell? But then again, maybe there are no records. Then, where was Darrell on May 1?

The ubiquitous publicity of Chandra Levy's disappearance caught up with Darrell. He was recognized by a Broward County Sheriff's Deputy checking into a motel in Dania Beach in the Ft. Lauderdale area at 3:30 am. Another arrest, this time the charges were resisting arrest without violence, false identification, driving with a suspended license, and a misdemeanor possession of marijuana, bond set at $50,000. He was driving a silver Toyota Previa minivan borrowed from his girlfriend.

None other than a former Watergate lawyer showed up. Johnny Diaz of the Miami Herald quotes him:

> "They have not kept up with each other," said attorney Jon Sale, who worked for Archibald Cox and Leon Jaworski during the investigation of Richard

Nixon. "He says he loves his brother but said he has not spoken to him in a long time."

Sale wouldn't say who hired him to represent Darrell Condit. [2]

A long time turned out to be about a year. Would that be in October when Condit started dating Chandra in D.C. and Darrell was arrested for cocaine and released despite being wanted in both Florida and California? Did Darrell owe Condit for getting out of jail again?

He would get out yet again. Someone paid his $50,000 bail, and it surely wasn't a bail bondsman who risked $50,000 on a six year fugitive because whoever put it up was bound to lose it. And they did. He was arrested again in March, 2002 after failing to appear for his November hearing.

In addition to jumping bail, the charges this time were resisting arrest without violence, driving with a suspended license, and marijuana possession. Why would somebody hire a Watergate lawyer and practically throw away $50,000 to keep Darrell out of jail? Whoever it was wasn't talking.

While a search had been on for Darrell, the D.C. police put a search on for Chandra in Rock Creek Park. It was mid-July, and areas near the Potomac and Anacostia Rivers had been searched and dragged earlier, but the information about computer web sites she had visited had just been belatedly given to them by the FBI. It showed that she looked up Rock Creek Park the day she disappeared.

The police were just now finding this out, two and a half months after she disappeared? How could that happen? Shouldn't they have known more like two and a half days after she disappeared?

With the Newport manager refusing to arrange for the D.C. police to check on Chandra's apartment despite frantic calls from Chandra's parents and worried calls from the landlord, it was a week before the police would check her apartment. It was another week before they removed her computer to give to the FBI. The FBI handles forensic analysis for D.C., and the police were expecting the information back in another three weeks, making the information more than a month old before they could respond to any revelations of what Chandra was doing on her computer before she disappeared.

The FBI sent the computer to a private laboratory, and it didn't come back in the expected three weeks. Lynn Sweet of the Chicago Sun-Times reports that Chief Gainer said the hard drive had crashed. They would get the information two months later instead.

Isn't the point of private laboratories to get timely processing? Why would it take three weeks to back up her hard drive and take a look at it? And if the hard drive crashed, and that's a big if, was it a hard crash with an embedded head, or just an excuse, but if the hard drive crashed, it doesn't take two months to retrieve the data. But it did for the FBI and their private laboratory.

But the D.C. police finally received the list of web sites, and the police were focused on Klingle Mansion. The Washington Post reports:

> Chandra Levy looked up a map site on the Internet for the Klingle Mansion in Rock Creek Park before logging off her laptop computer for the last time, a senior police official said yesterday. [3]

Klingle Mansion is an 1823 three-story, gray stone Pennsylvania Dutch-style building that is now the Rock Creek Park administration office. It is wired with modern security access keypads and is closed on Mondays and Tuesdays, including Tuesday May 1.

It sits at the end of a cul-de-sac with parking running up to it for park visitors. Visitors can walk from their parked cars onto backwoods, unmarked trails leading down to Rock Creek. It is conceivable that someone would drive here to meet, inconceivable to walk there to meet.

Klingle Mansion is not a well marked landmark with a paved walkway or trail leading up to it from Rock Creek jogging and walking trails. The administration building is set well back on a hill, out of sight and primarily accessed by driving up the driveway and parking before reaching the cul-de-sac. The cul-de-sac is basically for vehicles driving up to the front door to loop around to leave.

There is a small overgrown footpath leading up to it but someone coming down the Rock Creek jogging trail would probably not even see it, much less have any idea where it goes. There is also a jeep grade road that meanders up through the woods where one could get out to the Klingle Mansion drive, but in general you couldn't find Klingle Mansion from the Rock Creek Park trail running along the creek far below, map or no map.

Police seemed to understand this a year later, after Chandra was found, that any reference to Klingle Mansion was probably park related rather than a meeting spot. Steve Twomey and Sari Horwitz of the Washington Post write:

> Police officials said yesterday that Levy may not have been searching for directions to the mansion specifically, but seeking more general guidance. The Rock Creek Park Web site's home page included a photograph of Klingle Mansion at that time, so officials do not know "the precise connection," Gainer said. [4]

Much more troubling than focusing a search on Klingle Mansion were the reports that Chandra was a jogger in Rock Creek Park.

Thomas Fields-Meyer wrote in People that "police have…even brought cadaver-sniffing dogs to several locations, including the jogging path in Rock Creek Park, where Chandra regularly walked".

Newsday reports that this was "a park where Chandra Levy often jogged".

Tucker Carlson said on CNN's Crossfire that the police knew that "she frequently jogged in Rock Creek Park".

CNN again, despite all the information to the contrary, reported that a man reported finding a skull in "an area where Levy was known to go jogging".

WUSA-TV 9 in Washington reported from Associated Press and CBS that:

> The park is crisscrossed with running trails and was one of Levy's favorite jogging runs.

> Friends said Levy frequented the 1,754-acre park, located in Northwest Washington. [5]

Who was telling reporters that Chandra jogged in Rock Creek Park, and why? Why did only unnamed friends say that she jogged and walked in Rock Creek Park? Who had an agenda to set these reporters up to place Chandra jogging in

Rock Creek Park when she disappeared, and why were these reporters so oblivious to what her real friends with names were actually saying, over and over again?

Jennifer Baker told Jim Herron Zamora of the San Francisco Chronicle:

"She never went out alone," Baker said. "One reason she joined a health club is so she wouldn't have to jog in the streets there." [6]

Lisa DePaulo interviewed several named friends of Chandra for her Talk Magazine article, and she wrote: "Levy didn't smoke, had no pets, didn't jog (she was a fitness fanatic, but always at a gym)."

Sven Jones told Russ Mitchell of the CBS Early Show:

MITCHELL: Rock Creek Park is much like Central Park in New York, an—an—an oasis for city dwellers. Did she enjoy the park and how often did she go out there?

Mr. JONES: We didn't really talk about her visiting parks, and we didn't really talk so much about jogging, either. It was a little bit of a surprise for me, because we have not—neither one of us em—embraced jogging fully, so the park—I'm just not familiar. [7]

He told Bill O'Reilly of The O'Reilly Factor:

O'Reilly: "It looks like Mr. Jones that Ms. Levy was jogging, but you have said before that she wasn't an avid jogger. Any reaction to that?

Sven Jones: That's correct. As we spoke earlier, I didn't see her as somebody that would jog religiously. It was something that would be sort of out of character for her.

O'Reilly: Really, so she wasn't somebody who went out on a daily basis and ran around the park where she was discovered.

Jones: She may have done it on occasion, but certainly didn't embrace jogging as something that was personally enriching. [8]

Billy Martin, the Levy's lawyer, told the Washington Post:

Martin discounted the theory that Levy was abducted while jogging in the park.

"Her friends said she thought it was dangerous and she was very careful what she did," he said. "Rock Creek Park was a place that she knew was dangerous, and she discussed it with friends and family. All her friends knew she would not jog in the park." [9]

Internet site www.justiceforchandra.com admin Jayne posted:

On this week's America Most Wanted...were the two people closest to her, Jennifer stating that getting Chandra to jog was like pulling teeth—she said something to the effect that she couldn't imagine who would start such a preposterous story, while Sven Jones adamantly stated that jogging was "number one on their list of things NOT to do." [10]

And despite reporters quoting alleged unnamed friends to the contrary, the police understood this. Chief Terrance Gainer responded to Tucker Carlson on Crossfire:

But it is wrong to assume that she was a regular jogger in Rock Creek Park. That is not necessarily true. In fact, the information we have is that she did not often jog outdoors, that she used a treadmill more than Rock Creek. [11]

He told Bill O'Reilly:

O'REILLY: All right. Now, do—are you, in your opinion, is it a jogging incident? Could you possibly have jogged where she was found?

GAINER: You could have. She's not known to be an outdoor jogger, but she could have walked, she could have jogged. It was a beautiful day that day. And frankly, we have to look and see again with the cab drivers, if someone dropped her off, or whether she went up there to meet someone. [12]

And also told Dave Jones of the Modesto Bee:

Police know Levy "wasn't a real outdoor jogger," Gainer said. "We have more information that she used a treadmill more than she did a lot of outdoor running."

But he noted that Levy had canceled her gym membership the night before her disappearance.

"Maybe this was a way to get exercise that day," Gainer said. [13]

But the point of not being able to cancel her gym membership without a 30 day notice, as Washington Sports Club gym manager Errol Thompson told her, is that she had to pay another month and could still use the gym. Sure, he gave her a list of gyms in California that she could use if she returned to California during the month as planned, but she was not successful in canceling her gym membership. Any thought that she was forced out into Rock Creek Park against type to go jogging just has no basis.

No basis was needed though by Mark Geragos, Condit's third lawyer. He told CNN:

> Condit's attorney suggested on CNN last night, however, that the police had not done a thorough enough job searching for Levy. He noted that the remains were found near a jogging path that is on a direct line between Levy's Dupont Circle area apartment and Klingle mansion. [14]

Never mind that Chief Ramsey said that she was found "far from any jogging trail". [15] Or that Niles Lathem of the New York Post reports that there are "no real jogging paths there". A careful parsing of Geragos' statement is required to keep us from being led to believe that Chandra was murdered jogging to Klingle Mansion.

Yes, she was found on a line that runs from her apartment to Klingle Mansion, but a mile and a half farther beyond Klingle Mansion. It is just as accurate, and just as relevant or irrelevant, to say that Chandra was found on a direct line between Chandra's apartment and Condit's apartment, as Condit's apartment is a little more than halfway to Klingle Mansion from Chandra's apartment.

There obviously is no bearing on being found a mile and a half north of Klingle Mansion versus east or west of Klingle Mansion. Suffice to say that Chandra found on a jogging path between Chandra's apartment and Klingle Mansion is what Condit wants people to believe.

But Chandra had looked Rock Creek Park up on her computer for some reason, and with crack FBI efficiency, the police knew that within months. With luck, the police would be able to find her before her body had mummified completely. So the police sent 50 police recruits out to search Rock Creek Park. It was painful to watch.

They were looking for a body or for freshly dug ground that would indicate a burial spot. Andrew DeMillo of the Washington Post describes it:

> Twenty-seven police officers in training are scouring an area of Rock Creek Park near the Klingle Mansion, said Sgt. Bob Panizari of the D.C. police department's Special Investigations Division.
>
> For now, the recruits in Rock Creek Park are breaking into groups of two or three, searching mainly beaten paths and areas around the area of the mansion, rather than deep woods. Still, the federal park is huge, and the searchers face a daunting task. The park, which encompasses about 1,750 acres, is one of the country's largest urban sanctuaries and the mansion is used for office space for park administrators.
>
> "You know that saying about a needle in a haystack?" Panizari asked. "Well, this is a pretty big haystack." [16]

In fact, it was a national forest haystack. It was an impenetrable haystack. Steep and impenetrable. If the recruits had searched the hillside where Chandra was found—no disrespect to the victims of the Titanic tragedy, but remember the passengers sliding down the deck at the end of the movie? That would be the recruits searching the side of that hill. This was looking for a needle in a haystack you couldn't get to.

And who was going to leave Chandra within sight of a beaten path anyway? The recruits and possibly everyone else knew this. The Levys told Larry King:

> KING: What was it like for you looking at the search?
>
> S. LEVY: Oh, it's horrible. Just painful.
>
> KING: You want them to fail.
>
> S. LEVY: Well, want them to fail, and also, I sometimes think that they nonchalantly walk the grid and really, not really looking—I mean, that's kind of how I feel.
>
> B. LEVY: I know, I mean, I know a lot of people are out there, a lot of cadets, and you know, that was that was very late...
>
> KING: ...tried.
>
> B. LEVY: Well, in a way. [17]

Police did bring cadaver dogs to search portions of the park as well, but Chief Gainer said "there are not enough cadaver dogs in the United States to search Rock Creek Park". [18] Not a grid search of every square yard, anyway.

But if the FBI had returned the information on the computer over to the police within a few days or weeks at most, and the police were able to determine it was Rock Creek Park that Chandra looked up and not Klingle Mansion, then a thorough walk through with cadaver dogs over all the jogging and hiking trails and 11 miles of horse trails would have at least put the dogs within shot of having a chance to detect Chandra when there was something to detect. Especially if they had help.

In a www.washingtonpost.com online interview, that question was asked:

> Chantilly, Va.: …My question is, did you refuse the assistance of outside cadaver dogs when you were doing the search last year?

> Terrance W. Gainer: Actually we did not. I was present in Rock Creek Park when we used canines from Montgomery County. We had a lot of outside help and we welcome it. The whole park was not searched by cadaver dogs because they don't have enough stamina and there are not enough of them to search the whole park. [19]

Gainer talks about the assistance of some cadaver dogs from Montgomery County, but Susan Levine of the Washington Post reports there were several sources of search dogs:

> Some critics of how the department has conducted the Levy investigation say cadaver dogs should have been deployed extensively during officers' initial sweep of the park last summer. Given the animals' smarts and skills, many find it ironic that an untrained pooch, merely passing by, was the canine to find the Washington intern's remains…The men and women who own the search dogs are far too circumspect to voice such opinion.

> In fact, the nation's search-and-rescue network is overwhelmingly an unpaid force. The searchers buy their own dogs, cover their own expenses, do their own training and take their own work leave when their support is needed…. The greater Washington region has at least four prominent search-and-rescue organizations, including Mid-Atlantic D.O.G.S.,…. In 2001, members helped on 18 cases as far afield as the Midwest. [20]

And volunteer manpower for searching the park? In addition to the recruits walking their beat, William Ritchie, former D.C. Chief of Detectives, would have called upon those volunteers skilled at traversing the park terrain. He tells Bill O'Reilly:

> Well, first of all, I think if, based upon what they found on the computer, if you're going to commit to searching Rock Creek Park, then you need to cover all the areas and not just those areas adjacent to the normal thoroughfare.
>
> Now, I understand that resources are limited. I probably would have considered using volunteers, individuals who had experience in searching terrain areas, hikers, mountain climbers, rock climbers. And I would have paired possibly two or three of them with a police officer. [21]

Here are some search instructions. The "ridge", picnic areas #17/18, is the hillside where Chandra was found:

> There are several areas to explore. Best sites are the trails behind the Nature/Visitor Center, the Horse Center/Stables and Maintenance Yard areas, and the "ridge," known as picnic areas #17/18. The equestrian corral area by picnic area #25/26 could also be productive. Military Field, at the junction of Glover and Military Roads, is being restored as meadow habitat and the vegetation is thick. There is a mowed path running between the trees and the field edge which is worth careful attention.
>
> Start at dawn on the West Ridge, at picnic areas # 17/18, although the area directly around the Nature Center parking lot could also prove exciting. The blacktop path north of the Nature Center crosses a small meadow with a little pool which attracts migrants.
>
> The edge habitat around the stable, the indoor riding ring, and the horse paddocks should also be investigated. From the Horse Center follow the bridle trail which runs from the stable east along the fenced Maintenance Yard, cutting in by an obvious path into the open area beyond the fence. The stone blocks, columns and carved panels you see stacked here are from the original west front of the Capitol Building. The bridle trail continues down to Rock Creek.
>
> The woods edge near the equestrian corral by picnic sites #25/26 should also be investigated. Other areas: In Broad Branch check the bushes and areas along the creek. Explore the thicket around the Art Barn by Pierce Mill. Check the snags around Klingle House and the area around the barn. Walk through the woods and meadows around the House. You can explore the park further via trails that lead north to Pierce Mill up a shaded ravine or west to Connecticut Avenue. [22]

These search instructions are better than the instructions given to the police recruits, far better. They were given to birdwatchers.

Grand Jury

With the search of Rock Creek Park coming up empty, the FBI went to a crack cold-case team to solve Chandra Levy's disappearance. Susan Schmidt and Bill Miller of the Washington Post report on the new agents taking over:

> FBI officials shifted the investigation to the D.C. field office's major case squad, a signal that they were in for the long haul. The squad that initially worked on the case is intended to be reactive; the major case squad is set up for long-term investigations. The agent in charge of the case now is Melissa Thomas, a longtime investigator who consulted on the movie "Hannibal," a thriller about a female FBI agent who hunts a serial killer.
>
> Thomas is working with FBI agent Brad Garrett, whose biggest success came in 1997, when he helped capture a man who killed two federal employees four years earlier outside CIA headquarters in Virginia. In recent years, Garrett helped build the case that led to the conviction of Carl Derek Cooper in the 1997 slayings of three employees at a Starbucks coffee shop in Northwest Washington. Thomas and Garrett, who have training in profiling, are being aided by up to 12 members of their squad. [1]

Melissa Thomas was a specialist in profiling, and the FBI and D.C. police asked Condit for a fourth interview to build a profile on Chandra with what he could tell them. Niles Lathem of the New York Post described how investigators learned nothing new:

> During his last interview with investigators, Rep. Gary Condit was unable to recall all of his activities on the day Chandra Levy disappeared, The Post has learned.
>
> Law-enforcement officials said the congressman's fourth grilling by police and the FBI on Thursday failed to clear up a few lingering questions about his whereabouts on May 1, the last day police have been able to track the 24-year-old Bureau of Prisons intern.
>
> The officials told The Post that, in the 90-minute session in Condit lawyer Abbe Lowell's office, the California Democrat was pressed for more details of his movements that day.

The sources wouldn't reveal what specific questions were asked, but they said Condit was sometimes stumped and couldn't remember specifics of his activities.

There have been signs that investigators aren't totally satisfied with Condit's alibi for May 1, including the fact that police last Thursday interviewed a female ABC News reporter. [2]

Chief Charles Ramsey appeared on "Meet the Press" with Tim Russert and said that the police had not yet confirmed Condit's alibi nor checked his phone records for May 1. Steve Dunleavy of the New York Post talked to a veteran New York defense attorney about how this could be:

One of the most enduring presences in criminal and trial law for the past 25 years, Barry Slotnick, told me yesterday: "I wish I could have got the same deal for some of my clients in the past, but a lawyer in New York, Chicago, Los Angeles or any other city can't pull that act.

"Here a grand jury would have been impaneled ages ago, and even if Condit didn't appear or took the Fifth, a grand jury has wide powers of subpoena.

"All telephone records, all credit-card records, even his laundry records would have been firmly in hand of the police and investigators a long time ago."

Slotnick added: "You don't need Columbo on this case to do a basic investigation, but something has caused the D.C. cops to act with kid gloves, in a manner that couldn't happen anywhere else in the country.

"I would assume he has concerns, far beyond relations with his family, that he wants to hide." [3]

But the FBI didn't have anything to work with. Michael Isikoff of Newsweek quotes them: "The real issue is the body," says one law-enforcement source. "We have no clues. This case may not break until someday, somebody will be out walking in the woods or out fishing, and they'll find what we're looking for."

Sven Jones was asked to take a lie detector test, and after first agreeing refused to take it, a tell tale sign of talking to a lawyer. It's a travesty that lawyers as an industry advise everyone not to take lie detector tests so that the first thing you have to do to do the right thing is have the courage to ignore their industry pap advice.

Sure you could fail the test and raise suspicion, or you could refuse to take it and raise suspicion. Nice choice, with the lawyers no help to the victim in their blinders view of looking out for your interest. You have to care more about the victim than yourself to ignore them. Those who do do exactly that.

Not only does a person suffer the loss of a friend or loved one when someone they know disappears and is found murdered, but they must also suffer the scrutiny of police and public. Their offer to add insight into the tragedy by agreeing to fully answer questions and taking lie detector tests from the police to help solve the case should be recognized by all as admirable.

The logistics of Sven's situation was that he arrived back in D.C. the same day Chandra disappeared, and one of the last messages she left was asking to meet him in Georgetown for lunch. Certainly it is unfortunate but appropriate that the police looked at his whereabouts hard and asked him to take a lie detector test. Sven did the right thing. He took the test and passed it.

But it's sad that those who knew Chandra are necessarily pointed to with suspicion, at least in the beginning, and sad that even when they cooperate and try to help, some people remain suspicious. The words in their interviews should strike people as from the heart or not and should answer questions about any involvement. Sven's words were from the heart. That's all anyone can ask.

Another valuable lesson for us all was provided by an artist, Terry Aley of Overland Park, Kansas. Declan McCullagh in his Politech site provides this important reporting of a citizen fighting back for his rights and winning. Condit had requested eBay to end the auction of an artwork, "NEW ABSTRACT ART-CHANDRA LEVY & GARY CONDIT", under eBay's Verified Rights Owner (VeRO) Program, giving the reason that it violated Condit's "copyright, trademark or other rights."

The Los Angeles Times quoted eBay as reporting the basis of the complaint as the artwork being 'a violation of the congressman's right of publicity, based upon the use of his name or image' under California's "Right of Publicity" statute. Terry Aley responded with a vigor of intellect that would make our founders proud. He wrote Rep. Condit:

> Mr. Condit's name and likeness were not "directly connected with…commercial sponsorship or with …paid advertising" in my painting. I believe that

California Civil Code Section 3344 does not apply in this case, and is not sufficient cause for Mr. Condit's action.

I believe Mr. Condit violated my rights in a number of ways, and unless he publicly apologizes and retracts his attempt to suppress the sale of my painting, it is my intention to file suit under one or more statutes (see 18 USC 241 and 18 USC 242), and to release to the press information concerning the filing of that suit. Please let me hear from you by August 8, 2001. [4]

The statutes are explained further:

The two Federal Laws are both designed to protect Americans from being denied their rights.

The first makes it a crime for anyone acting as a public official, such as a US Congressman, to deny Constitutional and other rights to a US citizen. The Statute (18 USC 242—Deprivation of rights under color of law) provides specific penalties for violators: "…shall be fined under this title or imprisoned not more than one year, or both…."

The second Federal Law (18 USC 241—Conspiracy against rights) makes it a crime when "two or more persons conspire to injure, oppress, threaten, or intimidate…" any person from "…free exercise or enjoyment of any right or privilege secured to him by the Constitution or laws of the United States."

This statute also provides specific penalties for violators, "…shall be fined under this title or imprisoned not more than ten years, or both."

The action of Rep. Condit alone could be subject to Section 242, while the collective action of his staff could be considered a "conspiracy" under Section 241. [5]

A deadline to respond was given for August 8, and on August 7 Condit's office secretly had eBay restore the artwork auction. Terry Aley sums up the results of his action:

This announcement to the press is intended to show publicly that Rep. Condit recognizes that California Law does not protect him from being the subject of an artwork, and that the attempt to suppress or censor artwork is a potential violation of Federal Laws. [6]

The artwork suit was not the only setback for Condit. He had decided to break his silence after nearly four months, come out of seclusion, and give an interview. It was impossible for him to campaign in public and have fundraisers until he cleared the air. The two year re-election cycle of a member of the House of Representatives had forced his hand. Imagine if he had been early on in the six year cycle of Senator. It may have been years before anyone heard from him.

Connie Chung of ABC News got the highly sought after interview. Barbara Olson, as Larry King described her, former prosecutor and best-selling author, eloquently tells what she was looking for in Condit breaking his silence:

> ...It seems as though Gary Condit feels that things around him have gone on long enough, and—you know, it's interesting before you were talking about the political PR side.

> If you look back at people like Gary Hart, who refused to admit and refused to apologize, and look what happened to his career.

> And then you see people, I mean the famous, as obviously the checker speech with Nixon, or even Senator Kennedy, after what happened at Chappaquiddick, he went on television and he apologized and said that would live with him the rest of his life. Those kinds of things allow us to forgive.

> And if his talk tonight with Connie Chung, he says —we had a close friendship, and doesn't admit the relationship, doesn't answer whether he loved her, whether—if he denies that indeed he told her he would marry her, or that they would have children, then we've got this picture of Chandra must have been delusional. Anne Marie Smith is a liar and someone after money, and I guess Joeleen McKay whom he paid on his staff when he was having an affair must also be delusional. It's not a pretty picture. [7]

The interview was watched by 24 million people, about 30 percent of the U.S. television audience. His constituents were stunned at his responses. Petula Dvorak captured the essence of their reaction for the Washington Post:

> All summer long, the Hawaiian Days promotion at Perko's Cafe in Condit's home town of Ceres has dressed the waitresses in hula shirts and silk leis and has served waffles with paper umbrellas stuck in the pat of butter. The conversation there has been just as colorful throughout the summer—until yesterday.

> "I just don't know what to think anymore," said Charbonnie Blunt, 35, a waitress. "You want to believe Gary. Every day, we hold out a little hope that today, he'll clear it all up and explain everything. But he still hasn't done that. He didn't do it last night, and I stayed up late to watch it." [8]

Geraldo Rivera and his panel gave the most illuminating analysis of Condit's attempts to explain away his actions to Connie Chung:

(Excerpt from "Meet The Press")

RUSSERT: Two women, who've gone to the FBI, who've gone on national television, and said the pres—the—the congressman had an affair with them; concerned about their safety. Why would Congressman Condit lie about that?

Mr. LOWELL: Well, again, I realize that it's easy for you, as the interviewer, to say, 'Why did he lie about it?' I don't think the congressman lied about it. One of the things he's criticized for—and it's—could be a proper criticism. You know, when—when—when this woman named Joleen or Anne Marie Smith say that they had a relationship or they had a certain kind of relationship, I guess I understand that they're defining it the way they're defining it. I realize it drives people insane if the congressman says, 'I didn't deem that to be a relationship. Whatever we shared together, whatever we were, I don't think that's a relationship.'

(End of excerpt)

RIVERA: Oh, no, it's—it is—that is Clintonesque there.

Mr. ED ROLLINS (Republican Strategist): It's very Clintonesque.

RIVERA: I mean, 'Oral sex isn't a relationship,' but at least with oral sex, there was a survey that said many young people did not consider oral sex a relationship. What's he doing? I mean, try—is he trying to do a Clinton, trying to parse it this badly. How do you feel about it?

Mr. ROLLINS: Well—well, I—I feel this guy is the—is about the stupidest guy I've ever seen in—in American politics.

RIVERA: Oh, that—that good, huh?...

RIVERA: I want to go to Julian Epstein and Wendy Murphy. Julian, you first. I—I don't know—you—you obviously saw and heard Vince Flammini just now, the...

Mr. JULIAN EPSTEIN (Former House Democratic Counsel): Sure.

RIVERA: You heard a witness, who's standing in the wings ready to go in and weigh in: 25 rendezvous with Joleen McKay that Vince was present for, the—the initial meeting with Anne Marie Smith, the con—conversations with Gary Condit that—that followed. Isn't this exactly what—what was predicted and predictable after he said he had no relationship with these women...

Mr. EPSTEIN: Yeah. I...

RIVERA: ...that they would come forward with proof to prove him a liar?

Mr. EPSTEIN: Of course. I—I was surprised, Geraldo, you actually spent as much time as you did with them as—attempting to establish the case. I don't think there's anybody in the world that believes Gary Condit when he denies that there was a relationship, and I think this dancing on the head of a pin about defining what a relationship is is pathetic. I associate myself entirely with everything Ed Rollins said. I think it was the worst performance I've ever seen in American politics on Thursday night...

RIVERA: Putting aside the—the political just for a second, let me go to Wendy on the legal. Do—don't you think Flammini sounds convincing? Don't you think Gary Condit, were he under oath, committed perjury?

Ms. WENDY MURPHY (Attorney/Former Prosecutor): Well, Geraldo, how many times did he commit perjury is the question, I mean, assuming he was under oath. That was just pathetic. And it wasn't just that he lied about both women that he had relationships with...I think that he lied about so many things, including, you know, that Mrs. Levy was mistaken; that Chief Ramsey was causing confusion.

I mean, it was always everybody else's fault and he was telling the truth and this whole list of other folks, with, really, no motive to lie—they were all lying. I mean, that—I'm not sure who was advising him, but it was really, I think, a preposterous effort to—to expect anybody to believe, number one. I mean—and—and, really, so many of us thought that what he was going to do is say, 'I'm terribly sorry I did all these extramarital things. It was terribly humiliating. I couldn't admit it. And I'm sorry for the Levys that I didn't tell the truth.' And he didn't do it. I don't understand it....

RIVERA: Candice DeLong, we go to you now, the retired FBI profiler, the author of "Special Agent." You're the one who—who suggested that he shot himself in the foot, reloaded, then shot himself in the head. Why do you say that?

Ms. CANDICE DeLONG (Retired FBI Special Agent):
Well, shooting himself in the foot, I think, was all the ducking and dodging on Connie's initial questions about the affair, and then sh—reloading and shooting himself in the head was when he called these two women that he's known to have relationships with liars. I think the Titanic took longer to go down than Mr. Condit did as a result of that interview.

RIVERA: What is it, Candice, in your experience, that allows people to make mistakes that are easily provable to be—you know, make statement that are easily provable to be lies?

Ms. DeLONG: Well, Geraldo, one of the things that it reminded me of, in my 20 years of—of interviewing—working violent crimes and interviewing criminals—what kept going through my head, as I was watching Thursday night, was that this man seemed to be like so many sociopaths I've interviewed. And what—and what I mean by that, this is a clinical term, and these are people that do not feel guilt, as normal people do. They have an inability to empathize. I saw no empathy on—for the Levys. And then the next day, he essentially said they were confused…

As a result of his performance Thursday and subsequently on Friday, my level of suspicion regard hi—regarding his involvement in Chandra's disappearance is way up.

RIVERA: Do you think he believes she's alive or dead?

Ms. DeLONG: I thought he was acting like a man who believes there's no way in the world she's going to be found or walk into a police station and refute anything he said. I found it interesting that he volunteered to Connie, 'We never had a cross word. We never ha'—he said it three times. Yet according to the interview with Sven Jones, there certainly was a lot of far…

RIVERA: A pal of Chandra's from DC.

Ms. DeLONG: Yes, right. The—her confidante. There was a lot of fighting going on there. He know—Gary Condit, I thought, showed consciousness—in my opinion, showed consciousness of guilt by the things he said about Chandra. I thinks he—he knows she's not going to show up.…

Mr. ROLLINS: The thing that bothers me, for four months this man has shown absolutely no caring for this young girl that he obviously got involved with. He showed the other night no caring for these other women that he's been involved with, and—and I don't th—I don't see how—I mean, we've all been around political people who—who cast people away, but nowhere in that interview—and this was his—he set this interview up. Nowhere did he say, you know, 'My heart goes out to the family, but equally as important, I've lost a very dear friend. I d—I don't know where she is. I'm worried about it.' He doesn't feel that.

Ms. DeLONG: Another characteristic of a psychopath.

Mr. ROLLINS: And I think that tells you more than anything else about him.

Ms. MURPHY: It doesn't necessarily elevate the case to a prosecutable homicide or—at all…

Mr. EPSTEIN: Right, exactly.

Ms. MURPHY: …but it certainly will keep the police focused. They won't be looking at parallel investigations. They'll really see him as the key. And one of the things I think he said that I'd love to have an answer to is what's with this train trip thing? I mean, he said, basically, that he didn't call Chandra after May 1st for about four days…

RIVERA: Oh, just absurd. Just absurd. That's just—that's so lame. It's so lame.

Ms. MURPHY: …no, he didn't call her and—but—but—but, Geraldo, what's interesting…

RIVERA: He calls her on May 1st, and then he only realizes on May 6th, when Dad calls, that he hasn't heard from the woman he's been sleeping with two or three times a week.

Ms. MURPHY: But—but…

RIVERA: I mean, that's—that's too lame. That's too lame. I'm sorry.

Ms. MURPHY: But I want to know what he said to the police about that. What did he say to the police about his awareness of what her travel trai—her—her travel plans were? Because if he didn't tell them he thought she was going to take a train, if he didn't tell them he expected her to leave town on May 1st, that's a very new, very compelling, very self-serving statement. [9]

Chief Ramsey used the Connie Chung interview to describe to WUSA what it was like trying to get information from Condit about Chandra's disappearance:

"I think that people pretty much got a glimpse of what we've been going through over the last four interviews we've had with the congressman—a lot of conversation, but not a lot of substance," Ramsey said. [10]

And Chief Gainer added:

"He answered every question that Connie Chung put to him, and did you feel more informed after that?" Gainer asked. "Did he answer all her questions? Yeah. Did he answer all her questions to her satisfaction or the public's satisfaction? No." [11]

Clint Van Zandt told the Washington Post the next step that was required:

> Clinton R. Van Zandt, a former FBI profiler and president of Van Zandt and
> Associates, a behavior-oriented threat and crisis management company, said it
> may be time for police to ask the U.S. attorney to employ the kind of legal
> muscle often used in stalled investigations: a grand jury.
>
> "It's the most pressure at this point law enforcement can exert," Van Zandt
> said.
>
> Gainer doesn't dismiss the possibility but said it's more difficult to ask for a
> grand jury without physical evidence of a crime.
>
> "It's frustrating because you just can't quite find the smoking gun," Gainer
> said. [12]

The next step would have to wait. The Washington Post describes what happened through Chandra's mother's eyes:

> On Sept. 11, Susan Levy was preparing to fly to Chicago for the "Oprah"
> show, then to New York for the "Today" show. She never made it to the air-
> port. A friend from the East Coast called. She flipped on the television. The
> World Trade Center and the Pentagon were in flames.
>
> That was the last time the Levys were courted by media celebrities.
>
> For Susan Levy, "September 11 made all this much worse. I'm thinking about
> the grief that these families are going through. I know what they're going
> through." [13]

Barbara Olson was one of the brightest of shining stars that were added to
heaven's skies that day. She had provided some of the most insightful analysis of
the Chandra Levy case as a panelist on Larry King Live. And yet, with loss so
incomprehensible as occurred on September 11, what was one intern who
couldn't be found? Thousands could not be found now.

The coverage of Chandra Levy was panned as a mere sex scandal titillatingly
irresistible to the press, a trivial pursuit when more important things should have
been covered. But it wasn't just a sex scandal, it was a murder, and either a member of Congress being able to supress an investigation of murder or the disappearance of women without a trail of blood leaving police baffled and confused until
all potential evidence has deteriorated along with the body should have been the

focus of coverage, with sex merely establishing an intimate to investigate. That seemed too difficult a concept for the media to espouse, though.

In their attempt to undo excesses, Chandra was no longer even mentioned by name. She was now simply a Modesto woman who disappeared from Washington in May. Just one of many people who disappeared in 2001. This was true before September 11, and true after, but few under so mysterious conditions. There was greater loss elsewhere, but the mystery of Chandra's disappearance remained unsolved.

In November a D.C. Superior Court grand jury issued a subpeona to Condit. Normally secret, it became known because House rules require members of Congress to notify the Speaker when receiving a subpoena. Michael Doyle of the Modesto Bee reports on the grand jury action against Condit:

> As Rep. Gary Condit mulls a month-old grand jury subpoena, San Joaquin Valley law enforcement officials are lining up against him.
>
> So far, Condit hasn't given federal investigators what they demanded in a subpoena issued around Nov. 13. His new lawyer, Mark Geragos, says Condit's compliance is still being worked out with federal investigators.
>
> Condit told the Los Angeles Times Monday that the subpoena covered items such as phone message pads, newspaper articles and other things he already was prepared to turn over.
>
> Grand jury subpoenas can be sensitive for members of Congress, in part because of separation-of-powers concerns, and some legal experts say Condit's response time may not be unusual....
>
> In a Nov. 14 letter to House Speaker Dennis Hastert, required under House rules, Condit said he will determine whether the subpoena issued by the District of Columbia Superior Court is consistent with congressional rules. Many members of Congress make this response. [14]

While clearly members of Congress are victims of numerous nuisance suits, it is shameful that House rules allow members of Congress to delay or avoid responding to Federal court grand jury subpeonas as urgently as the citizens they represent. Justice was not served while Condit and Geragos studied a grand jury subpeona related to a missing woman to see if it was consistent with congressional rules.

How can Congress possibly justify using the Constitution to shelter members of Congress from criminal inquiries? It is exactly this attitude which is in question throughout the alleged investigation of a member of Congress in the disappearance of Chandra Levy.

It is not in the interests of the grand jury for someone who doesn't want to respond to decide if they should. If they can't decide as fast as a citizen would be required to, then make the decision for them, as fast as a citizen would be required to. Justice should not be delayed because a member of Congress is involved. A citizen would hope justice would be better served by Congress, not less.

Michael Doyle of the Modesto Bee reports on the grand jury process:

> The District of Columbia Superior Court grand jury investigating the Levy case and its aftermath convenes on the second floor of a building five blocks from the Capitol. Sixteen to 24 grand jurors sit in what looks much like a terraced classroom, save for a witness box.

> Defense attorneys are not in the room during grand jury questioning, but they can be consulted outside. Typically, three grand juries are meeting in Washington at any one time. [15]

Jim Keary of the Washington Times expands upon it, establishing that the grand jury changes every month requiring the sitting panel to come up to speed on action to date:

> The records were subpoenaed by a D.C. Superior Court grand jury that meets for a month at a time. Because the investigation of the disappearance of Miss Levy has been ongoing since May, at least five different panels could have heard evidence.

> Normally, before a grand jury would issue an indictment, the sitting panel would read the transcripts of past grand jury panels that investigated the case. [16]

This defies imagination of how a group of people could come up to speed in such a complex case and then question more witnesses within a month, much less hear additional cases as well. At least, it should have been a complex case by then.

In January, 2002, it looked like the grand jury would act as Allan Lengel of the Washington Post reports:

A D.C. grand jury probing the Chandra Levy case is reviewing documents that it subpoenaed from Rep. Gary A. Condit and soon plans to call witnesses, a law enforcement source said.

The development comes as investigators continue to look for clues in Levy's disappearance and probe allegations of obstruction of justice involving Condit (D-Calif.). Levy vanished May 1.

WUSA-TV (Channel 9) reported last night that the grand jury plans to call Condit, members of his staff, Levy's former co-workers from the U.S. Bureau of Prisons, residents of her D.C. apartment building, acquaintances from her health club and a flight attendant who contends that she had a 10-month affair with Condit.

In November, the grand jury subpoenaed telephone message slips, calendars and constituent mail from Condit's office. [17]

Condit continued his re-election efforts to win the Democratic primary. Helen Kennedy of the New York Daily News laid out how far Condit had fallen:

Condit's run has been full of indignities:

He couldn't get enough signatures to get on the ballot without paying a fee.

The House subcommittee on homeland security cropped him out of online photos showing members touring Ground Zero.

A local folk band penned a song called "Dear Congressman Condit," which features the refrain: "I wish it was you that was missin'."

The Washington Post toured his D.C. condo and reported on his mirrored closets, numerous bedside candles and the "elaborate set of wooden foot massagers."

The loyal supporter who lent the use of his living room for the Chung interview endorsed Cardoza, and local papers in Condit's district favor dumping him.

When Condit hit the streets to talk with voters, he mistakenly spent time chatting up people in the wrong district. One voter, in earshot of trailing reporters, asked point-blank, "Where'd you bury the body?"

Still, Condit soldiered on. [18]

Condit lost the March primary to his former key aide Dennis Cardoza. He no longer had to answer questions to try to win re-election, and he didn't.

Probably for political reasons, Condit had not been scheduled to appear before the grand jury until the primary elections were over. Now that they were, Condit was scheduled to appear in early April. He postponed it. Given the secrecy of grand juries, only the most minimal of information was available concerning grand jury actions. On April 12 it was known that Condit appeared at the federal courthouse for a short while, but unknown if he had postponed again, briefly testified, or declined to testify by invoking his Fifth Amendment rights against self-incrimination.

The following month, May 2002, Randy Groves, Condit's former legislative aide and press secretary, was called before the grand jury and testified.

A source close to Condit later said that Condit invoked his Fifth amendment rights in mid-April. [19] He would not be answering any questions about what happened to Chandra Levy. He had pretended to until he lost re-election. Now he no longer even pretended.

In April Geragos told Condit that Chandra would probably be found in May. Joyce Chiang had washed up out of the Potomac River in April, 1999, so it couldn't have been based on Joyce Chiang. Whatever it was based on, Geragos was right. Chandra was found just as he predicted.

Found

A man was poking into leaves where his dog was sniffing, looking for a turtle. He found a skull instead. Soon the world would know that Chandra had been found. Steve Twomey and Sari Horwitz of the Washington Post describe the moment:

> The skeletal remains had been scattered, perhaps by the weather, maybe by animals. They were surrounded by the minutiae of someone who might have been intent on exercise, perhaps a run or brisk walk. There was a jogging bra. There were two Reebok tennis shoes. There was a Walkman-like radio. There were running tights tied in a knot, suggesting that this unknown human being might have been bound and killed. There was a sweat shirt.
>
> It bore the name of the University of Southern California.
>
> The D.C. medical examiner's office is on the grounds of D.C. General Hospital in Southeast Washington, and on Wednesday afternoon, the medical examiner himself, Jonathan L. Arden, brought back the single most important find from the Rock Creek Park site, the skull. Teeth do not decompose. And they are practically as unique to a person as fingerprints. The root canals, the spacing, the fillings and the crowns add up to a personal signature.
>
> Arden X-rayed the skull. He hung the exposed film on a light screen, beside the X-rays collected months ago from the Levys. He stepped back, then stepped forward, then stepped back again, comparing the two jawlines, comparing the fillings. Then Arden turned to the half-dozen police and federal investigators who had crowded into his small office.
>
> "It's her," he said. [1]

Twomey and Horwitz with more on the scene of Chandra's discovery:

> Detectives believe the body was not in any kind of grave, but was simply left on the forest floor, where dirt and leaves eventually covered it, said law enforcement sources who spoke on condition that they not be identified. Police found "less of the body than more," they said, possibly because of animals.

The bones were very deteriorated and had no tissue or hair, the sources said. The skull, which was not complete, was cracked, although the cause was unclear. All the bones that were discovered were found within five yards of the skull. [2]

The side of the steep hill where Chandra was found was a mile and a half beyond Klingle Mansion, a hill running from a picnic area, grove 18, on Ridge Road to a small creek at the bottom running along Broad Branch Road. It looks like any other steep hill, with gullys formed by water runoff and erosion. Chandra was found in a depression midway down the slope, a carefully selected spot to hide her body covered with leaves.

Ted Williams, former D.C. homicide detective, tells Greta Van Susteren:

I was out at the crime scene this afternoon, by the way. And it's such a steep incline that, if in fact there was a sexual assault at that venue, at that location, I can tell you, the guy would have to have been very acrobatic. And I say that simply because of the manner in which that there's an incline.

Now, everything I saw there this afternoon led me to believe that Chandra possibly was killed somewhere else, brought to this location. And I now believe—and I may very well be wrong—but I do believe that it could have been possibly two people involved in this and not just one person, in light of the location. [3]

Western Ridge horse trail is a dirt trail running in the woods along Ridge Road at the top of the hill, splitting at grove 18 to a gravel horse trail that continues on up the hill and a branch that veers inward into thicker forest. The dirt trail branch, barred to horses, meanders deeper into the forest and meets up again with the horse trail at Rock Creek Park's Nature Center farther up Ridge Road. The steep hill where Chandra was found is in a corner with grove 18 above to the right, conveniently with a place to pull a vehicle back up to the horse trail, and a dirt trail veering inward from there across the top and to the left.

The winding two lane road below, Broad Branch, runs through a cavernous valley at the bottom along a small tributary of Rock Creek. Passing cars can barely be seen through thick leaves and branches, but they are not far away. A deep ravine slices down the hill to the left, cutting off access to all but the most determined. A path on the other side of the ravine runs down to the top of a cliff facing Broad Branch Road and on down to the creek. Thick, impenetrable brush cuts off access from the road below.

Her broken sunglasses were found near the trail, her Walkman farther downhill. Unlikely as it was for Chandra to be here, it was a murder on a horse trail. Was she really on a suicidal death march on a horse trail deep in a forest, without her cell phone to call for help, without her wallet or even her pepper spray she always carried, or was the death scene staged to look that way? Had she decomposed here for a year with no one noticing, just downhill from picnic sites on the main park road? The Washington Times reports:

> Because only skeletal remains were found, police will search for samples of Miss Levy's DNA among the brush to determine whether she died there or somewhere else, a police source said. If officers find large samples of her DNA in one location, it can be assumed her body decomposed there. [4]

The police assembled a forensic team to conduct an "archaeological dig" in a 50 by 70 yard area. [5] They mapped the locations of bones, searched the area with metal detectors and cadaver dogs, and brought in the recruits again to search a wider area surrounding the site. They found nothing with her bones and clothes, no evidence whatsoever, no DNA or fiber evidence, no bullet holes, no stab marks, no blood, not even the concentration of DNA that would indicate she decomposed there. Dr. Cyril Wecht tells Newsweek:

> "After 13 months, I just have great doubts about whether the crime scene will yield anything of a definitive nature," said Dr. Cyril Wecht, a leading forensic pathologist. "If there's no evidence of bone injury from a beating, a skull fracture, or a gunshot or stab wound, then you have nothing to work with. You've just got bones." [6]

CBS reports the medical examiner's findings:

> Medical examiner Dr. Jonathan Arden ruled Levy's death a homicide Tuesday but said there was not enough evidence to say conclusively how she died, or whether she was killed in the park where the remains were found last week.
>
> Arden said Levy's skull, which police reported was damaged, was fractured after she died. Among other potential causes of death, Arden said, "I did not see the evidence of a gunshot, stab wound or beating."
>
> Other medical examiners said the lack of those telltale signs makes strangulation a more likely cause of death. Arden said strangulation is difficult to diagnose when examining only bones. [7]

Mark Sherman of the Associated Press quotes further:

> "There's less to work with here than I would like," Arden told reporters who peppered him with questions. "It's possible we will never know specifically how she died."

> "There's nothing else that can be done," as part of his work, he said. [8]

Niles Lathem of the New York Post reports on shutting down the search:

> But while there is still a lot of work to do, police are satisfied that there is nothing left to find at the scene.

> Before the area of Rock Creek Park was reopened, police cadets raked the leaves back on the wooded hillside in an attempt to restore the grim scene back to its natural state.

> "They tried to restore it as if we had never been there. Or, more importantly, as if she had not been laid to rest there," Washington Assistant Police Chief Terrence Gainer told reporters. [9]

The police opend up the site again, and Greta Van Susteren and Ted Williams took a look:

> VAN SUSTEREN: Here with me in Washington is former D.C. homicide detective Ted Williams....

> Ted, I want to talk about the actual location where the remains were found. We struggled to get up to that area. Very difficult to get at it. And what surprised me the most of all is how many other things we found there a couple of days after that the police didn't see. Your thoughts?

> TED WILLIAMS, FORMER D.C. HOMICIDE DETECTIVE: Well, I'll tell you it was amazing that, once we got up to the area and the vicinity of the—actually where the skeletal remains were found, I was just surprised at all of the information that I believe and—that could be considered physical evidence that was in that area.

> VAN SUSTEREN: Well, let's show some of our collection. We have—just as an aside—I mean, obviously, we have a loafer shoe that we found that the police never picked up, obviously. Hold up some of these other things.

> WILLIAMS: Sure. Ropes that certainly could have been utilized to tie someone up. We have a woman's stocking that was found in that area. A rubber glove possibly from the crime scene search. Beer cans.

VAN SUSTEREN: You know what the interesting thing is? I mean, this was all within about a hundred yards at least of where the remains were found.

We even found an empty condom wrapper, and I think we have a photo of that to show. That was probably within a hundred yards of where the remains were.

But what's so extraordinary is just how much junk there was that the police didn't seize. Does that bother you as a former homicide detective?

WILLIAMS: Oh, absolutely it troubles me. You know, I would have anticipated that the police department would have gone with a grid search in that area.

They would have picked up every piece, every object in that area, and then they would have started with what I define as a process of elimination, to eliminate some of these items.

Greta, we could very well be sitting here with some of the evidence that the police officers need to...

VAN SUSTEREN: Or it could simply be just a bunch of litter that people left behind. But, nonetheless, we saw an awful lot of stuff out there that was never collected that was rather surprising. [10]

A woman's stocking, a condom wrapper, a shoe, beer cans, all left within yards of Chandra's skeleton, and no one saw her or her clothes being dragged all over the side of the hill for a year? No dog was curious and pulled their owner that way? Yet a dog came off Broad Branch and up the side of the hill to find her skull? Very odd, unless the bones weren't there the previous summer.

This is as difficult to comprehend as Chandra on a horse trail, dragged fighting down the side of a hill, losing her sunglasses as she went, and attacked on a steep incline and left there. Yet who would stage her death this way, and why?

The Levys were hoping for an answer. Their private investigators, working for their lawyer Billy Martin, followed up at the site with a Washington Post reporter in tow. Allan Lengel's trip report is shocking:

> [A 12- to 14-inch tibia, or shinbone,] was found by Dwayne A. Stanton and Joe McCann, the two private detectives working for the Levy family. Armed with a shovel, an ax and two rakes, the two former D.C. homicide investigators arrived about 11 a.m. Thursday, parked at Grove 17 and then walked

down a narrow, rocky horse path into a wooded area with dense foliage that leads toward Grant Road NW. About three minutes down the path, they turned left and headed down a steep incline toward the creek and Broad Branch Road. About 238 feet down, they stopped and began their search.

Stanton and McCann had hiked around the area before. They returned with rakes this time because they had seen leaves around the crime scene that appeared not to have been disturbed. They cut through three of the fallen trees nearby to see if an animal could have deposited any of the remains inside but found nothing.

Then they began raking elsewhere. They spotted a police flag that said "shoe," and another flag in a different area that said "lipstick." Stanton found a piece of twisted wire looped in a figure eight—with one large loop and one narrower one—under a thin pile of leaves. The wire is being analyzed, though police have theorized that it may have been used by the National Park Service to secure young trees.

About 1½ hours into their search, McCann's rake tapped against the bone. It had been under a thin pile of leaves and embedded in the ground.

The bone was about 50 feet from part of the crime scene area where skeletal remains had been found, in a patch of the park that had been cleared of leaves and brush during the first search. It was damaged—as if chewed by an animal—on both ends. Ramsey later said the bone was 25 yards from where the skull had been found.

When they discovered the bone and the wire, Stanton and McCann stopped their search and called police and the Levys' lawyers. They declined to comment on what they had found and told a reporter accompanying them to leave the area because it had again become a crime scene.

Jonathan L. Arden, the District's chief medical examiner, studied the bone and ruled it "consistent in every way" with Levy's remains. The find offered no new insights into the Levy case, and the cause of death is still undetermined. [11]

Stanton and McCann also found a hard contact lens later and gave to the police for DNA testing. There was no word on whether the police gained any insight from this and checked if any suspects used to wear glasses, which can sometimes be determined by looking at old news photos. Still missing were bones from her pelvis, thigh, and left foot, but found was wire twisted into a figure eight. The police theorized it was used to support saplings, but the Park Service told the Washington Post:

"We would use heavier gauge wire, and we definitely have garden hose [around] the wire to protect the trunk of a tree," Cynthia Cox, assistant superintendent for Rock Creek Park, said, adding that the service has not planted trees in that area of the park for at least five years.

"I think this wire is significant, and I don't think it belongs here," Joe McCann, one of the two investigators working for the Levy family, said when the wire was discovered under a pile of leaves. [12]

Was Chandra restrained with rope that one ex-D.C. detective with Greta found and a wire twisted into two loops that two other ex-D.C. detectives working for the Levys found? The question is just as puzzling as why everyone who seems competent is an ex-D.C. detective.

Things could not seem to get more bizarre, but they did. Police came back to search the site a second time and found money with red dye on them from a bank robbery. This wasn't an isolated spot on a side of a hill, this was Grand Central Station. It isn't possible to both be torn apart by animals with your body spread around for dozens of yards and be buried from sight at the same time, is it?

The police by now were assisted in their search by the Fraternal Order of Police Search and Rescue Team, a group of volunteer federal and local police officers trained and certified by the National Association of Search and Rescue. They told the Washington Post:

Lou Cannon, president of the association, which represents 38 law enforcement agencies in the city, said he was "grateful" that the department "finally called us in, but we would have appreciated it if they had called us a year ago." [13]

Three forensics experts, quoted often throughout the case, offered their services to the Levys to perform a private investigation on Chandra's remains. Dr. Henry Lee, Dr. Cyril Wecht, and Dr. Michael Baden visited the hillside and then the medical examiner's office. They hoped to review her clothing as well.

A month later they were still waiting. Into the fall they were still waiting. Arden refused to release her body. This has serious implications for those of the Jewish faith, where the body must be intact for burial. A year after Chandra was found, Michael Doyle of the Modesto Bee reports:

Arden said through a spokesman Friday that he is working on returning the remains to the Levy family; Katz said she has heard that it could happen within weeks.

Three high-profile experts who offered their services to the Levy family looked at the bones, but could not conduct a microscopic examination and were not given access to other evidence, such as her clothing.

'We never did really review the whole file,' said Dr. Henry Lee, one of the experts. [14]

The medical examiner apparently decided a year was long enough to keep anyone from examining her. He released her body and the Levys were finally able to bury her. The nationally renowned forensic experts never were allowed to conduct their tests. Why did the Washington medical examiner keep Chandra's evidence from being independently examined?

Her spandex leggings, or leotards, turned inside out and knotted at the bottom of both ends, were the most prominent piece of evidence to examine. These are cited as jogging clothes by many, and used as proof that Chandra was jogging on the horse trail and attacked by someone lurking along the way. Were they casual clothes that she would wear on a Tuesday afternoon to meet someone?

A neighbor at the Newport said she had often seen Chandra on the way out wearing jogging clothes and her Walkman. [15] Internet poster libra1009 wrote:

> I just want to respond about the spandex leggings being casual wear. I seem to remember in one of the home videos that was shown on the news, the one where Chandra is discussing some classes and a paper she had written, she was wearing a sweatshirt over black leggings. I'm sure you've seen the home video. I believe it is the one released where we all heard her voice for the first time. She was sitting in her parents' house in an ulphostered chair, talking about a paper she had written. She then got out of the chair, apparently to retrieve the paper to show her parents. It was then you could definitely see her dressed in the sweatshirt and leggings. I'm sure this video has been played over and over on all the news channels. [16]

She actually wasn't dressed like a jogger. She was just wearing her usual outfit which she also wore to the gym. Were the leggings used to tie her up during a sexual assault? Isn't that rather elaborate and difficult for an unplanned attack on a passerby? www.justiceforchandra.com member Rita posted an informative summary of USA Today's Tom Squitieri being interviewed on Fox News:

> Squitieri reiterated that Chandra was not a jogger, she obviously was going to the park to meet someone and was waiting for someone to call. When they did, she got up and left.
>
> Out of all that he said, a theory he had about the tights were interesting, he said they could have been used to restrain her but also, to get her where she was, the tights could have been used as a carrying device. He said she was in a ravine, so the tights could have been used to help carry her there.
>
> Squitieri believes this was a hastily planned affair because of the shallow grave, his point being that had it been planned longer, it would have been better planned.
>
> He was asked about the fact Anne Marie Smith saw evidence of tying up under Condit's bed, and Squitieri said that several women had reported this to him independent of her, they didn't even know she existed at that time, so it was not a copy cat type of thing for them to report bondage with Condit. [17]

Along with the tights was the USC sweatshirt seen in the video. At Chandra's memorial in Modesto just after she was found, her friend Mike Vanden Bosch told the audience, according to the San Jose Mercury News:

> She wore it everywhere, he told more than 1,000 people at her public memorial. Even in the oppressive heat of Central Valley summers, Levy insisted on wearing that sweatshirt, he said, laughing. [18]

The sweatshirt is inconclusive to some degree. While too hot to be jogging in it, she always wore it even in hot weather. It can't be used to rule her out as walking during the day. How far she would walk and how deep into the forest is another matter altogether.

Along with the jogging clothes was her Walkman. It was described as "a portable radio, which did not include a cassette tape" and "an empty portable cassette player and headset". It could have been something like this model:

Sony WMGX322 Walkman Digital AM/FM Stereo Cassette Player ($89.85, Amazon.com)

Features:

Stereo cassette recording and playback
Built-in stereo speakers
Manual speed control
Supplied microphone and stand
AM/FM stereo tuner [19]

Internet poster JenX wrote this about jogging with a Walkman:

> Well, two things—a cassette Walkman is generally a lot smaller than a CD Walkman (unless you are using a fancy MP3 player) and a lot of people still use them. She could have taped CD's onto a cassette and used that for walking—I do it all the time, and use a CD Walkman for running. So they aren't necessarily outdated for that purpose.
>
> However, that doesn't really explain a missing cassette. That seems weird to me.
>
> I can't see "jogging" with a cassette Walkman. They are too shifty. Your basic Walkman barely stays in place. I think if she was actually jogging she'd be wearing a nicer style CD Walkman or at least something that stays in place better throughout the 'run'—if she was running. [20]

According to the police, she wasn't wearing shoes "made for serious running". [21] Was she doing serious walking? At the crossroads of grove 18 is a gravel horse trail that comes up from Beach Drive which had she walked it would surely drive gravel into the traction patterns of her shoes. The Western Ridge horse trail that comes up Ridge Road is a dirt trail and likewise could leave some dirt in the traction patterns.

Pristine traction patterns would be consistent with her being carried from a car backed into grove 18 rather than her walking miles on horse trails to get there. Chandra's running shoes should be examined for gravel or dirt in the soles if they haven't been already.

What wasn't found with Chandra? Guy Taylor of the Washington Times quotes the police:

> "We did not find a bracelet that she may have worn or her keys, and we have not found the ring," police spokesman Sgt. Joe Gentile said.

The ring, with two diamonds and the initials "C" and "L" engraved on the outside, wasn't found in Rock Creek Park, where Miss Levy's remains were discovered May 22.

Police obtained a sketch of the ring yesterday from the Modesto, Calif., jeweler who sold the ring to Miss Levy's family in 1998. Investigators will take the sketch to pawnshops across the city and the region, hoping that if the ring was pawned, it may lead to a suspect, Sgt. Gentile said. [22]

Helen Kennedy of the New York Daily News described the lost jewelry as:

Missing were Levy's size 4 gold signet ring, set with two diamond chips and her intertwined initials —a $416 custom-designed gift from her mother—her apartment key and a thin gold bracelet. [23]

And then there was this also from the New York Daily News:

Sgt. Joe Gentile said the disappearance of the items does not automatically point to robbery: Animals and birds sometimes make off with shiny objects. [24]

So we have wildlife running around with a keyring, bracelet, and a pinky ring with CL on it? Perhaps a fox is wearing the pinky? I saw a fox wearing a pinky just the other day. I do agree wildlife and foxes have a way of making you lose your ring and keys, but I don't believe that's what happened here.

For a bracelet, ring, and keys to go downhill never to be seen again would require the equivalent of a small landslide, after a clean separation of the jewelry from the bones as well. In being washed downhill there would not be a clean separation but instead a trail of bones that would lead downhill.

The missing keys, ring, and bracelet appear to look like a robbery. To not take the jewelry leaves too much consideration for a murder of passion and leaves out the far more prevalent scenarios of an attack for rape and robbery or just robbery. But to make it look like a robbery there is a dilemma. The jewelry must be pawned. They weren't.

That is a fatal flaw, not as definitively fatal as that which killed Chandra, but potentially just as fatal. Unless the jewelry enters the pawn and trade market of a robber, it is not a robber who killed her. In fact, it is someone who dares not reveal the jewelry to complete the crime scene, someone who knows her and someone who risks too much to try to pawn it.

While taking the jewelry to make it look like a robbery, a person would not want to do what a normal robber would do right away, that is pawn the jewelry. There is too much risk. They did not kill her for the money that a gold ring, bracelet, and possibly watch would bring, yet they must take it. If they pawn it, it leaves vital clues about her killer. To keep it is a death sentence, once found in their possession.

There is only one recourse for such a murderer who is setting her up as being attacked on a horse trail. They must hide the jewelry, bury it someplace that won't be linked to them, far away.

And the keys? She had no id to give her address. Only someone who knew her could use them.

Horse Trail

How did Chandra end up on a horse trail deep in a forest? Picnic area #18 is next to Western Ridge horse trail, which runs for miles to Maryland before looping back and coming back down the east side of Rock Creek Park as Valley Trail.

Chandra was found just off a crossroads of sorts of horse trails and a road with a place to pull back into the woods and unload. You're supposed to unload horses, though, not bodies.

andrew, a poster who bikes and hikes in Rock Creek Park, wrote by e-mail:

> The Western Ridge trail is essentially for horses. I assume people run on it, and it is listed (part of it) as part of some running trails in DC, but it's really not in the realm of most runners. In fact, of the "serious" runners I'd say 99 out of 100 wouldn't even take it. It's not in a part of the park that people run in nor is it of the condition you would want to run on (it's more a path than a trail). It's not a main trail for hikers or bikers. The majority of them (that even get up that far) opt to take Beach Drive (beautiful) or Glover Road (hilly, but smooth). I've never seen anyone running on Broad Branch. [1]

If they were, they're suicidal, which is for some reason what a few people want us to believe about Chandra. Walking or jogging, she was miles from home, far beyond Klingle Mansion, with no protection or even a cell phone. Sven even walked her home down the street in Dupont Circle!

She would have essentially gone completely against character, in terms of security, to walk halfway to Maryland on a horse trail while, in terms of time, still not having a ticket to go home or indications she knew what to tell her landlord the next day about her move out date.

Niles Lathem wrote of this mystery in the New York Post:

> How Chandra got there remains one of the biggest mysteries of the case.

One possibility is that someone accosted her while she was jogging or walking.

But the area, near a nature center, is 4 miles away from Levy's downtown Washington apartment, and there are no jogging trails leading there.

Another possibility is that Chandra was killed somewhere else and her body was dumped in the wooded hillside.

The roads leading to the area are fairly well-traveled, making it a risky proposition for a killer to take a body out of the trunk of a car and carry it into the woods without being spotted.

Police think it's also possible that this was the death scene.

"It is possible that she walked in there [with the killer] and was killed there," said one law-enforcement source. [2]

Sari Horwitz and Allan Lengel write further on that in the Washington Post:

Investigators also say Levy was probably killed there, rather than dumped after being slain, according to sources. They think there is a good chance she was killed in daylight, partly because of her sunglasses and clothing. The T-shirt and Spandex leggings she was wearing would have been suitable during the day, when the temperature rose to 82 degrees, but not at night, when the temperature hovered about 50 degrees.

It is unclear, however, why Levy would have been walking on that trail, four miles from her Dupont Circle apartment. Her friends and relatives say she was not a jogger, was not familiar with the park and had expressed safety concerns about being in Rock Creek Park by herself.

The most obvious attraction near the trail, the Nature Center, was closed May 1 last year, as it is every Tuesday. The stables were open, but employees there said records do not show that she rode the horses, and no one remembers her coming there that day. Levy's friends also say she didn't like horses, even though her mother owned two. [3]

Could Chandra have jogged there? Western Ridge trail is part of an extended trail system through Rock Creek Park down into downtown Washington. andrew describes by e-mail:

Anyway, heading north on Rock Creek Parkway from downtown DC, you pass Georgetown, Dupont Circle, the Zoo, and then the Klingle Mansion (including a big tunnel under the zoo's vet clinic). You eventually, I mean eventually (because this road curves all over) come to a split where Beach

Drive goes deep into the park and Branch road skirts along the edge. About a hundred feet after this split is a another split, between Branch Road and this MASSIVE uphill switchback road. It really blows when you are biking. You cross the creek and then peddle uphill until you are a third of the way up and then turn around 180 and peddle up some more and then turn 90 and peddle up some more until you get up this monster. It's pretty rough (as far as DC hills go).

It is about 1/10 of a mile north (barely 1/10th) of the Branch/Beach intersection. I think it is called Glover Road. This road is blocked off at Branch by a police cruiser. It works it's way up the hill until it runs along the top (parallel to the Western Ridge). This hill is pretty tall. When you are on top of it, you look down on the tops of the trees at the bottom (and these are old, huge Oaks, Elms, etc).

Something that isn't being reported is the fact this is NOT a jogger's area, certainly not for some girl from California looking for an evening run. Joggers use the park EXTENSIVELY but by and large, I'd say 80% of them NEVER go past the Zoo. They run between the Lincoln Memorial and the Zoo. After the zoo, the number of runners drops to a minimum and bikers and roller bladers really take over.

Don't look at a "crow flies" measurement of this. Rock Creek pathways can take probably three miles to do what a "crow flies" in one or two.

I've biked that hill a number of times (both up and down). I rode up there the other day and police have closed the road at the Beach/Branch split (you can drive on Beach) and on the North side it is closed at Abelmarle & Branch.

A lot of the "DC Media" never, ever cross that split in the road (Beach & Branch). In fact, many never go past the zoo. Unfortunately a lot of the reporting (including the "talking heads") are based on this idea that Rock Creek is this tiny, highly populated little park through downtown DC (that's all they ever see). It isn't—It's huge. Just huge and thick.

The area where Levy was found, if what I can make out of the maps, is not a jogging area by any stretch of imagination. On the lower side, Branch Avenue, it is a very narrow dark street with tight corners and very little room on either side. I don't even like to bike on it because commuters come ripping around on it at all hours of the night. It basically runs north-south with the creek on the east side of the road.

I am 100% convinced she did not run up to where they found her. There are so many quality bike and jogging paths in DC NEARER her home and more interesting that this place. Basically, for her to get up to the Western Ridge would have required about a four + mile run, a 1/2 mile uphill, and then having her decide "hey, after all this, I'm going off road and cross country." The main bike running trails on Rock Creek run parallel to the road (you can always see the cars) but the Western Ridge is very cross country.

Rock Creek has a paved, six to ten foot wide bike path that runs from the Lincoln Memorial up to Beach/Branch drive, then "continues" on Beach drive (they close it to traffic on the weekend) and then picks up with other suburban bike trails. From the Lincoln Memorial you can cross the bridge and connect with the Mt. Vernon trail (16 miles) or take the trail along I-66 past Dulles (20+ miles). You can also connect to the Georgetown C&O Canal (crushed gravel) which runs nearly 100 miles to PA or the Capitol Crescent trail (paved) that runs nearly 10 miles upto suburban DC.

The point is: There are hundreds of miles of dedicated running/biking paths in the DC area (as a biker, it's great). Even the super runners (skinny, granola eating marathoners) just wouldn't run up here, let alone at night, especially their last night in DC.

She was brought here or lured here. In fact, if someone said "meet me at the Klingle Mansion" and then let's go for a drive in the park" I can see that happening very easily. It's a short drive. It probably offered one of the first picnic areas available as you drove up Glover. We won't know until they open up the scene. [4]

Rita Cosby and Bill O'Reilly also discussed this:

O'REILLY: The evidence that I've locked in on yesterday and today are the computer records that show that she looked at this park and a mansion within the park before she left the house.

COSBY: Immediately before.

O'REILLY: Immediately before, the police know that. Now, you don' t believe she was jogging, do you?

COSBY: No, I don't, and police do not believe she was jogging. That area was so thickly wooded, so many rocks in that area, it's not a common place to jog. So they're saying she must have been brought there, or that could be a secondary site, even.

At the top of the, it's interesting, there's a grove area, as they're describing, a place where even a car could park. So it is possible that either she was lured to that area or that part was just the location where maybe they dropped the body off. [5]

Could Chandra have gone to Klingle Mansion to meet someone? Greta Van Susteren discussed with ex-D.C. homicide detective Ted Williams:

> WILLIAMS: But I can tell you, after having been over to Chandra's apartment, it is highly unlikely that Chandra walked all the way from her apartment.
>
> I believe the department—the police department is doing the right and proper thing trying to determine if cab drivers brought her to this venue. [6]

And in fact, there are no taxi dispatch records of picking her up, and no taxi drivers remember it. Even though Condit drove Anne Marie Smith around in an older red Ford Fiesta or Escort, Chandra never mentioned to Linda Zamsky riding in his car. She said they took a taxi.

Chandra could have taken the metro train from Dupont Circle, past the Woodley Park Station at Calvert St. and the Adams Morgan area where Condit lived, to the Cleveland Park Station at Porter St. It's not an easy walk to Klingle Mansion from there to Williamsburg Lane which has no sidewalks and is uphill at the end.

www.justiceforchandra.com member James Forrester posted about the walk to Klingle Mansion from the metro station:

> The Klingle Mansion (KM) is on Williamsburg Lane directly off Porter St. The closest subway stop for Chandra would have been Cleveland Park which is just two stops on the "Red" Shady Grove line from Dupont Circle. Porter is one block from the Metro station but when you turn on Porter its probably 15 or 20 minutes to Williamsburg Lane (WL). Turning on WL you pass some very expensive houses. I later checked on who lived there and its a real who's who of media, government and business leaders.
>
> You walk past a paved parking area to reach the circular driveway in front of the KM. There is also an extension of the paved road that goes behind the KM where there are about 8 parking spaces.
>
> The front of the Klingle Mansion faces the woods which lead down to Rock Creek toward the East! Not the West. There are walking trails and some steep parts. Below, the view includes Rock Creek in one of its deeper and wider points, a jogging trail on the opposite side, and several roads. [7]

I arrived at Klingle Mansion one Friday morning in the conventional manner of park goers there. I drove up early and parked in a Williamsburg Lane parking lot leading up to Klingle Mansion. I wanted to walk from Klingle Mansion to grove 18 on Ridge/Glover Road, the "ridge", to see if I could get a sense of what following Western Ridge Trail would have been like had Chandra jogged there as some suggest. It's a mile and half from Klingle Mansion. Exercise experts who don't know the terrain say the four miles from her apartment to where she was found, establishing at a minimum an eight mile run, is normal for a person in Chandra's excellent shape.

This doesn't take into account that there was no obvious destination for Chandra as to where she would start her return. Western Ridge Trail runs to the end of Rock Creek Park miles away. A closed Nature Center is mentioned as a destination simply because there is nothing else. She was four miles from home on a trail to nowhere, no end in sight.

And an idyllic eight mile run on a paved jogging path? Hardly. I ventured downhill from Klingle Mansion, looking for a sign for Western Ridge Trail, actually, looking for a sign for anything. A small unmarked footpath brought me out to a paved trail along Rock Creek. I turned northward, venturing toward what I knew from previously looking at a map would be Pierce Mill.

At a turn in the path was one of those signposts with signs sticking out in different directions. I saw Western Ridge Trail. I thought it pointed straight ahead but maybe my eyes were still bleary in the early morning. Anyway, I should have zigged when I zagged.

The trail started out nicely enough. I envisioned Chandra walking on the trail, enjoying a nice early May afternoon. Then the trail petered out to a footpath, then barely discernible concentrated wear and tear, then nothing. I was facing a bank with loose rocks as stairsteps. Horse trail? You'd have to help a llama up these rocks.

Hoisting my laptop bag securely over my shoulder, I clambered up the rocks to a new ridge. Time and again the ridge would thin to nothing. When in doubt, which was most of the time, I climbed another level to a new ridge. I came across a giant tree laying on its side, too thick around to climb over, so lengthy I had to debate whether to go up or down the hill to get around it.

It was at this point that I knew not only horses but Chandra had not come through here. I knew not where I was or where I was going, but knew going forward into the unknown was preferable to returning through the known.

At times I could see buildings high above. Large dogs would come out of brush above me and bark menacingly. I was sure I had stumbled onto private property of something formerly known as the Soviet Union and would be dealt with accordingly. Instead, I stumbled out of trees onto a busy sidewalk, looking for all the world like a disoriented homeless person with his belongings in a bag over his shoulder out foraging for breakfast.

People looked at me with some pity, not entirely a novel experience, averting their eyes lest I be a panhandler. I looked around, seeing a park sign. I had walked through Hazen Park and found myself on Connecticut Ave. I got the attention of a young man and asked where Pierce Mill was, explaining I had come through Hazen Park. He was somewhat surprised, and I don't blame him, but directed me on up Connecticut to Tilden Street and down to Rock Creek again. I was back on track, still in search of Western Ridge Trail.

From Pierce Mill I kept going north, here undoubtedly an idyllic paved jogging path running along Rock Creek. Suddenly, it came to a halt at a major intersection, Broad Branch and Beach Drives. Western Ridge Trail? Maybe, somewhere over there.

It is telling that experienced riders didn't think Chandra made the trip I was taking. Sari Horwitz and Allan Lengel of the Washington Post report:

> Dwight Madison, supervisory ranger for the National Park Service, said police officers have interviewed him, asking what route Levy would have taken if she had walked or jogged from Klingle Mansion to where her remains were found. A section of the Western Ridge trail runs between Grove 17 and the mansion at the end of Williamsburg Lane, he said.
>
> A longtime rider at the stables said she and other riders think Levy was killed elsewhere and dumped in the woods. They believe that their horses would have picked up the scent of a decomposing body or that riders would have seen animals attracted to a corpse. [8]

I crossed and found a sign for horses pointing on up a hill. It didn't exactly say Western Ridge Trail, but it was a horse trail. I started climbing, looking for picnic areas 17 and 18. After a long trek uphill, past a large equestrian field, I was sitting at picnic table 18 facing Ridge Road. Where Chandra was found was behind me and over the hill.

As you pass picnic area 18 the horse trail becomes a gravel trail and continues on uphill. The dirt Western Ridge Trail becomes hiking only, or No Horses, as it dips downward just before turning sharply uphill.

It is at that point that Chandra was found at least 200 feet straight downhill from the No Horses path. I found an orange stake and three orange flags marking about a 45 foot long by 15 foot wide rectangle on the side of the hill, about 300 feet in from Broad Branch Road.

The site is a large naturally hollowed out spot below a tree on a steep incline. A log lays to one side, and there the left orange flag is planted. The flags are very small, planted in the ground with small stiff wires. Yet I saw the flags from a path looking across the ravine. Any clothes not covered with leaves would have been seen just as easily.

I believe the skull was found further downhill, probably at the orange flag below the stake. I estimated the flag at being about 45 feet downhill from the stake. There was no gully or ditch that the skull would have washed down, just a rocky slope downhill. The slope is so steep that the foot deep hollow wouldn't do much to hold anything from being washed on downhill.

I was amazed to see the lack of underbrush on that entire slope. Acres of trees on steep, rocky, leaf covered slopes with no bushes to speak of. It's not as if where Chandra was found has been cleared or is in a clearing, the entire side of the hill is the same way.

There are large deep ravines on both sides, but it is not the most inaccessible spot. For example, the area between there and grove 18 is very rough. But it appears to have been chosen based on the ability to drop downhill from the path and get back up fairly quickly. The more inaccessible sides of the ravines on both sides would take much longer to traverse.

The location was in my opinion picked by someone very familiar with the park who knew they could drive up to the entrance to the path, even pull off the road into the trees, and go straight downhill between two large ravines and deposit her on the steep side of the hill a hundred feet high above the busy road. This section between the two ravines and guarded nearby at the base by a sheer 70 foot cliff would never be traversed by a casual passerby.

For this reason I think it is possible that she lay there on the other side of the ravine from the top of the cliff since she was murdered, if covered well the whole time. The path to the top of the cliff and then on up to Western Trail Ridge is too well trodden to have missed seeing her clothes strewn about on the side of that hill across the ravine for a year, but if covered well so few would have traversed the side of the hill between those two ravines that she would likely have gone undetected.

However, a dog would not miss that site whatsoever. For us to believe she lay there a year, we have to believe that the turtle hunter is the first dog walker to follow their dog across the ravine to see what it had found. That is hard to believe.

There are walking paths up the side of the hill from Broad Branch. Path is a generous term here. It is little more than worn down footprints around logs and rocks. The start of the path is at the corner of Grant Road and Broad Branch. The creek channel running along Broad Branch is very wide and deep, but the water is that of a small creek. The path runs along the hill above the creek like walking on a wall above a sidewalk. The path is just wide enough to walk on and ten feet above the creek. It is also in plain view of traffic on the road.

One walks along the top of the creek for at least 300 feet before coming to a sheer cliff where the path goes uphill sharply. Another path comes up from the other side. The path stops alongside the creek below where Chandra was found. That is how inaccessible Chandra's site was from below at the creek.

The cliff is sheer and at least 70 feet high. The ground below is soft, though. The footing is treacherous. At the top of the cliff the path heads on uphill at a slant across the side of the hill. It is not an easily seen path to follow.

Any thoughts of someone bringing Chandra up the path from the corner of Broad Branch and Grant are totally offbase. Not only is there no parking down there, a person wouldn't even be able to walk along the road to get there. Entering at the corner of these country roads and walking on the path along the creek is in plain view of cars on Broad Branch and narrow and treacherous.

There is an almost invisible branch of the path that goes up the hill beside the cliff but it is little more than footholds for climbing straight up the hill. It is inconceivable doing this at night or carrying someone up the hill this way at anytime, even two people.

Did someone come up this hill to wait for a passing woman to attack? You have to see how high this hill is, how isolated from the streets it is, how one would be run over should they venture down to Broad Branch Road and cling to the side of the mountain as cars whizz around the curves, to see how unlikely anyone would be to venture up Western Ridge Trail and hang out in the woods to attack someone.

Just because it's unlikely doesn't mean it didn't happen, but if it did, the person had a long way to get back to his regular haunts. He would stick out like a sore thumb if he ventured on foot up that mountain. It certainly would have been isolated for a sexual predator.

I saw two couples with dogs in an entire Friday on Western Ridge Trail at grove 18. There were many groups of riders riding along Ridge Road just outside the trees and stopping at the picnic area, but none ventured into the darkness of forest. It is intensely silent. A sex predator would have a long silent wait in the forest for a lone woman to come by on that shadowy trail.

Of course a stalker could follow a woman up the mountain. With Chandra wearing headphones he wouldn't have to be particularly stealthy either, just stay back out of sight and follow. That's quite a distance to wait to attack, but if Chandra turned inward and walked into the No Horses branch of Western Ridge Trail it would have been an attack soon after she had ventured further away from the road and people who could help. Closing the distance between them without alarming the woman would require a cheetah like rundown, though.

Another suggestion of an attacker is that of a homeless person, a vagrant, perhaps a hobo if you will living in a tent. The same reasoning applies. It is so remote from food and water that a person would have to trek up and down the mountain on horse trails for supplies. In addition, they would be very noticeable and dealt with by the Park police if not reported first by the many horse riders.

As a result, I didn't see the usual bottles and rags that one sees in remote areas of metro parks. There were two beer cans laying next to the trail between where you drop straight down the hill to where Chandra was found and where the path that slants downhill to the top of the cliff starts. Quite frankly the trail is not an inviting spot to sit and party. I tried to sit on logs to type but everything was so slanted on the steep slope that I kept sliding off. And that was sober.

I would expect people to walk back there from picnic area 18 as you see people do in any state or national park. You have to expect the occasional beer can from picnicers being tossed. But the lack of parking and police chasing people out of there after dark would keep it from being a party spot.

It is exactly that isolation that makes it possible to drive up, pull into the trees at picnic area 18, and carry a body down the trail and then downhill and dump it and get back out of there in a hurry undetected. Greta discussed this with Ted Williams, the ex-D.C. homicide detective:

GRETA VAN SUSTEREN, HOST: Ted, your thoughts. You're a homicide detective in D.C., you come upon a scene and you see that. What do you do with that when you discover that?

WILLIAMS: …Listen, Greta, let's be very realistic. When you're talking about rapists who murder, people who rob, who kill, those individuals will rob, kill, and get out of there. They will rape, kill, and move out in a hurry. They don't take time to try to get rid of a body. Somebody methodically attempted to get rid of the body of Chandra Levy, as far as I'm concerned.

VAN SUSTEREN: Ted, how far or how close can you actually drive an automobile to the place where the body could then be pushed over this sort of hilly area?

WILLIAMS: It's a distance. It is quite a distance away, I would say at least 200–300 yards or even more from where you could drive an automobile. Now, if you came in from one side, where you would have to actually cross the creek and go up the incline, as I did this afternoon, you would be closer to the area where this crime took place, or where they found the skeletal remains. But it's very difficult.

So, my theory on this is, it is difficult to believe one person took that body through the woods, came to this cliff-like area, and then dropped it. I just don't see it happening that way. [9]

The difficulty has to do with the lack of sunlight because of the trees and the rocky, sandy soil which makes footing so treacherous. For example, with brush one can hang on to something as they gingerly traverse downhill. There's nothing to hang on to.

But it's not impossible to walk up and down the hill. I did it carrying a heavy laptop case over my shoulder. A person could carry or drag Chandra down that hill. It's not necessary for her to have walked it. In fact, in my opinion it would be far more difficult to force her down that hill than it would be to carry her.

When you take a look at what she was supposed to have done to get here to be attacked, how isolated this spot is when the Nature Center is closed, and how many people, horses, and dogs would have had to be totally oblivious to the corpse over the side of the hill, not only is it difficult to believe that Chandra jogged here, it is difficult to believe she was here at all throughout the summer Rock Creek Park was searched.

Somebody could back a vehicle off the road right to the path. The road to the Nature Center is open day and night, and there's next to no traffic on it. If you back off the road at grove 18 it even has marker posts to show where to stop backing up.

The thought of moving her body around is morbid, but consider the murdered Sacramento lawyer who was moved by his wife and buried in a vineyard after being kept in a refrigerator for a few months, and during the same year Chandra was murdered. It's morbid, but not inconceivable.

The perfect spot for driving up at night, hauling the bodybag across a field to a path, and then down the side of a hill to make it look like she had been sexually assaulted and robbed, then hidden in a ravine.

A little too perfect. While the ideal remote location for access by car, it was an impossible location for her to have gone to by herself that afternoon, four miles into wilderness, off jogging paths, off the horse trail, off into wilderness.

Chandra's body was not seen for a year even as condoms, beer cans, trash, tree markings, a lipstick, and, if she were there, even her bones littered the area. However, her body was not seen.

The logistics of someone encountering Chandra on that trail, subduing her, silencing her, controlling her, moving her down the hill, sexually assaulting her, and strangling her, are certainly doable as it does happen all too often, but it would be pretty tough to do with one person if there much resistance at all.

Over and over we come to the conclusion of her trusting someone even to be there, and then being betrayed as she was subdued and killed. Yet it is difficult to believe that a killer would risk parking a vehicle in broad daylight at the picnic area to betray Chandra in the woods. The risk is unimaginable.

She was at the end of a trail, and meant to look like she met her end there, hiking without a cell phone, without money or a credit card, without id, hiking to the ends of the earth until she died.

She was supposed to be distraught, obsessed, unable to take no for an answer, suicidal. That was the way she was left in the park. Suicidal, with her wish granted.

Officially, the police say that the elements have destroyed the crime scene and say both that she could have been there all along and that she could have been brought there later.

There is no forensic basis whatsoever for her death occurring at that site. Had there been such evidence, thinking would be oriented to an assault by a stranger or a betrayer at that site.

I would not expect such evidence, and there isn't any according to the police. On top of all other improbabilities of how she would come to die there, one must also add that the proof of her decomposition has been destroyed. The list of improbabilities is improbably long.

Guandique

On May 7, 2001, six days after Chandra disappeared, Ingmar Guandique, 19, was arrested for breaking into a neighboring apartment. His apartment building was on Somerset Place NW, about two miles up Blagden and 16th St. from the intersection of Broad Branch, Beach, and Ridge Roads where one can trek up Western Ridge horse trail to grove 18.

Michael Doyle of the Modesto Bee describes what happened:

> A woman in the red-brick apartment building next to his, close to Rock Creek Park, had come upon him hiding in the corner of her bedroom.
>
> "She started to scream," the police report stated, "which caused (him) to flee out the front door."
>
> Police who subsequently searched Guandique found him with one large screwdriver, two small screwdrivers and a gold ring that belonged to his neighbor. They found that the woman's deadbolt had been "destroyed," and they charged Guandique with attempted burglary and released him. [1]

Guandique was a Salvadoran, and friends and family say that he came to America illegally a year and half earlier. Illegal or not, he was arrested, charged with attempted burglary, and released from custody. Is there any reason to think he would behave differently and could now be trusted among us? No, there is not. It is only asking for trouble, and trouble we got.

A week later, May 14, with only the first glimmer of a report of Chandra's disappearance having made it to print, an obviously unchastened Guandique was hanging out near the Broad Branch and Beach intersection. Matthew Cella and Jim Keary of the Washington Times report:

> [About] 6:30 p.m. Halle R. Shilling, 30, was jogging at the Pierce Mill Road parking lot. She was running north on Beach Drive when she saw Guandeque sitting on the curb on the west side of the Broad Branch parking lot.

He began running after her, then caught her. He pulled a knife on her after grabbing her around the neck. She screamed, pushed his face with her hand and fled. [2]

Niles Lathem of the New York Post added this:

She said Guandeque bit her when she tried to push him away and he fled. [3]

The Washington Post and Modesto Bee quoted a victim impact statement she wrote a year later:

"I began screaming as loud as I could," wrote the first victim, 30, who had taken a self-defense course. "We continued to wrestle. He shushed me. I continued to scream, knowing that the cars driving by on Beach Drive…well hidden from view by the trees, were drowning out my voice…,. I do not doubt for a minute that he purposefully stalked me as a hunter tracks his prey." [4]

"I know, in my gut, that given a chance he would not hesitate to repeat his crime on some other woman, and it scares me to think what would happen if she was not prepared with some sort of self-defense."

At 5-foot-10 and 160 pounds, Shilling was larger than Guandique. She fought back and, "inexplicably," she said, he ran away. [5]

And he did strike again. Matthew Cella and Jim Keary of the Washington Times describe it:

Christy C. Wiegand was similarly assaulted by Guandeque on July 1 about 7:30 p.m., court records showed. She was jogging on Beach Drive when she saw Guandeque standing beside the trail. He began to run after her and grabbed her from behind. He then pulled her off the trail.

He took out a knife as he held Miss Wiegand, a 26-year-old lawyer originally from Pittsburgh, by the chin and covered her mouth because she was screaming. She freed herself when she felt him lose his grip. [6]

Helen Kennedy of the New York Daily News adds:

In the second attack, he came up behind the victim as she reached the crest of a hill. He grabbed her and they fought, rolling down the hill into a ravine, where he held a knife to her throat before she ran away.

"I was terrorized by the knowledge that my life might end in a ravine in Rock Creek Park," the woman testified. [7]

Sari Horwitz and Allan Lengel of the Washington Post quoted her court statement:

> According to court records, including written statements from Guandique's victims, the park assaults were remarkably similar. He went to Rock Creek Park, fell in behind the women as they were jogging in isolated sections of the park, jumped them and pulled them to the ground. In both attacks, he brandished a knife.
>
> In the second attack, Guandique pulled the woman off the trail.
>
> "When my attacker dragged me into the ravine, holding a knife against my throat and covering my mouth, I thought and still think today that he was going to rape me or try to kill me," the woman, 26, wrote. "I feared for my life…
>
> Her assailant "was extremely strong, and with his hand cutting off my air and the knife at my throat I didn't feel I could struggle for very long. He was a bold and practiced attacker…[who] waited until he thought I was fatigued from jogging up a hill and purposely selected a secluded spot right next to a deep ravine."
>
> As in the first attack, the woman was able to break away and flee. Cut and bruised, she flagged down a motorist and reported the incident to the U.S. Park Police, who arrested Guandique about 45 minutes later at Joyce Road and 16th Street NW. She identified him. Under questioning, he told police about the earlier incident. [8]

Michael Doyle of the Modesto Bee adds more of her statement:

> "What struck me most was that within 10 seconds, I was off the jogging path in the woods, struggling to scream and out of sight of any passers-by," recalled the woman, who at the time was a 26-year-old recent law school graduate. "Until that day, I never realized how quickly someone with the advantage of surprise and a weapon can put a person in a position of total isolation and helplessness." [9]

This coming from a woman who was a former varsity rower and stood 5 foot 11, weighing 175 pounds. The two women escaped Guandique's attacks, but they were both tall and strong. Chandra was in superb condition and had taken self defense training, but was much more petite than these women at 5 foot 3 and 110 pounds, just one of many good reasons not to be out in the middle of a forest to start with. These women Guandique attacked were running within sight of the heavily travelled Beach Drive.

The second attack was two weeks before the FBI would finally get back to the D.C. police with the information that Chandra had looked up a map of Rock Creek Park on her computer and the subsequent search of the park by police. According to the Washington Post:

> D.C. police first spoke to Guandique about the Levy case in the summer of 2001 after U.S. Park Police alerted them to his arrest in the jogger assaults, according to court records. But law enforcement sources said they found nothing to indicate he was involved in her disappearance, especially since, at the time, they weren't aware that her body was in the park. [10]

They would question Guandique again with a report of one of those infamous "cellmate confessions" that prosecutors trot out when all else is in doubt. Anybody that has ever been in jail knows that instead everyone there claims to be innocent, no one is ever guilty. You would think we live in a crime free society listening to them.

Sari Horwitz and Allan Lengel of the Washington Post wrote of the cellmate confession:

> After Guandique's arrest, an inmate at the D.C. jail told authorities that Guandique had confided in him that he stabbed Levy and left her body in the park, law enforcement sources said. The inmate didn't try to trade the information for a lighter sentence, saying he came forward because he felt bad for the Levy family.

> In September 2001, the inmate failed a polygraph test, also administered through an interpreter. Guandique, who denied involvement in the Levy case, passed, the sources said, and authorities felt comfortable that he was not their man. [11]

Guandique may have passed a polygraph test concerning Chandra, but that same month he pleaded guilty to two counts of assault with intent to commit robbery. The Washington Post quotes the court:

> In a pre-sentencing memorandum, Assistant U.S. Attorney Kristina L. Ament called Guandique "a predator" who, armed with a knife, used the isolated por-

tions of the park "as a hunting ground, waiting beside popular running trails, selecting victims and stalking them."

Guandique, in a plea bargain agreement, admitted trying to rob the joggers, one on May 14, 2001—two weeks after Levy disappeared—and the other on July 1, 2001. At his sentencing Feb. 8, D.C. Superior Court Judge Noel A. Kramer said the attacks appeared to be more than attempted robberies.

Guandique "went out of his way for a physical encounter that ended up, at least in one instance, out of sight, in a ravine in Rock Creek Park," the judge said, according to a transcript. "This is not a run-of-the-mill robbery...,. Mr. Guandique is ready to terrorize people, ready to have a physical encounter...,. [H]e is highly dangerous." [12]

Let there be no doubt. How dangerous? A man in Minnesota served 23 years for stabbing and trying to kidnap a woman, this with a previous conviction of rape. Did he spend 23 years thinking of ways he could make amends to his fellow citizens once he was released? No. He apparently spent 23 years figuring out better ways to get away with rape and murder. He was out only seven months before kidnapping Dru Sjodin, 22, from a North Dakota mall parking lot. She has still not been found as of this writing.

A man in Florida was arrested 13 times in 10 years, including kidnapping and false imprisonment charges. CNN reports on the incident, of which the man was acquitted a year later:

According to records from the Manatee County Sheriff's Department, a woman said Smith grabbed her as she was walking along a street and threatened to "cut her if she failed to remain quiet."

A passing vehicle stopped and intervened, allowing her to flee, the record said.

The records also said Smith told authorities "he had been in an altercation earlier" that evening "and wanted somebody to walk with."

A few months before the incident in Manatee, Smith was convicted of carrying a concealed weapon—a knife, according to his arrest record from the Florida Department of Law Enforcement.

Smith has faced numerous drug charges, and in 2001 was convicted of heroin possession, possession of controlled substances, and attempting to obtain controlled substances by fraudulent means. He served a little more than a year in prison. He was on probation when he was arrested Tuesday. [13]

On probation, but roaming around looking for prey. A video surveillance camera caught him kidnapping 11 year old Carlie Brucia walking through a car wash parking lot. I think a little bit of life got sucked out of this country when we saw the evil of a man kidnapping a little girl walking home. I know it did from me. And our hearts sank further when she was found behind a church on a nearby highway.

Both men that killed Dru Sjodin and Carlie Brucia had been charged with assault earlier where the women got away. So now has Guandique. Guandique was sentenced to 10 years in prison. Will he or other men who attack women kidnap a woman and make her disappear when they get out of prison like these men did? Do we dare let these predators roam free unmonitored to find out?

After Chandra was found, the proximity of time and place of her disappearance to Guandique's attacks refocused attention on him, and rightfully so. However, although Beach Drive is on one side of a hill with grove 18 near the top, and Broad Branch Road runs around to the other side of the hill, there is a hill in between, a rather large hill.

It has been suggested that Guandique may have walked up Broad Branch Road from the site of his later attacks and then entered the path at Grant along the creek in the hopes of finding a passing woman on Western Ridge trail above to attack.

A person would have to dodge so much traffic on Broad Branch as they walked along the side of the road that they would have to fear being seen and remembered by several drivers when the victim was found and the crime reported. He would have to walk in traffic for more than a mile, then enter off the road, uphill at 45 degrees for hundreds of yards, then lay in wait on a path seldom used.

Not likely, especially when he would be passing Western Ridge trail at Ridge Road and could walk up that instead. Assuming Chandra actually was on an isolated horse trail deep in a forest, did Guandique follow her up from the intersection of Broad Branch, Ridge, and Beach?

If he had, he would have gone from a man who attacked a woman on a trail, subdued her, tied her up with her own leggings, then murdered her and stole her jewelry to a man six days later who ran out of a neighbor's apartment with a ring when she caught him and screamed. Quite a change in behavior for a cold blooded killer who ties leggings into knots.

His family said he had a serious drug problem. He was a petty thief, with pending charges of attempted burglary even as he assaulted two women joggers. A petty thief would have pawned the jewelry or given them to his girlfriend.

The police put out a national APB on Chandra's ring for the entire public, including pawnbrokers, to keep a lookout for the ring and report it if seen. It has not been found.

Guandique had also taken a lie detector test, administered by the U.S. Attorney's Office, and passed. The inmate to whom Guandique allegedly confessed heard Guandique say that he stabbed Chandra and left her in the park, this of course after the highly publicized searches of Rock Creek Park. Now that Chandra was found, it could be seen that her clothes had no blood on them from her being stabbed. Just one of many reasons the inmate had failed his lie detector test, one can imagine.

Some new information became available, though, and the Washington Post reported:

> A grand jury has subpoenaed friends of a man who is now the focus of the Chandra Levy investigation, among them an apartment manager who has told The Washington Post that the man had facial scratches and a cut, swollen lip around the time the former federal intern disappeared.
>
> Sheila Cruz, the manager of a building on Somerset Place NW where Ingmar Guandique lived, said she can place the time she saw the facial abrasions as late April or early May because it was shortly before Guandique, then 19, was arrested May 7, 2001, for breaking into an apartment in the complex.
>
> Levy, whose remains were found in Rock Creek Park this spring, disappeared May 1, 2001.
>
> Guandique blamed his wounds on his girlfriend, saying she had hit him, Cruz said. But the former girlfriend, in an interview, said she had not caused the injuries to his face. She said she never saw the scratches and swollen lip. She described a relationship that was on and off and had become tumultuous by May 2001.

Cruz was subpoenaed late Wednesday night, hours after she was interviewed by The Post. Her boyfriend, one of Guandique's friends, also was subpoenaed.

Guandique's former girlfriend, Iris Portillo, and her mother said in an interview that they were called to the U.S. attorney's office last month. Portillo, 20, said she took detectives to a spot in Rock Creek Park where she had gone with Guandique, less than a mile from where Levy's remains were found. She said investigators took a gold bracelet, which she said was a gift from Guandique in early 2001, and a necklace....

Portillo said she and Guandique had several fights during the months he lived with her in early 2001, including one in which he bit her just above the breast. Another time, she said, he put his hands around her neck, in a choking manner. Once, she said, he punched her in the nose.

In late May or early June 2001, she said, Guandique moved out of the Somerset Place building and began staying with a friend in Maryland.

"He hit me a lot, and I was scared of him," Portillo said. "But I don't believe he killed anyone." [14]

Chandra disappeared May 1, and Guandique was arrested May 7 for burglary. His landlady pinpointed his arrest as when he had facial injuries. This was a few days after Chandra disappeared and is used to make Guandique a suspect. If this is true, such memorable facial injuries should appear in Guandique's May 7 mugshot.

True, Guandique is a predator, but a predator who didn't know Chandra. Whoever took her jewelry didn't pawn it, and they hid her body. That sounds like a predator all right, but a predator who knew Chandra.

Woman Missing

"Woman missing in Modesto." With these words, www.justiceforchandra.com admin benn alerted us to yet another Modesto women who had disappeared, Laci Peterson.

Thus began thousands more posts on another missing woman even as we waited for a grand jury in Washington to start investigating Chandra's murder. We waited futilely.

Here is a post I made during those futile days:

What a time for my main posting computer to crash. I spent all night last night trying to replace the C: drive, get it to boot, etc., forgoing sleep as usual. I was falling asleep at traffic lights again today.

So it ended up being far worse than a hard disk crash, and I took the computer in to where I bought it. I'm thinking I can post without my research for at least a couple of days, and the only other thing I use the computer for is e-mail, mainly to get 20 spams for every e-mail from somebody I know, so I thought no big loss if I can't check e-mail for a couple of days.

Well, the computer had to go into the shop so I checked with the ISP and found I could read and reply to my e-mail through a web page just like Yahoo, Hotmail, and the others. Yahoo! I said, as I put my PC in the shop. Bring on the spam.

So I'm clunking through this kludgy web page interface for e-mail, and I see something about Chandra. It turns out to be a response from Chief Ward of USC, and I almost missed it buried in the spam. So I post the response and dive back into the spam.

Whoa, lo and behold, I am told DO NOT RESPOND. Well, that can't be spam, that's the exact opposite of spam. Strange. I look at the address. Mike Dayton. I'm thinking, don't I know a Mike Dayton from somewhere?

Wait. I just call the guy Dayton. I didn't even know his first name. Mike Dayton sends me an e-mail but tells me not to respond. So of course I think spoofing. But I look the e-mail over and it's got a legitimate tone.

I would post the text of the e-mail to decide yourself because there is so much spoofing going on, but it isn't a polite thing to do and I usually don't. Other information could change my mind, of course, but the wording is legitimate and straight forward, and I'm confident it's him. Spoofing the e-mail address alone rules out trivial pranks.

Someone asked if he was married awhile back, but no information was posted on it. For the record, he says, he's been happily married for the last six years. He adds that my "false, defamatory, and malicious posts are being 'collected' by his attorneys. [plural, I guess he figures he'll need more than one].

Well, to be honest with you all, I think I'm the only one on the whole internet that thinks he's clueless about what happened to Chandra, and have said so all along. Because of that, it wasn't a concern to me what all has been said about him. I mean, if he's collecting names of people who have made mean and malicious remarks about him, he'll need a full time staff of lawyers!

Well, I stand by my posts over the last year. I think he thought he was helping Condit get rid of a link to a past mistress of Condit's, Joleen McKay, his "assignment" so to speak, while Lynch's assignment was Anne Marie Smith. To Condit, the question is, where's the watch? He didn't want anybody asking that, and now it's on the tip of everybody's tongue. I don't think he wanted Anne Marie to know he was calling from Luray that night either, but soon it will be on the tip of the public's tongue, as soon as it starts getting press.

I also hope I get my main posting computer back up again soon with data intact. I have backups but starting over and getting the backups into place and figuring out what I've lost is a major pain. This looks like a motherboard failure, but only a year after my last one. They just don't make PC's like they used to.

In the meantime, if I disappear, I'm as grouchy and distraught as ever, but mainly because my PC crashed, which tends to cause me to want to throw it in the river rather than myself.

rd

Such as our posts went. The grand jury had tried to talk to Condit in April, after he lost his primary re-election and before Chandra was found. He didn't spend much time with them. They then talked to his Washington spokeman, Randy Groves, just before Chandra was found, and talked to his Modesto spokesman, Mike Lynch, a couple of weeks later.

Whatever the grand jury was seeking, they seemed sated. No one else heard from them through the summer and fall of 2002.

By December, the Levys made a trip to Washington. They talked to Greta Van Susteren about it:

> VAN SUSTEREN: Mrs. Levy, you're here on business here in Washington, right?

> SUSAN LEVY: Yes, we are.

> VAN SUSTEREN: And the business is?

> SUSAN LEVY: To be at the grand jury.

> VAN SUSTEREN: And also with us is Billy Martin, who has been assisting you on this case. And of course, Billy I've known for—I shouldn't say 100 years, Billy, but I sure have known you a long time. Billy, what's going on in the investigation?

> BILLY MARTIN, LEVY FAMILY ATTORNEY: Well, Greta, we're pleased to learn that the investigation is still very much an active and it's alive...

> VAN SUSTEREN: You know, Mrs. Levy, I was very disappointed in the police here. And Billy and I have, you know, been in the criminal court system together for years. But I was very disappointed that it took a year to find your daughter's remains because, you know, that's—that search, that grid search is not far from where I live.

> SUSAN LEVY: It's unacceptable.

> VAN SUSTEREN: Well, you know, because there's so many clues there. That's the problem. And as time goes by, the clues—do you share—I mean...

> SUSAN LEVY: Yes.

> VAN SUSTEREN: Frankly, I'm scandalized.

SUSAN LEVY: Yes. I'm disappointed.

VAN SUSTEREN: Billy, why'd that happen? Why did they —why did they not find the remains for almost a year? Because you know all the clues disappear over time like that.

MARTIN: Yes. Greta, there—every crime scene has either DNA or other active ingredients that would add to an investigation. We don't know why it took so long. There were times when there were offers from some of the search-and-rescue teams who go out to some of the disasters across the world, who asked to go into Rock Creek Park and help in the grid search.

And we were told that the grid search had been completed. So you can imagine the pain and the frustration on behalf of the Levys that we felt a year later when Chandra was discovered, her remains were found in an area that we had been led to believe had been searched.

VAN SUSTEREN: And I'll one-up you, one, Dr. Levy, is because after they searched the area where her remains were found, they unsealed it. I went in there, found a lot of suspicious items myself. I mean, I—you know, I walked the land myself with two others. And then, of course, Billy had investigators go in...

ROBERT LEVY: Yes.

VAN SUSTEREN: ...and more remains were found. I mean, how can you have a level of confidence in this police department?

ROBERT LEVY: Well, it just was pretty tough. The way they—you know—you know, it was just—you know, they weren't looking anymore.

They weren't looking in that area. You know, it was just by fate that she was found. [1]

No sooner did they return to Modesto than Laci disappeared, on Christmas Eve. Yet another family to share pain with right in their hometown. It was all too easy for a careful murderer to trust that any stray forensic evidence would be destroyed by the time a woman was found, if she ever was found. In this case, Laci's unborn baby Conner disappeared with her. Some think Chandra may have been pregnant when she disappeared, too.

By spring, two years had passed since Chandra disappeared. Michael Doyle of the Modesto Bee talked to Chandra's aunt and godparents about it:

Fran Iseman also wonders why a Washington-based grand jury never called her to testify, though she was close to Chandra Levy, who, with her parents, spent her 24th birthday at the Isemans' place about two weeks before the disappearance.

Levy's aunt, Linda (Zamsky) Katz, likewise said she was not called to testify, even though she said Chandra Levy confided in her about an affair with then-Rep. Gary Condit of Ceres. Condit, defeated for re-election last year, has stopped denying published reports that he told police about the affair.

Charles Iseman said it is his fervent hope that the Justice Department perseveres in the case.

"The cry for justice for Chandra screams out to the heavens," Fran Iseman said. [2]

"When this first happened, we were all pretty numb," said Linda Katz, Levy's aunt by marriage formerly known as Linda Zamsky. "Now I'm angry, and I'm frustrated that we haven't gotten any answers."

A grand jury has heard testimony about Ingmar Guandique, now in prison for attacking two women in Rock Creek Park, and investigators told The Washington Post last month that they are interested in several dozen sex offenders. But without any indication of progress, Washington police employ a rote description of the case. [3]

Where was the FBI that was supposed to have taken over the case long ago? Washington's NBC4 followed up with them:

The disappearance and murder of Chandra Levy remains one of this area's most notorious mysteries.

In a News4 exclusive, the lead investigators speak candidly about the case with Joe Krebs.

"It appears that she was on her computer early afternoon of May 1, and then she logs off. Then it's, of course, a year and three weeks later that we find her remains in Rock Creek Park," recalled FBI Agent Brad Garrett....

"In actuality, we don't know exactly what happened to her, what precipitated her death," said Sgt. J.C. Young.

In fact, they don't even know how she died.

"Well, we've been in constant contract with the medical examiner's office and we're still attempting to get the actual autopsy report from the medical examiner's office," said Young.

"Is it someone she knew? Maybe. Is it someone she didn't know? Maybe. It could go either way," said Garrett.

Still, investigators insist, they are making progress.

"The public's got to be patient because everything doesn't happen overnight. Watching CSI and Homicide these people believe that these crimes can be solved in a day or so, and that doesn't happen," said Young.

They need help from someone who knows something or someone who saw something.

"Someone sees something happen on every crime scene, believe it or not, and all they have to do is report it," said Young.

"We will eventually solve this case at the end, whatever the truth is, because there's been a lot of speculation about what this case might be, and I always like to bring the truth out, and we will at the end," said Garrett. [4]

The FBI is working on Chandra's case, but they haven't got the autopsy report from the Medical Examiner's office after a year and a half?

The Levys had three renowned forensic specialists who weren't allowed to examine her body closely or look at the forensic evidence. The Levys couldn't even get their daughter back for a year for burial. And then, as a final nail in the coffin, Chandra's resting place for a year as her parents and their forensic experts anxiously sought access was described by Sewell Chan of the Washington Post:

Behind the walls of the District's morgue, even death is put on hold.

Unclaimed bodies, awaiting public burial, have been decomposing on fiberglass trays in refrigerated storage rooms, some for up to three years. The cause and manner of death for roughly 400 people who have died since 1999 are "pending," the details of their demise left unresolved. Paper case files—the morgue's records are not computerized—are stored in unlocked rooms where workers, visitors and funeral directors wander freely. [5]

Chandra's body laid amongst this while the medical examiner refused to let the Levys get a professional opinion on her death, stress on professional. I suppose the Levys are lucky. They at least got Chandra back. Four hundred other families have been waiting years while their loved ones are decomposing. It is really too tragic for words.

Just as tragic is that two years after Chandra disappeared, police were still interested in investigating several dozen sex offenders. There are too many to investigate. We cannot continue to tolerate defense lawyers saying everyone is innocent because so many could be guilty.

Convicted felons should be monitored until they have completed probation. It makes no sense to think they don't. Until we put an electronic monitoring system in place, we will continue to lose innocent women to predators, predators that have already been caught time and again on lesser offenses and are on parole. These are the people that must be watched, not the entire population or children.

There are several technologies already in place and being used, if we can get to a point in our society of deciding which approach to use we will have achieved something great. If we use more than one of these technologies it has to be part of a unified national system is my only requirement.

The minimum requirement is that it records GPS locations of the person's whereabouts and is periodically uploaded to police. What this does is eliminate the anomynous roaming of the wolves to strike at will on a stray lamb without anyone knowing who could have done it. The GPS locations recorded will show who was at the location. GPS locations are accurate to a few yards.

The recording doesn't stop an abduction, but it ensures that we can tell who was there. If the device is removed or broken without coming in to a police station to report it, then that is the same as breaking out of jail. It means immediate return to incarceration.

If felons know that they cannot get away anomynously with a crime, then it changes their entire psychology. Sure, someone could go berserk, break the device and kill someone, but they know they will not get away with it. Now these felons think they will get away with it.

I say probation instead of life because the length of probation is based on the severity of crime. Registered sex offenders would be life, for example, as that is a type of permanent probation. But if someone had a five year probation and didn't commit another crime, then we need to focus our attention on those who are committing crimes.

www.justiceforchandra.com admin jane posted these statistics on GPS monitoring from Heather Hayes of fcw.com:

> When a convict with a 10-year history of abusing and stalking his ex-wife made parole in Scott County, Minn., last year, the only thing between him and his victim was an inconspicuous bracelet prison officials had attached to his ankle. He paid it no mind and headed straight for his ex-wife.
>
> But before he came within five miles of her, corrections officers were all over him.
>
> That was the last time that convict underestimated his high-tech ankle gear.
>
> Police now can keep tabs on criminals like this one by using Global Positioning System (GPS) satellites, the same technology the military uses to target bomb sites and the U.S. Justice Department uses to zero in on drug traffickers....
>
> In Florida, offenders monitored by GPS have not committed a single felony while on parole. By contrast, 27 percent of offenders tracked with traditional electronic monitoring commit felonies within 18 months. And nationally, 30 percent of all crimes are committed by people under community supervision....
>
> In Fresno County, for example, probationers who once paid $7 to $10 a day for the electronic ankle bracelet system now pay up to $16 a day for GPS monitoring. If the convicts were to remain in jail, the state and county could pay as much as $75 a day for adults and $100 a day for juveniles. [6]

The criminals, drug addicts, sex predators, wolves roaming to strike, have stolen goodness from our live's story and replaced it with fear. We need to drop them in cages in the desert, and replace our fear with their fear. Drop food in. Give them a treadmill, although they don't deserve to be treated as well as hamsters.

Women are dead basically because we don't have enough cages for these thugs. Our message to the legal system should be, catch all you want, we'll build more cages.

Pipe sea water into the desert and convert it to fresh water, put solar arrays on top of the cages to shade and power the cages. Who cares if someone gnaws through a bar, the dogs need a workout occasionally anyway.

Once out of their cages, I think Homeland Security has to include monitoring sex offenders and people on parole. They will strike like wolves at a lamb any chance they get. It's either the wolves or the lambs that need constant monitoring, we have to make a choice.

Maybe a little girl's impending death caught on tape will do it. Something must move us to act. Surely we cannot wait for the wolves to strike aqain.

In closing, why pursue the logic to recreate what happened in those last days of Chandra's life? Because some people care about Chandra and what happened to her, and what happened wasn't determined by the police investigation. The FBI is waiting for someone to drop a dime. Maybe the information here will enable someone to connect some dots and make a call. Maybe it won't. But we cared.

I hope Chandra is able to know how many good people put so much effort into helping find her. The good people will move on, but none will forget the disappearance of Chandra Levy.

Bibliography

Hunting Turtles

Doyle, Michael. "Intern may have had keys made, Dianne Feinstein says Condit lied to her about his affair with Levy." Modesto Bee 1 Aug. 2001.

Doyle, Michael. "Medical examiner can't tell how ex-intern was killed." Modesto Bee 29 May 2002.

Twomey, Steve and Sari Horwitz. "Skeletal Remains Found." Washington Post 23 May 2002.

Twomey, Steve and Sari Horwitz. "With Levy case going nowhere, chance stepped in." Washington Post 26 May 2002.

Paid Intern

1. Levy, Chandra. "HOLOCAUST MEMORIAL: A student's view of Wiesenthal Center." Modesto Bee 27 Aug. 1993.

2. Lehmann, John and Cynthia Bournellis. "Friends had been telling Chandra Levy for years: Quit falling in love with older men." New York Post 12 Aug. 2001.

3. Fagan, Kevin and Jim Herron Zamora. "Family and friends call Chandra Levy the girl least likely to vanish without a trace." San Francisco Chronicle 1 July 2001.

4. St. George, Donna, Allan Lengel and Petula Dvorak. "DC Intern Lived On Edge of Secrecy." Washington Post 8 July 2001.

5. Melley, Brian. "Acquaintances say Levy was a good student, fitness nut." Union Tribune 14 July 2001.

6. "Missing Intern Case Still a Mystery." Los Angeles Times 20 May 2001.

7. Harnden, Toby. "Fears for missing intern linked to congressman." Telegraph U.K. 18 May 2001.

8. Flammini, Vince Interview with Geraldo Rivera. Geraldo. NBC. 17 July 2001. Transcript.

9. Flammini, Vince. Interview with Sean Hannity and Alan Colmes. Hannity and Colmes. Fox News. 27 Feb. 2002. Transcript.

10. Williams, Ted, Michael Doyle, and Vincent Flammini. Interview with Greta Van Susteren. On the Record. Fox News. 29 Apr. 2002. Transcript.

11. Miller, Jim. "Condit, Davis ties run deep." Modesto Bee 24 Dec. 2000.

12. Murray, Frank J. "Who is Chandra Levy?" Washington Times 29 July 2001.

13. Ibid.

14. DePaulo, Lisa. Talk Magazine article on Chandra Levy. Excerpt. London Times U.K. 12 Aug. 2001.

15. Lauerman, Kerry. "The congressman, the missing intern and the mother." Salon 22 June 2001. <www.salon.com>.

16. Thermos, Wendy. "Student Vanishes Without a Word." New York Times 12 May 2001.

Arax, Mark and Stephen. "Days of Torment for Interns Parents." Los Angeles Times 7 July 2001.

"Condit children quit California governor's staff." CNN 28 Aug. 2001.

"D.C. Police, FBI, interview parents, Condit." WJLA 16 May 2001.

Dart, Bob. "Mystery of the missing intern has Washington abuzz." Atlanta Journal-Constitution 20 May 2001.

"Disappearance casts new light upon missing intern Chandra Levy." Associated Press 13 July 2001.

Doyle, Michael. "Anxiety deep, answers few in Levy case." Modesto Bee 12 May 2001.

Dvorak, Petula. "Washington Lifestyle Dazzled Intern: Missing Daughter's Hopes, Accomplishments Comfort Parents Keeping Vigil." Washington Post 22 May 2001.

"FBI Joins Missing Intern Case." Modesto Bee 19 May 2001.

"Friends fill in details of missing woman's personality." Dallas Morning News 25 May 2001.

"Intern Told Friend of Relationship With Congressman." Fox News 18 May 2001.

Jackson, Robert L. "Police Dogs Search Woods for USC Student." Los Angeles Times 17 May 2001.

Jardine, Jeff. "Condit faces new allegations." Modesto Bee 4 July 2001.

Jardine, Jeff and Michael Doyle. "Chandra Levy: A Closer Look." Modesto Bee 1 July 2001.

Jeffreys, Daniel. "The Vanishing." London Daily Mail 12 July 2001.

Levy, Susan. Interview. Newsweek. 13 Aug. 2001.

McCray, Kerry and Michael Doyle. "Levy stands out." Modesto Bee 24 May 2001.

Santana, Arthur. "Lack of Information Leaves Family Frustrated." Washington Post 16 May 2001.

Yost, Pete. "Police to Search Missing Woman's Apt." Associated Press 18 May 2001.

Secrecy

1. Jardine, Jeff. "Condit faces new allegations." Modesto Bee 4 July 2001.

2. Herendeen, Susan. "Congressman's wife keeps low profile; friends offer support." Modesto Bee 4 July 2001.

3. Frey, Jennifer. "Lady of the House." Washington Post 6 Aug. 2001.

4. Lathem, Niles. "Fly Gal: Condit Didn't Want To 'Pull a Newt'." New York Post 29 June 2001.

5. "Chandra's Aunt's Statement." Fox News. 9 July 2001.

6. St. George, Donna, Allan Lengel and Petula Dvorak. "DC Intern Lived On Edge of Secrecy." Washington Post 8 July 2001

7. Frey, Jennifer. "Lady of the House." Washington Post 6 Aug. 2001.

8. Smith, Anne Marie. Interview with Tony Snow and Rita Cosby. Fox News. 11 July 2001. Transcript.

9. Smith, Anne Marie and Jim Robinson. Interview with Sean Hannity and Alan Colmes. Hannity and Colmes. Fox News. 28 May 2002. Transcript.

10. Riechmann, Deb. "The Contrasts of Condit." Associated Press 13 July 2001.

Arax, Mark and Stephen Braun. "Condit: From Success to Scandal." Los Angeles Times 16 July 2001.

"Condit children quit California governor's staff." CNN. 28 Aug. 2001.

Depaulo, Lisa. Interview with Geraldo Rivera. Rivera Live. CNBC. 6 Aug. 2001. Transcript.

Dvorak, Petula and Allan Lengel. "Condit Denies Asking Woman Not to Assist Levy Inquiry, Former Driver Alleges Lawmaker Had Affair." Washington Post 4 July 2001.

Flammini, Vince Interview with Geraldo Rivera. Geraldo. NBC. 17 July 2001. Transcript.

Flammini, Vince. Interview with Sean Hannity and Alan Colmes. Hannity and Colmes. Fox News. 27 Feb. 2002. Transcript.

Kennedy, Helen. "Condit Wove a Web of Lies, Say Ex-Lovers." New York Daily News 5 Aug. 2001.

Kennedy, Helen. "D.C. Cops Mystified As Intern Vanishes." New York Daily News 16 May 2001.

Lengel, Allan and Petula Dvorak. "Aunt Linda Details Chandra's Affair with Gary." Washington Post 6 July 2001.

Levy, Robert and Susan. Interview with Stone Phillips. NBC News. 10 Aug. 2001. Transcript.

"Levy Relative Details Condit Affair." ABC News. 6 July 2001.

"Levy's parents say Chandra admitted affair." CNN. 31 July 2001.

Lochhead, Carolyn. "A Power Broker Comes Of Age." San Francisco Chronicle 18 Dec.1996.

Mattix, Cheryl. "Levy's aunt speaks out." Port Herman. 2 Aug. 2001.

Mooney, Michael G. "Smith details alleged Condit affair." Modesto Bee 6 Sept. 2001.

Olson, Barbara, Mark Geragos, Cynthia Alksne and Julian Epstein. Interview with Roger Cossack. Larry King Live. CNN. 2 Aug. 2001. Transcript.

Olson, Barbara, Mike Geragos, Cynthia Alksne, Julian Epstein, and Lisa DePaulo. "Will Chandra Levy ever be found?" Interview with Larry King. Larry King Live. CNN. 30 July 2001. Transcript.

"Police Keep Quiet on Levy Investigation." Washington Times 23 Aug. 2001.

Robinson, Jim. Interview with Paula Zahn. The Edge. Fox News. 11 June 2001. Transcript.

Smith, Anne Marie and Jim Robinson. Interview with Larry King. Larry King Live. CNN. 13 July 2001. Transcript.

Friendships

1. St. George, Donna, Allan Lengel and Petula Dvorak. "DC Intern Lived On Edge of Secrecy." Washington Post 8 July 2001.

2. Doyle, Michael. "Anxiety deep, answers few in Levy case." Modesto Bee 12 May 2001.

3. Doyle, Michael. "Condit's gift giving could be an issue." Modesto Bee 22 July 2001.

4. Lauerman, Kerry. "The congressman, the missing intern and the mother." Salon. 22 June 2001. <www.salon.com>.

5. Levy, Susan. Interview. Newsweek. 13 Aug. 2001.

6. Leiby, Richard and Petula Dvorak. "The Wait of Their Lives." Washington Post 26 Aug. 2001.

7. Ibid.

8. Thermos, Wendy. "Student Vanishes Without a Word." New York Times 12 May 2001.

9. "Campaign Finance Reports and Data" at http://www.fec.gov, 5 Sep. 2002.

10. "Chandra's Aunt's Statement." Fox News. 9 July 2001.

11. Harnden, Toby. "Fears for missing intern linked to congressman." Telegraph U.K. 18 May 2001.

12. "Police Keep Quiet on Levy Investigation." Washington Times 23 Aug. 2001.

13. St. George, Donna, Allan Lengel and Petula Dvorak. "DC Intern Lived On Edge of Secrecy." Washington Post 8 July 2001.

14. Lengel, Allan and Petula Dvorak. "Intern Mentioned A 'Boyfriend', Landlord Says: Levy Briefly Considered Move, He Says." Washington Post 21 June 2001.

15. Smith, Anne Marie and Jim Robinson. Interview with Larry King. Larry King Live. CNN. 13 July 2001. Transcript.

16. Santana, Arthur. "Lack of Information Leaves Family Frustrated." Washington Post 16 May 2001.

17. Dvorak, Petula. "Washington Lifestyle Dazzled Intern: Missing Daughter's Hopes, Accomplishments Comfort Parents Keeping Vigil." Washington Post 22 May 2001.

18. Dvorak, Petula and Allan Lengel. "Minister Says Daughter, at 18, Had an Affair With Condit." Washington Post 12 July 2001.

19. Lehman, John and Edmund Newton. "Pol's Teen-Wed Shame." New York Post 14 July 2001.

Arax, Mark and Stephen Braun. "Condit: From Success to Scandal." Los Angeles Times 16 July 2001.

Arax, Mark and Stephen Braun. "Days of Torment for Interns Parents." Los Angeles Times 7 July 2001.

Brazil, Eric. "Relationship with congressman questioned." San Francisco Chronicle 18 May 2001.

Burger, Timothy J. and Helen Kennedy. "Police hunt for Chandra's body; Condit balking at taking lie test." New York Daily News 13 July 2001.

"Condit passes private polygraph, lawyer says." CNN 13 July 2001.

"Congressman Meets With Police: Police Call Meeting 'Productive'." ABC News 23 June 2001.

DePaulo, Lisa. Talk Magazine article on Chandra Levy. Excerpt. London Times U.K. 12 Aug. 2001.

Drake, John. "California assists D.C. in case." ABC News. 15 May 2001.

Doyle, Michael. "Levy's remains to be returned to Modesto, godparents say." Modesto Bee 22 May 2003.

Doyle, Michael. "Private dicks search toss intern's apartment." Scripps-McClatchy Western Service 27 June 2001.

Fagan, Kevin and Jim Herron Zamora. "Family and friends call Chandra Levy the girl least likely to vanish without a trace." San Francisco Chronicle 1 July 2001.

Hosenball, Mark and Michael Isikoff. "A Capital Mystery Heats Up." Newsweek 2 July 2001.

Jacoby, Mary. "Missing intern; media frenzy." St. Petersburg Times 23 June 2001.

Jardine, Jeff. "Levys keep their hopes alive." Modesto Bee 1 Aug. 2001.

Jardine, Jeff. "Minister: Daughter had affair with Condit." Modesto Bee 12 July 2001.

Kennedy, Helen. "Condit Lawyer: Lie Test OK: If FBI asks, congressman should do it, he's advised." New York Daily News 30 May 2002.

Lathem, Niles. "Fly Gal: Condit Didn't Want To 'Pull a Newt'." New York Post 29 June 2001.

Lathem, Niles, Steve Dunleavy, Edmund Newton and Andy Gellar. "Condit's 'Affair' Teen Had Baby." New York Post 13 July 2001.

Lengel, Allan and Petula Dvorak. "Aunt Linda Details Chandra's Affair with Gary." Washington Post 6 July 2001.

"Levy case opens door on secret life: The search for missing former intern Chandra Levy has focused the spotlight on U.S. Rep. Gary Condit." CNN 1 June 2002.

Murray, Frank J. "Who is Chandra Levy?" Washington Times 29 July 2001.

Serrano, Richard A. and Robert L. Jackson." D.C. Puzzles Over Missing USC Student." Los Angeles Times 19 May 2001.

Smith, Anne Marie. Interview with Tony Snow and Rita Cosby. Fox News. 11 July 2001. Transcript.

"Where In The World Is Chandra Levy" at http://www.geocities.com/redd_herring.geo/chandra/chandralevy_main.html under "Q & A session with Denis Edeline.", 3 Aug. 2001.

Explanation

1. Wright, Brad and Paul Courson. "Levy's former neighbors don't recall much." CNN 27 July 2001.

2. DePaulo, Lisa. Talk Magazine article on Chandra Levy. Excerpt. London Times U.K. 12 Aug. 2001.

3. Cowan, Lee. Interview with Tom Bergeron. The Early Show. CBS. 8 July 2001. Transcript.

4. DePaulo, Lisa. Talk Magazine article on Chandra Levy. Excerpt. London Times U.K. 12 Aug. 2001.

5. Olson, Barbara, Mark Geragos, Cynthia Alksne and Julian Epstein. Interview with Roger Cossack. Larry King Live. CNN. 2 Aug. 2001. Transcript.

6. Levy, Robert and Susan and Billy Martin. Interview with Larry King. Larry King Live. CNN. 30 Apr. 2002. Transcript.

7. Isikoff, Michael and Evan Thomas. "From Bad to Worse." Newsweek 3 Sept. 2001.

8. Isikoff, Michael. "Interview with Gary Condit and Abbe Lowe." Newsweek 3 Sept. 2001.

9. Isikoff, Michael and Evan Thomas. "From Bad to Worse." Newsweek 3 Sept. 2001.

10. Isikoff, Michael. "Interview with Gary Condit and Abbe Lowe." Newsweek 3 Sept. 2001.

11. Levy, Robert and Susan. Interview with Stone Phillips. NBC News. 10 Aug. 2001. Transcript.

12. "Chandra's Aunt's Statement." Fox News 9 July 2001.

13. Lengel, Allan and Petula Dvorak. "Aunt Linda Details Chandra's Affair with Gary." Washington Post 6 July 2001.

14. Arax, Mark and Stephen. "Days of Torment for Interns Parents." Los Angeles Times 7 July 2001.

15. "Levy Relative Details Condit Affair." ABC News 6 July 2001.

16. Levy, Robert and Susan. Interview with Stone Phillips. NBC News. 10 Aug. 2001. Transcript.

17. St. George, Donna, Allan Lengel and Petula Dvorak. "DC Intern Lived On Edge of Secrecy." Washington Post 8 July 2001.

18. Murray, Frank J. "Mom won't judge Chandra." Washington Times 29 July 2001.

19. Doyle, Michael and J. N. Sbranti. "D.C. police reject local assistance in search for missing Modesto woman." Modesto Bee 15 May 2001.

Burger, Timothy J. and Helen Kennedy. "Police hunt for Chandra's body; Condit balking at taking lie test." New York Daily News 13 July 2001.

"Chandra's Brother Talks." Los Angeles Times 21 June 2001.

Depaulo, Lisa. Interview with Matt Lauer. Today. NBC News. 3 Aug. 2001. Transcript.

Doyle, Michael. "Levy's remains to be returned to Modesto, godparents say." Modesto Bee 22 May 2003.

Fields-Meyer, Thomas, Champ Clark, Michael Fleeman, Macon Morehouse and J. Todd Foster. "Searching For Chandra." People 25 June 2001: 87.

Jardine, Jeff. "Minister: Daughter had affair with Condit." Modesto Bee 12 July 2001.

Jones, Sven. Interview with Bill O'Reilly. The O'Reilly Factor. Fox News. 24 May 2002. Transcript.

Kennedy, Helen "D.C. Cops Mystified As Intern Vanishes." New York Daily News 16 May 2001.

Lathem, Niles and Cathy Burke. "Condit Wife's Mystery Phone Call." New York Post 27 July 2001.

Leiby, Richard and Petula Dvorak. "The Wait of Their Lives." Washington Post 26 Aug. 2001.

"Missing Intern Left Clue." Fox News 18 May 2001.

"Nonexistent Phone Calls (and Other False Tales)." Newsweek 29 July 2001.

Olson, Barbara, Mike Geragos, Cynthia Alksne, Julian Epstein, and Lisa DePaulo. "Will Chandra Levy ever be found?" Interview with Larry King. Larry King Live. CNN. 30 July 2001. Transcript.

"Police Dismiss Private Test." 9 Eyewitness News 14 July 2001.

Squitieri, Tom and Kevin Johnson. "Flight attendant questioned for second day." USA Today 13 July 2001.

BOP

1. St. George, Donna, Allan Lengel and Petula Dvorak. "DC Intern Lived On Edge of Secrecy." Washington Post 8 July 2001.

2. Hosenball, Mark and Michael Isikoff. "A Capital Mystery Heats Up." Newsweek 2 July 2001.

3. "Cops Want to Interview Condit's Wife." Fox News. 25 June 2001.

4. Kennedy, Helen. "Cops Have More Questions for Calif. Pol." New York Daily News 21 June 2001.

5. Arax, Mark and Stephen. "Days of Torment for Interns Parents." Los Angeles Times 7 July 2001.

6. Cowan, Lee. Interview with Tom Bergeron. The Early Show. CBS. 8 July 2001. Transcript.

7. Kennedy, Helen. "Cops Have More Questions for Calif. Pol." New York Daily News 21 June 2001.

8. Doyle, Michael. "Levy lawyer to start own probe." Modesto Bee 21 June 2001.

9. "USC Political Science Syllabus" at http://www.usc.edu/dept/polsci/unruh/syllabus.htm, 17 Jan. 2002.

10. "Post from H.F." at http://www.bannerofliberty.com/OS7-01MQC/7-27-2001.1.html, 27 July 2001.

11. "Student Jobs FAQ" at http://www.studentjobs.gov/faqs.htm, 17 Jan. 2002.

12. "Minority Recruitment" at http://www.ed.gov/offices/OIIA/Hispanic/fr/Agencies/fy1998/98agencies/dj.html, 17 Jan. 2002.

13. "Do Your Career Justice" at http://www.studentjobs.gov/agency-fedprison-allenwood.htm, 17 Jan. 2002.

Britton, Kimberly. "Search continues for USC student" USC Tojan 21 May 2001.

DePaulo, Lisa. Talk Magazine article on Chandra Levy. Excerpt. London Times U.K. 12 Aug. 2001.

Doyle, Michael. "Condit's gift giving could be an issue." Modesto Bee 22 July 2001.

Fagan, Kevin and Jim Herron Zamora. "Family and friends call Chandra Levy the girl least likely to vanish without a trace." San Francisco Chronicle 1 July 2001.

"FBI Joins Missing Intern Case." Modesto Bee 19 May 2001.

Fields-Meyer, Thomas, Champ Clark, Michael Fleeman, Macon Morehouse and J. Todd Foster. "Searching For Chandra." People 25 June 2001: 87.

Levy, Robert and Susan. Interview with Larry King. Larry King Live. CNN. 15 Aug. 2001. Transcript.

"Levys said to refuse Condit's calls." MSNBC 20 June 2001.

Murray, Frank J. "Who is Chandra Levy?" Washington Times 29 July 2001.

Serrano, Richard A. and Robert L. Jackson. "D.C. Puzzles Over Missing USC Student." Los Angeles Times 19 May 2001.

Shannon, Elaine. "Why the FBI's Missing Guns and Computers Mess Isn't—and Is—as Bad as it Looks." Time. 18 July 2001.

Big News

1. Smith, Anne Marie. Interview with Tony Snow and Rita Cosby. Fox News. 11 July 2001. Transcript.

2. Robinson, Jim. Interview with Paula Zahn. The Edge. Fox News. 11 June 2001. Transcript.

3. Sperry, Paul. "Hunt For Missing Intern: Smith shares intimate Condit details; Mistress says congressman fantasized about 'bunch of guys' during phone sex." WorldNetDaily 20 July 2001.

4. Smith, Anne Marie and Jim Robinson. Interview with Sean Hannity and Alan Colmes. Hannity and Colmes. Fox News. 28 May 2002. Transcript.

5. Sperry, Paul. "Hunt For Missing Intern: Smith shares intimate Condit details; Mistress says congressman fantasized about 'bunch of guys' during phone sex." WorldNetDaily 20 July 2001.

6. Robinson, Jim. Interview with Paula Zahn. The Edge. Fox News. 11 June 2001. Transcript.

7. Mooney, Michael G. "Smith details alleged Condit affair." Modesto Bee 6 Sept. 2001.

8. Isikoff, Michael. "Interview with Gary Condit and Abbe Lowe." Newsweek 3 Sept. 2001.

9. Isikoff, Michael. "The Battle Over Chandra." Newsweek 23 July 2001.

10. Isikoff, Michael. "Interview with Gary Condit and Abbe Lowe." Newsweek 3 Sept. 2001.

11. Jardine, Jeff and Michael Doyle. "Chandra Levy: A Closer Look." Modesto Bee 1 July 2001.

12. Dvorak, Petula and Allan Lengel. "Second Condit Interview Sheds Little Light." Washington Post 25 June 2001.

13. Leiby, Richard and Petula Dvorak. "The Wait of Their Lives." Washington Post 26 Aug. 2001.

14. Olson, Barbara, Mark Geragos, Cynthia Alksne and Julian Epstein. Interview with Roger Cossack. Larry King Live. CNN. 2 Aug. 2001. Transcript.

15. "Campaign Finance Reports and Data" at http://www.fec.gov, 5 Sep. 2002.

16. Bier, Jerry. "Carolyn Condit, Enquirer settle suit." Fresno Bee 10 July 2003.

17. Doyle, Michael. "P.M. Update: Missing Modesto woman's parents meet with police." Modesto Bee 17 May 2001.

18. People. 23 July 2001.

19. DePaulo, Lisa. Talk Magazine article on Chandra Levy. Excerpt. London Times U.K. 12 Aug. 2001.

20. "Lost in a Washington mystery." Baltimore Sun 26 May 2001.

21. Arax, Mark and Stephen. "Days of Torment for Interns Parents." Los Angeles Times 7 July 2001.

22. Lengel, Allan and Petula Dvorak. "Intern Mentioned A 'Boyfriend', Landlord Says: Levy Briefly Considered Move, He Says." Washington Post 21 June 2001.

23. Lengel, Allan and Petula Dvorak. "Aunt Linda Details Chandra's Affair with Gary." Washington Post 6 July 2001.

"Condit submits to fourth interview." NBC News. 27 July 2001.

"Condit's Calendar." ABC News. 29 June 2001.

"Cops Want to Interview Condit's Wife." Fox News. 25 June 2001. <www.foxnews.com>.

Cowan, Lee. Interview with Tom Bergeron. The Early Show. CBS. 8 July 2001. Transcript.

Doyle, Michael. "Condit aide denies cover-up: He says he never tried to stop a woman from disclosing alleged affair." Modesto Bee 27 July 2001.

Doyle, Michael and J. N. Sbranti. "D.C. police reject local assistance in search for missing Modesto woman." Modesto Bee 15 May 2001.

Drake, John. "California assists D.C. in case." ABC News. 15 May 2001.

Edeline, Denis. Interview with Geraldo Rivera. Geraldo. CNBC. July 2001. Transcript.

Jones, Sven. Interview with Jane Clayson. The Early Show. CBS. 18 May 2001. Transcript.

Kennedy, Helen. "Cops Comb Condit's Apartment." New York Daily News 11 July 2001.

Kennedy, Helen. "D.C. Intern Was Smitten: She told landlord she wanted to move in with beau." New York Daily News 20 June 2001.

Lathem, Niles and Cathy Burke. "Condit Wife's Mystery Phone Call." New York Post 27 July 2001.

Levy, Robert and Susan and Billy Martin. Interview with Larry King. Larry King Live. CNN. 30 Apr. 2002. Transcript.

Levy, Susan. Interview. Newsweek. 13 Aug. 2001.

Levy, Susan. Interview with Katie Couric and Matt Lauer. Today. NBC. 17 May 2001. Transcript.

Marshall, Joshua Micah. "Chandra's contested calls to Condit: It's the New York Post vs. Newsweek. Or could the truth lie somewhere in between?" Salon 1 Aug. 2001.

"Nonexistent Phone Calls (and Other False Tales)." Newsweek 29 July 2001.

Robinson, James and Terry Lenzer. Interview with Paula Zahn. The Edge. Fox News. 19 July 2001. Transcript.

Robinson, Jim, Britt Hume, Juan Williams, Ceci Connolly and Bill Kristol. Interview with Rita Cosby. Fox News Sunday. Fox News. 26 Aug. 2001. Transcript.

Sherman, Mark. "Chandra Levy Had Untold 'Big News'." Associated Press 6 July 2001.

Smith, Anne Marie and Jim Robinson. "I was hurt." Interview with Diane Sawyer. Good Morning America. ABC. 28 Aug. 2001. Transcript.

Squitieri, Tom and Kevin Johnson. "Flight attendant questioned for second day." USA Today 13 July 2001.

"Where In The World Is Chandra Levy" at http://www.geocities.com/redd_herring.geo/chandra/chandralevy_main.html under "Q & A session with Denis Edeline.", 3 Aug. 2001.

Whitney, David. "Missing intern's parents: Condit knows more." Scripps-McClatchy Western Service 14 June 2001.

Wiegand, Steve. "Facts are few in Levy mystery." Sacramento Bee 3 Sept. 2001.

The Scream

1. Cosby, Rita. "Flight Attendant Says Condit Asked Her to Lie." Fox News. 3 July 2001.

2. Dvorak, Petula and Allan Lengel. "Missing Intern's Parents Back in D.C.—With new attorney." Washington Post 20 June 2001.

3. Marshall, Joshua Micah. "Chandra's contested calls to Condit: It's the New York Post vs. Newsweek. Or could the truth lie somewhere in between?" Salon 1 Aug. 2001.

4. Condit, Gary. Interview with Sun-Star. Merced Sun-Star 24 Aug. 2001. Transcript.

5. Isikoff, Michael. "Interview with Gary Condit and Abbe Lowe." Newsweek 3 Sept. 2001.

6. "She Was Going Back Home': New Description of Chandra's Mindset Seems to Make Suicide Less Likely." ABC News 19 July 2001.

7. "Thread Archives." at www.justiceforchandra.com/forums, 5 Sep. 2002.

8. Martin, Billy. Interview with Bill O'Reilly. The O'Reilly Factor. Fox News. 24 Jan. 2002. Transcript.

9. Isikoff, Michael; Klaidman, Daniel; Clift, Eleanor; Murr, Andrew. "An Affair to Remember." Newsweek. 16 July 2001: 20.

10. Press Release. "Oxon Hill man sentenced in murder of Omni Shoreham employee." U.S. Department of Justice. 4 Dec. 2001.

11. Ramsey, Charles. "Is Private Lie Detector Test Taken by Rep. Gary Condit Good Enough for D.C. Police?" Interview with Bob Scheiffer. Face the Nation. CBS. 16 Jul. 2001. Transcript.

"Bethesda Red Line train." at http://www.wmata.com/metrorail/Stations/station.cfm?station=12, 5 Sep. 2002.

"Chandra's Brother Talks." Los Angeles Times 21 June 2001.

"Condit submits to fourth interview." NBC News. 27 July 2001.

Doyle, Michael. "Anxiety deep, answers few in Levy case." Modesto Bee 12 May 2001.

Dvorak, Petula and Allan Lengel. "Second Condit Interview Sheds Little Light." Washington Post 25 June 2001.

Fagan, Kevin. "A Life Suspended." San Francisco Chronicle 28 Apr. 2002.

Fahrenthold, David A. and Arthur Santana. "Lots of Attention but Little News As Search for Intern Continues." Washington Post 18 May 2001.

Franken, Bob. "Bob Franken on the Levy disappearance probe." CNN. 16 Jul. 2001. Transcript.

Jardine, Jeff. "Condit faces new allegations." Modesto Bee 4 July 2001.

Kennedy, Helen "D.C. Cops Mystified As Intern Vanishes." New York Daily News 16 May 2001.

Lehmann, John and Cynthia Bournellis. "Friends had been telling Chandra Levy for years: Quit falling in love with older men." New York Post 12 Aug. 2001.

Lengel, Allan and Sari Horwitz. "Levy Was on Internet on May 1, Police Say Intern Looked Up Rock Creek Map, Other Sites." Washington Post 16 July 2001.

Murray, Frank J. "Who is Chandra Levy?" Washington Times 29 July 2001.

"New Details Emerging About the Morning Chandra Disappeared." Associated Press 15 July 2001.

"Omni-Shoreham Hotel." at http://www.omnihotels.com/hotels/default.asp?h_id=6, 17 Jan. 2002.

Santana, Arthur and Cheryl W. Thompson. "Street Crimes Probed in Intern's Case." Washington Post 19 May 2001.

Squitieri, Tom and Kevin Johnson. "Police again want to talk with Calif. Congressman." USA Today 21 June 2001.

Sweet, Lynn. "Levy 'jubilant' at last sighting." Chicago Sun-Times 20 July 2001.

"Trader Joe's Bethesda." at http://www.traderjoes.com/locations, 5 Sep. 2002.

On Her Computer

1. Arax, Mark and Stephen. "Days of Torment for Interns Parents." Los Angeles Times 7 July 2001.

2. DePaulo, Lisa. Talk 8 Aug. 2001.

3. Ramsey, Charles, Michael Doyle and Tom Squitieri. Interview with Bob Schieffer. CBS. 29 July 2001. Transcript.

4. "Chandra Levy Website Addresses." WJLA 20 July 2001.

5. "Missing Intern." CNN 21 July 2001.

6. Ibid.

Doyle, Michael. "Condit's schedule checks out." Modesto Bee 22 July 2001.

Lengel, Allan and Sari Horwitz. "Levy Looked Up Map Of a Rock Creek Site." Washington Post 16 July 2001.

Levy, Susan. Interview with Katie Couric and Matt Lauer. Today. NBC. 17 May 2001. Transcript.

"Lost in a Washington mystery." Baltimore Sun 26 May 2001.

Murray, Frank J. "Who is Chandra Levy?" Washington Times 29 July 2001.

Ramsey, Charles. "Is Private Lie Detector Test Taken by Rep. Gary Condit Good Enough for D.C. Police?" Interview with Bob Scheiffer. Face the Nation. CBS. 16 Jul. 2001. Transcript.

Stites, Roxanne and Lori Aratani. "Levy may have tracked Condit via Web the day she disappeared." San Jose Mercury News 19 July 2001.

Sweet, Lynn. "Police: Missing intern no 'trollop'." Chicago Sun-Times 19 July 2001.

Klingle Mansion

1. Stites, Roxanne and Lori Aratani. "Levy may have tracked Condit via Web the day she disappeared." San Jose Mercury News 19 July 2001.

2. "Thread Archives" at www.justiceforchandra.com/forums, 5 Sep. 2002.

3. Van Zandt, Clint. "The FBI Profile." Interview with Greta Van Susteren. The Point. CNN. 25 July 2001. Transcript.

4. "Thread Archives" at www.justiceforchandra.com/forums, 5 Sep. 2002.

5. "Klingle Mansion" at www.nps.gov/rocr/, 17 Jan. 2002.

6. "Rock Creek Park" at http://www.mdbirds.org/dcbirds/ccorridor.html, 2000.

"Condit Has an Alibi." Newsweek. 20 July 2001.

Fahrenthold, David A. and Arthur Santana. "Lots of Attention but Little News As Search for Intern Continues." Washington Post 18 May 2001.

Jacoby, Mary. "Clues to missing intern sought in park." St Petersburg Times 17 July 2001.

Johnson, Kevin and Tom Squitieri. "D.C. police retrace steps in their search for Levy." USA Today 17 July 2001.

Kennedy, Helen. "Cops on Intern Net Trail: Computer shows Levy may have been lured to path." New York Daily News 16 July 2001.

Lengel, Allan and Sari Horwitz. "Levy Looked Up Map Of a Rock Creek Site." Washington Post 16 July 2001.

Lochhead, Carolyn. "A Power Broker Comes Of Age." San Francisco Chronicle 18 Dec.1996.

Frantic

1. Condit, Gary. Interview with Connie Chung. PrimeTime Live. ABC. 23 Aug. 2001. Transcript.

2. Levy, Robert and Susan and Billy Martin. Interview with Larry King. Larry King Live. CNN. 30 Apr. 2002. Transcript.

3. Douthat, Ross. "Condit Watch." National Review 9 Aug. 2001.

4. Levy, Robert and Susan. Interview with Larry King. Larry King Live. CNN. 15 Aug. 2001. Transcript.

5. "Congressman Meets With Police: Police Call Meeting 'Productive'." ABC News 23 June 2001.

6. "Where In The World Is Chandra Levy" at http://www.geocities.com/redd_herring.geo/chandra/chandralevy_main.html under "Q & A session with Denis Edeline.", 3 Aug. 2001.

7. DePaulo, Lisa. Talk Magazine article on Chandra Levy. Excerpt. London Times U.K. 12 Aug. 2001.

8. Olson, Barbara, Mark Geragos, Cynthia Alksne and Julian Epstein. Interview with Roger Cossack. Larry King Live. CNN. 2 Aug. 2001. Transcript.

9. Douthat, Ross. "Condit Watch." National Review 9 Aug. 2001.

10. Condit, Gary. Interview with Connie Chung. PrimeTime Live. ABC. 23 Aug. 2001. Transcript.

11. "Police Keep Quiet on Levy Investigation." Washington Times 23 Aug. 2001.

12. Levy, Robert and Susan. Interview with Larry King. Larry King Live. CNN. 15 Aug. 2001. Transcript.

13. Levy, Robert and Susan. Interview with Stone Phillips. NBC News. 10 Aug. 2001. Transcript.

14. Ibid.

"Chandra Levy Timeline." ABCNews. 2002.

Dvorak, Petula. "Washington Lifestyle Dazzled Intern: Missing Daughter's Hopes, Accomplishments Comfort Parents Keeping Vigil." Washington Post 22 May 2001.

Jardine, Jeff and Michael Doyle. "Chandra Levy: A Closer Look." Modesto Bee 1 July 2001.

Kennedy, Helen "D.C. Cops Mystified As Intern Vanishes." New York Daily News 16 May 2001.

Lengel, Allan and Jamie Stockwell. "Search for IRS Worker Broadens." Washington Post. 19 June 2003.

Lengel, Allan and Petula Dvorak. "Intern Mentioned A 'Boyfriend', Landlord Says: Levy Briefly Considered Move, He Says." Washington Post 21 June 2001.

Miller, Bill. "Miles Between Missing and Murdered." Washington Post 30 July 2001.

Novak, Viveca. Interview with McEdwards. Just in Time. CNN. 18 June 2001. Transcript.

Ortega, Ralph. "Without a trace." New York Daily News. 6 March 2003.

Walsh, Mary, Ariane DeVogue, Pierre Thomas and Brian Hartman. "Losing Hope." ABC News 21 June 2001.

Woolfolk, John and Roxanne Stites. "MODESTO HOUSE SEALED OFF AS FBI AIDS INVESTIGATION." San Jose Mercury News 28 December 2002.

The Newport

1. Zamora, Jim Herron. "Modesto woman is missing in Washington, D.C.: Police begin bicoastal search for grad student." San Francisco Chronicle 13 May 2001.

2. Levy, Susan. Interview with Katie Couric and Matt Lauer. Today. NBC. 17 May 2001. Transcript.

3. Keary, Jim. "Missing intern's trail quickly growing cold." Washington Times 24 May 2001.

4. Dvorak, Petula and Allan Lengel. "Second Condit Interview Sheds Little Light." Washington Post 25 June 2001.

5. St. George, Donna, Allan Lengel and Petula Dvorak. "DC Intern Lived On Edge of Secrecy." Washington Post 8 July 2001.

6. Franken, Bob. "Bob Franken on the Levy disappearance probe." CNN. 16 Jul. 2001. Transcript.

7. "D.C. Police To Interview Members Of Condit's Family." WUSA 26 June 2001.

8. Kennedy, Helen. "Condit Lawyer: Lie Test OK: If FBI asks, congressman should do it, he's advised." New York Daily News 30 May 2002.

9. Levy, Robert and Susan and Billy Martin. Interview with Larry King. Larry King Live. CNN. 30 Apr. 2002. Transcript.

10. Jardine, Jeff and Michael Doyle. "Chandra Levy: A Closer Look." Modesto Bee 1 July 2001.

11. "Parents: Chandra never made return plane reservation." CNN 14 July 2001.

12. Lang, Laura. "THE GIRL NEXT DOOR." Washington City Paper 20 July 2001.

13. "Where In The World Is Chandra Levy" at http://www.geocities.com/redd_herring.geo/chandra/chandralevy_main.html under "Q & A session with Denis Edeline.", 3 Aug. 2001.

14. Dvorak, Petula and Allan Lengel. "Second Condit Interview Sheds Little Light." Washington Post 25 June 2001.

15. "D.C. police chief says video was useless in Levy case." Courttv.com 25 June 2001.

"California woman missing in Washington, D.C." Associated Press 10 May 2001.

"CHANDRA MYSTERY SOLVED." National Enquirer. 9 April 2002.

Coles, Joanna. "Have you seen this woman?" London Times U.K. 28 May 2001.

"Condit Has an Alibi." Newsweek. 20 July 2001.

Douthat, Ross. "Condit Watch." National Review 9 Aug. 2001.

Doyle, Michael. "P.M. Update: Missing Modesto woman's parents meet with police." Modesto Bee 17 May 2001.

Doyle, Michael. "Private dicks search toss intern's apartment." Scripps-McClatchy Western Service 27 June 2001.

Fahrenthold, David A. and Arthur Santana. "Lots of Attention but Little News As Search for Intern Continues." Washington Post 18 May 2001.

Kennedy, Helen "D.C. Cops Mystified As Intern Vanishes." New York Daily News 16 May 2001.

Leiby, Richard and Petula Dvorak. "The Wait of Their Lives." Washington Post 26 Aug. 2001.

Levy, Robert and Susan. Interview with Larry King. Larry King Live. CNN. 15 Aug. 2001. Transcript.

Murray, Frank J. "Who is Chandra Levy?" Washington Times 29 July 2001.

O'Donnell, Norah and Stone Phillips. "Vanished: Investigation Continues Into Disappearance of Washington Intern Chandra Levy." Dateline. NBC. 28 May 2001. Transcript.

Santana, Arthur and Cheryl W. Thompson. "Street Crimes Probed in Intern's Case." Washington Post 19 May 2001.

Sbranti, J.N. "Search is on for woman from valley." Modesto Bee 11 May 2001.

Serrano, Richard A. and Robert L. Jackson. "D.C. Puzzles Over Missing USC Student." Los Angeles Times 19 May 2001.

Yost, Pete. "Police to Search Missing Woman's Apt." Associated Press 18 May 2001.

Investigation

1. Brazil, Eric. "Relationship with congressman questioned." San Francisco Chronicle 18 May 2001.

2. Zamora, Jim Herron. "Modesto woman is missing in Washington, D.C.: Police begin bicoastal search for grad student." San Francisco Chronicle 13 May 2001.

3. Santana, Arthur. "Lack of Information Leaves Family Frustrated." Washington Post 16 May 2001.

4. Lathem, Niles and Dan Mangan. "Mystery Beau Paid For Missing Intern's Airfare." New York Post 19 May 2001.

5. Santana, Arthur. "Search Intensifies for Missing Intern." Washington Post 17 May 2001.

6. Honawar, Vaishali. "Missing woman's mother speaks out." Washington Times 25 May 2001.

7. Ramsey, Charles. "Is Private Lie Detector Test Taken by Rep. Gary Condit Good Enough for D.C. Police?" Interview with Bob Scheiffer. Face the Nation. CBS. 16 Jul. 2001. Transcript.

8. Honawar, Vaishali. "Missing woman's mother speaks out." Washington Times 25 May 2001.

9. "D.C. Police To Interview Members Of Condit's Family." WUSA 26 June 2001.

10. Fagan, Kevin. "A Life Suspended." San Francisco Chronicle 28 Apr. 2002.

11. Sbranti, J. N. "Reward, hot line are set up for tips." Modesto Bee 12 May 2001.

12. Doyle, Michael and J. N. Sbranti. "D.C. police reject local assistance in search for missing Modesto woman." Modesto Bee 15 May 2001.

13. Kennedy, Helen "D.C. Cops Mystified As Intern Vanishes." New York Daily News 16 May 2001.

14. Isikoff, Michael. "Interview with Gary Condit and Abbe Lowe." Newsweek 3 Sept. 2001.

15. "Chandra Levy Timeline." ABC News 2002.

16. Smith, Anne Marie. "CITIZEN COMPLAINT COMMITTEE STANIS-LAUS COUNTY GRAND JURY MODESTO, CALIFORNIA THE PEOPLE OF THE STATE OF CALIFORNIA, v. GARY A. CONDIT, MIKE LYNCH and DON THORNTON Defendants." AFFIDAVIT OF MS. ANNE MARIE SMITH, IN SUPPORT OF A CITIZEN COMPLAINT FOR CRIMINAL INDICTMENTS FOR OBSTRUCTION OF JUSTICE AND SUBORNA-TION OF PERJURY. 26 Aug. 2001.

17. Cosby, Rita. "Condit in trouble, has to disappear." Fox News 4 July 2001.

18. Condit, Gary. Interview with Jodi Hernandez. KOVR. 23 Aug. 2001. Transcript.

"Chandra's aunt speaks out." Fox News 1 Aug. 2001.

"Condit Has an Alibi." Newsweek 20 July 2001.

Doyle, Michael. "Anxiety deep, answers few in Levy case." Modesto Bee 12 May 2001.

Doyle, Michael. "Family, friends try to move on." Modesto Bee 28 Apr. 2002.

Dvorak, Petula. "Washington Lifestyle Dazzled Intern: Missing Daughter's Hopes, Accomplishments Comfort Parents Keeping Vigil." Washington Post 22 May 2001.

Hostein, Lynne. "Search widens for missing USC student." KTLA-TV 22 May 2001.

Jacoby, Mary. "Clues to missing intern sought in park." St Petersburg Times 17 July 2001.

Kennedy, Helen. "Intern Visited Pol." New York Daily News 17 May 2001.

"Levy friends show support for D.C. intern." Modesto Bee. 19 May 2001.

"Police Keep Quiet on Levy Investigation." Washington Times 23 Aug. 2001.

Wiegand, Steve. "Facts are few in Levy mystery." Sacremento Bee 3 Sept. 2001.

Stonewalling

1. Santana, Arthur. "Lack of Information Leaves Family Frustrated." Washington Post 16 May 2001.

2. Ibid.

3. Doyle, Michael and J. N. Sbranti. "D.C. police reject local assistance in search for missing Modesto woman." Modesto Bee 15 May 2001.

4. Whitney, David and J.N. Sbranti. "Levys navigate 'tricky' media encounters." Modesto Bee 15 May 2001.

5. Ibid.

6. Doyle, Michael and J. N. Sbranti. "D.C. police reject local assistance in search for missing Modesto woman." Modesto Bee 15 May 2001.

7. Ibid.

8. Doyle, Michael "Levy's parents field D.C. media barrage." Modesto Bee 18 May 2001.

9. Doyle, Michael. "Condit's gift giving could be an issue." Modesto Bee 22 July 2001.

10. Ibid.

11. Lauerman, Kerry. "The congressman, the missing intern and the mother." Salon. 22 June 2001. <www.salon.com>.

12. Levy, Robert and Susan. Interview with Larry King. Larry King Live. CNN. 15 Aug. 2001. Transcript.

13. Burger, Timothy J. "Solid Rep as Partier." New York Daily News 20 May 2001.

14. Sbranti, J.N. and Michael Doyle. "Condit still has valley's trust." Modesto Bee 20 May 2001.

15. Olson, Barbara, Mike Geragos, Cynthia Alksne, Julian Epstein, and Lisa DePaulo. "Will Chandra Levy ever be found?" Interview with Larry King. Larry King Live. CNN. 30 July 2001. Transcript.

16. Santana, Arthur. "Search Intensifies for Missing Intern." Washington Post 17 May 2001.

17. Ibid.

18. Dvorak, Petula and Allan Lengel. "Absent evidence, Levy probe stalls." Washington Post 9 Sept. 2001.

19. "Police Keep Quiet on Levy Investigation." Washington Times 23 Aug. 2001.

20. Fields-Meyer, Thomas, Champ Clark, Michael Fleeman, Macon Morehouse and J. Todd Foster. "Searching For Chandra." People 25 June 2001: 87.

Baker, Jennifer. Interview with Greta Van Susteren. The Point. CNN. 17 May 2001. Transcript.

"Condit's neighbors surveyed." Modesto Bee 19 May 2001.

Depaulo, Lisa. "Have the Media Devoted Too Much Coverage to Chandra Levy's Disappearance?" Interview with Tucker Carlson. Cross Fire. CNN. 18 Jul. 2001. Transcript.

Doyle, Michael. "P.M. Update: Missing Modesto woman's parents meet with police." Modesto Bee 17 May 2001.

Fahrenthold, David A. and Arthur Santana. "Lots of Attention but Little News As Search for Intern Continues." Washington Post 18 May 2001.

"Intern Told Friend of Relationship With Congressman." Fox News 18 May 2001.

Jackson, Robert L. "Police Dogs Search Woods for USC Student." Los Angeles Times 17 May 2001.

Kennedy, Helen "D.C. Cops Mystified As Intern Vanishes." New York Daily News 16 May 2001.

Kennedy, Helen. "Intern Visited Pol." New York Daily News 17 May 2001.

Lathem, Niles and Dan Mangan. "Mystery Beau Paid For Missing Intern's Airfare." New York Post 19 May 2001.

Lengel, Allan and Andrew DeMillo. "Flight Attendant Spends 6 Hours With Investigators." Washington Post 12 July 2001.

Lengel, Allan and Petula Dvorak. "Mother asks for help to find missing daughter." Washington Post 18 May 2001.

Mitchell, Andrea. "Parents of Missing Student arrive in D.C. to look for answers." NBC News 16 May 2001.

"Police Find Pair of Running Shoes." 9 Eyewitness News 17 July 2001.

Yost, Pete. "Police to Search Missing Woman's Apt." Associated Press 18 May 2001.

Zamora, Jim Herron. "Modesto woman is missing in Washington, D.C.: Police begin bicoastal search for grad student." San Francisco Chronicle 13 May 2001.

Luray

1. Fintz, Stacy and Kevin Fagan. "Mill Valley woman says Condit aide sought her silence: New details on watch-giver." San Francisco Chronicle 28 July 2001.

2. Squitieri, Tom and Kevin Johnson. "Condit inquiry gets new twist." USA Today 25 July 2001.

3. Blomquist, Brian. "Who Was Condit's Mystery Driver?" ABC. 24 July 2001.

4. "Woman Who Gave Condit Watch Dated Mike Dayton First." New York Post 31 Aug. 2001.

5. Condit, Gary. Interview with Connie Chung. PrimeTime Live. ABC. 23 Aug. 2001. Transcript.

6. Doyle, Michael. "Staffer romance revealed: Woman's affair with Condit mirrors Levy's." Modesto Bee 25 July 2001.

7. Keller, Amy and Damon Chappie. "Condit Campaign Amends FEC Forms." Roll Call.

8. Brazil, Eric. "Relationship with congressman questioned." San Francisco Chronicle 18 May 2001.

9. Smith, Anne Marie and Jim Robinson. Interview with Larry King. Larry King Live. CNN. 13 July 2001. Transcript.

10. Olson, Barbara, Mark Geragos, Cynthia Alksne and Julian Epstein. Interview with Roger Cossack. Larry King Live. CNN. 2 Aug. 2001. Transcript.

11. Ibid.

12. Fahey, Todd Brendon. "Luray, Virginia: Key In Condit/Levy Case." Ether Zone 15 June 2001.

13. "alt.true-crime." at http://www.google.com/groups, 19 July 2001.

14. Smith, Anne Marie. "CITIZEN COMPLAINT COMMITTEE STANIS-LAUS COUNTY GRAND JURY MODESTO, CALIFORNIA THE PEOPLE OF THE STATE OF CALIFORNIA, v. GARY A. CONDIT, MIKE LYNCH and DON THORNTON Defendants." AFFIDAVIT OF MS. ANNE MARIE SMITH, IN SUPPORT OF A CITIZEN COMPLAINT FOR CRIMINAL INDICTMENTS FOR OBSTRUCTION OF JUSTICE AND SUBORNA-TION OF PERJURY. 26 Aug. 2001.

15. Dart, Bob. "Flight Attendant Asks Grand Jury To Indict Condit." Cox News 28 Aug. 2001.

Blomquist, Brian. "Levy Kin: Investigate Condit Bro." New York Post 19 July 2001.

"Chandra Levy mystery: A timeline." USA Today 2001.

Flammini, Vince, George Lewis, Ed Rollins, Julian Epstein, Wendy Murphy, Candice DeLong, Don Vance, Dominick Dunne. "Backfiring of Congressman Gary Condit's media blitz." Rivera Live. CNBC. 27 Aug. 2001.

Iander, John. "What was Condit like in the 1980's?" KOVR 13 News 23 Oct. 2001.

Sbranti, J.N. and Michael Doyle. "Condit still has valley's trust." Modesto Bee 20 May 2001.

Serrano, Richard A. and Robert L. Jackson. "D.C. Puzzles Over Missing USC Student." Los Angeles Times 19 May 2001.

Zamora, Jim Herron. "Modesto woman is missing in Washington, D.C.: Police begin bicoastal search for grad student." San Francisco Chronicle 13 May 2001.

Obsessed

1. "Lost in a Washington mystery." Baltimore Sun 26 May 2001.

2. Lengel, Allan. "Intern Spent Night With Condit." Washington Post 7 June 2001.

3. "Grand jury used in intern's case." MSNBC 14 June 2001.

4. Olson, Barbara, Mike Geragos, Cynthia Alksne, Julian Epstein, and Lisa DePaulo. "Will Chandra Levy ever be found?" Interview with Larry King. Larry King Live. CNN. 30 July 2001. Transcript.

5. Jardine, Jeff. "Minister: Daughter had affair with Condit." Modesto Bee 12 July 2001.

6. Squitieri, Tom and Kevin Johnson. "Condit inquiry gets new twist." USA Today 25 July 2001.

7. Smith, Anne Marie and Jim Robinson. Interview with Sean Hannity and Alan Colmes. Hannity and Colmes. Fox News. 28 May 2002. Transcript.

8. "Levy's Parents Drop Bombshell." New York Post 15 June 2001.

9. "Levy's Parents Ask 'Mysterious Boyfriend'." ABC News 15 June 2001.

10. "Levys said to refuse Condit's calls." MSNBC 20 June 2001.

11. Cosby, Rita. "The second interview." Fox News 28 June 2001.

12. Lathem, Niles and Andy Geller. "New Chandra Twist." New York Post 28 June 2001.

13. Dvorak, Petula and Allan Lengel. "Missing Intern's Parents Back in D.C.—With new attorney." Washington Post 20 June 2001.

14. "Grand jury used in intern's case." MSNBC 14 June 2001.

15. Dvorak, Petula and Allan Lengel. "Missing Intern's Parents Back in D.C.—With new attorney." Washington Post 20 June 2001.

16. Cosby, Rita. "The second interview." Fox News 28 June 2001.

17. Keary, Jim and Audrey Hudson. "Condit to be questionsed again about intern." Washington Times 20 June 2001.

18. Marshall, Joshua Micah. "Chandra's contested calls to Condit: It's the New York Post vs. Newsweek. Or could the truth lie somewhere in between?" Salon 1 Aug. 2001.

19. Levy, Susan. Interview. Newsweek. 13 Aug. 2001.

Bazinet, Kenneth R. "Pol Pager Got Many Intern Hits." New York Daily News 18 June 2001.

"Chandra's Brother Talks." Los Angeles Times 21 June 2001.

"Condit Talking With TV Networks." New York Post 17 June 2001.

Doyle, Michael "Levy's parents field D.C. media barrage." Modesto Bee 18 May 2001.

Kennedy, Helen. "Cops Have More Questions for Calif. Pol." New York Daily News 21 June 2001.

Kennedy, Helen. "Pol Told Cops He Rejected Intern." New York Daily News 28 June 2001.

Lathem, Niles. "Condit Coming Clean." New York Post 23 June 2001.

Lathem, Niles. "Cops Fear Intern May Have Done Herself In." New York Post 21 June 2001.

Lehmann, John and Cynthia Bournellis. "Friends had been telling Chandra Levy for years: Quit falling in love with older men." New York Post 12 Aug. 2001.

Lengel, Allan and Petula Dvorak. "Intern Mentioned A 'Boyfriend', Landlord Says: Levy Briefly Considered Move, He Says." Washington Post 21 June 2001.

Levy, Robert and Susan. Interview with Larry King. Larry King Live. CNN. 15 Aug. 2001. Transcript.

"No Leads: Police Pan Focus on Missing Intern's Lifestyle." ABC News 8 June 2001.

"Nonexistent Phone Calls (and Other False Tales)." Newsweek 29 July 2001.

Novak, Viveca. Interview with McEdwards. Just in Time. CNN. 18 June 2001. Transcript.

Solly, Dale. "Chandra Levy's Parents Set To Return To Washington." WJLA 18 June 2001.

Sweet, Lynn. "Levy 'jubilant' at last sighting." Chicago Sun-Times 20 July 2001.

Smith, Anne Marie and Jim Robinson. Interview with Larry King. Larry King Live. CNN. 13 July 2001. Transcript.

"Where In The World Is Chandra Levy" at http://www.geocities.com/redd_herring.geo/chandra/chandralevy_main.html under "Q & A session with Denis Edeline.", 3 Aug. 2001.

Alibi

1. Burger, Timothy J. and Helen Kennedy. "Pol Has a Time Line Alibi: Busy on Hill, with wife when intern disappeared." New York Daily News 29 June 2001.

2. "Police to return to parks in Levy case; Experts: Condit damaged own reputation." CNN 22 July 2001.

3. Lathem, Niles. "ABC Reporter Dated Condit." New York Post 7 July 2001.

4. "Condit's Calendar." Good Morning America. ABC News. 9 July 2001.

5. Tapper, Jake. "Police ignore Condit's faulty alibi." Salon 18 July 2001. <www.salon.com>.

6. Dayton, Mullen, Mejia, Moore, Austin. "Gary Condit's Staff Speaks Out." Interview with Larry King. Larry King Live. CNN. 30 Aug. 2001. Transcript.

7. Cooper, Matthew. "Under the Hot Lights: Gary Condit's Cowboys." Time 29 July 2001.

8. "to Have a Chiropractor Appointment." at http://www.geocities.com/gypsygal14/Slang.html, 5 Sep. 2002.

9. Dayton, Mullen, Mejia, Moore, Austin. "Gary Condit's Staff Speaks Out." Interview with Larry King. Larry King Live. CNN. 30 Aug. 2001. Transcript.

10. Frank, Thomas. "Condit Labors On." Newsday 18 July 2001.

11. Lathem, Niles. "Chandra Probers Easing Up On Condit." New York Post 1 July 2001.

Campbell, Duncan. "Cheney could be Condit witness." Guardian 23 July 2001.

"Condit Gives Police Timeline, Police Officials Negotiate To Interview Wife." ABC News 29 June 2001.

"Condit Has an Alibi." Newsweek 20 July 2001.

"Condit: Questions to Mrs. In Advance." New York Times 30 June 2001.

Doyle, Michael. "Anxiety deep, answers few in Levy case." Modesto Bee 12 May 2001.

Doyle, Michael. "Condit's schedule checks out." Modesto Bee 22 July 2001.

Isikoff, Michael. "The Battle Over Chandra." Newsweek 23 July 2001

Marshall, Joshua Micah. "ABC's messy role in Condit affair." Salon. 13 July 2001. <www.salon.com>.

Sherman, Mark. "Rep. Gary Condit subpoenaed for documents related to missing intern." Associated Press 15 Nov. 2001.

The Watch

1. Kennedy, Helen. "She Claims Affair With Pol: Flight attendant says Condit wanted her to lie, stall FBI." New York Daily News 3 July 2001.

2. Ibid.

3. Pean, Hervey. "Missing intern's aunt asks Rep. Condit for full account." Cox News Service 7 July 2001.

4. Lengel, Allan and Petula Dvorak. "Aunt Linda Details Chandra's Affair with Gary." Washington Post 6 July 2001.

5. Lengel, Alan and Petula Dvorak. "Police Want to Talk With Condit Again." Washington Post 7 July 2001.

6. Dvorak, Petula and Allan Legel. "Levy Family Seeks Condit Polygraph." Washington Post 9 July 2001.

7. Burger, Timothy J. "Kin: Give Condit Lie Detector." New York Daily News 9 July 2001.

8. "Man who claims he saw Condit dump a watch case." Interview with Paula Zahn. The Edge. Fox News. 25 July 2001. Transcript.

9. Squitieri, Tom and Kevin Johnson. "Investigators reportedly focus on Condit staffers." USA Today 25 July 2001.

10. Flammini, Vince, George Lewis, Ed Rollins, Julian Epstein, Wendy Murphy, Candice DeLong, Don Vance, Dominick Dunne. "Backfiring of Congressman Gary Condit's media blitz." Rivera Live. CNBC. 27 Aug. 2001.

11. Larry King Live. "Panelists Discuss Gary Condit's Interview With 'Vanity Fair'." 23 August 2001. Transcript.

12. Condit, Cadee. Interview with Larry King. Larry King Live. CNN. 5 Sept. 2001. Transcript.

13. Condit, Gary. Interview with Larry King. Larry King Live. CNN. 25 Feb. 2002. Transcript.

14. Franke-Ruta, Garance. "THE NEIGHBORS, THE HANGERS-ON, AND THE CREEPY WOODS." Washington City Paper 20 July 2001.

15. Kennedy, Helen. "Cops Comb Condit's Apartment." New York Daily News 11 July 2001.

16. Dart, Bob. "Levy Visited Condit-Related Sites Just Before Vanishing." Cox News 19 July 2001.

17. Lengel, Allan and Petula Dvorak. "Condit Passes Private Polygraph Lawyer Says." Washington Post 14 July 2001.

18. "Police scour D.C. park in Levy search." CNN 17 July 2001.

19. "Expert Panel Discusses Elizabeth Smart Case." Interview with Larry King. Larry King Live. CNN. 12 June 2002. Transcript.

20. Kennedy, Helen. "Cops on Intern Net Trail: Computer shows Levy may have been lured to path." New York Daily News 16 July 2001.

Burger, Timothy J. and Helen Kennedy. "Police hunt for Chandra's body; Condit balking at taking lie test." New York Daily News 13 July 2001.

"Campaign Finance Reports and Data" at http://www.fec.gov, 5 Sep. 2002.

Doyle, Michael. "Condit aide denies cover-up: He says he never tried to stop a woman from disclosing alleged affair." Modesto Bee 27 July 2001.

Dvorak, Petula and Allan Lengel. "D.C. Police Question Condit For A 4th Time." Washington Post 27 July 2001.

Isikoff, Michael. "The Battle Over Chandra." Newsweek 23 July 2001

Isikoff, Michael. "The Story Changes." Newsweek 7 July 2001.

Lathem, Niles and Cathy Burke. "Condit Wife's Mystery Phone Call." New York Post 27 July 2001.

Lengel, Allan and Petula Dvorak. "Woman Says Condit Asked Her to Lie." Washington Post 3 July 2001.

"Levy Aunt Speaks." ABC News 2 Aug. 2001.

"Newsweek, NBC confirm Levy affair." MSNBC Washington 7 July 2001.

"Police Seek Condit Phone Records." ABC News 6 July 2001.

"'Significant' chance Levy won't be found." USA Today 19 July 2001.

Sisk, Richard and Leo Standora. "Pol Threw Out Watch Case." New York Daily News 20 July 2001.

"The Heat Goes On: The Levy team uses the media spotlight to keep Chandra's case from going cold." CNN 23 July 2001.

Exposed

1. Lengel, Allan and Petula Dvorak. "Minister recants story about Condit, daughter" Washington Post 21 July 2001.

2. Lengel, Allan and Petula Dvorak. "FBI Concludes Minister Invented Tale About Condit." Washington Post 31 July 2001.

3. Jardine, Jeff. "Minister: Daughter had affair with Condit." Modesto Bee 12 July 2001.

4. Burger, Timothy J. and Helen Kennedy. "Police hunt for Chandra's body; Condit balking at taking lie test." New York Daily News 13 July 2001.

5. "Letter denies alleged affair with Condit." CNN 12 July 2001.

6. Burger, Timothy J. and Helen Kennedy. "Police hunt for Chandra's body; Condit balking at taking lie test." New York Daily News 13 July 2001.

7. Jardine, Jeff. "Condit Denies Affair With Teen." Modesto Bee 13 July 2001.

8. Ibid.

9. "Feds open criminal inquiry into whether Condit obstructed justice." Associated Press 12 July 2001.

10. Burger, Timothy J. and Helen Kennedy. "Police hunt for Chandra's body; Condit balking at taking lie test." New York Daily News 13 July 2001.

11. Jardine, Jeff. "Condit Denies Affair With Teen." Modesto Bee 13 July 2001.

12. Jardine, Jeff and Michael G. Mooney. "Save Mart: 'Explicit' coverage goes too far." Modesto Bee 17 July 2001.

13. Ibid.

14. Dvorak, Petula and Allan Lengel. "Minister Says Daughter, at 18, Had an Affair With Condit." Washington Post 12 July 2001.

15. Lengel, Allan and Petula Dvorak. "Minister recants story about Condit, daughter" Washington Post 21 July 2001.

16. Ibid.

17. Lengel, Allan and Petula Dvorak. "FBI Concludes Minister Invented Tale About Condit." Washington Post 31 July 2001.

18. Ibid.

19. Olson, Barbara, Mike Geragos, Cynthia Alksne, Julian Epstein, and Lisa DePaulo. "Will Chandra Levy ever be found?" Interview with Larry King. Larry King Live. CNN. 30 July 2001. Transcript.

20. Levy, Susan. Interview. Newsweek. 13 Aug. 2001.

Brazinet, Kenneth R. and Helen Kennedy. "D.C. Park Combed For Clues." New York Daily News 18 July 2001.

"Condit takes polygraph." ABC News 13 July 2001.

Jardine, Jeff. "Levys keep their hopes alive." Modesto Bee 1 Aug. 2001.

Kennedy, Helen. "Condit Evidence Dumping Probed." New York Daily News 21 July 2001.

Lathem, Niles, Steve Dunleavy, Edmund Newton and Andy Gellar. "Condit's 'Affair' Teen Had Baby." New York Post 13 July 2001.

Rock Creek Park

1. Blomquist, Brian. "Levy Kin: Investigate Condit Bro." New York Post 19 July 2001.

2. Diaz, Johnny. "Condit brothers not close." Miami Herald 23 July 2001.

3. Lengel, Allan and Sari Horwitz. "Chandra Levy Spectacle Comandeers Media Stage." Washington Post 16 July 2001.

4. Twomey, Steve and Sari Horwitz. "Park Slope Went Unsearched: Area Where Levy's Remains Were Found Fell Between Sweeps." Washington Post 24 May 2002.

5. "More Evidence Points to Murder in Levy Case." WUSA-TV 9 2002.

6. Zamora, Jim Herron. "Modesto woman is missing in Washington, D.C.: Police begin bicoastal search for grad student." San Francisco Chronicle 13 May 2001.

7. Jones, Sven. Interview with Ross Mitchell. The Early Show. CBS. 23 May 2002. Transcript.

8. O'Reilly, Bill. "Sven Jones after Chandra found." 24 May 2002. Transcript.

9. Horwitz, Sari and Allan Lengel. "Levy Possibly Bound By Leggings: Knotted Garment Sharpens Suspicion of Foul Play." Washington Post 25 May 2002.

10. "Thread Archives" at www.justiceforchandra.com/forums, 5 Sep. 2002.

11. Gainer, Terrance. "Do D.C.'s Police or Gary Condit Deserve More Respect?" Interview. Cross Fire. CNN. 23 May 2002. Transcript.

12. Ritchie, William. Interview with Bill O'Reilly. The O'Reilly Factor. Fox News. 28 May 2002. Transcript.

13. Jones, Dave. "Mood inside Levy home one of tears." Modesto Bee 26 May 2002.

14. Twomey, Steve and Sari Horwitz. "Skeletal Remains Found." Washington Post 23 May 2002.

15. Kennedy, Helen. "Chandra Cops Stymied." New York Daily News 24 May 2002.

16. DeMillo, Andrew. "Police Searching Parks for Levy" Washington Post 16 July 2001.

17. Levy, Robert and Susan. Interview with Larry King. Larry King Live. CNN. 15 Aug. 2001. Transcript.

18. Twomey, Steve and Sari Horwitz. "Park Slope Went Unsearched: Area Where Levy's Remains Were Found Fell Between Sweeps." Washington Post 24 May 2002.

19. "MPD Chief Gainer online interview." washingtonpost.com 23 May 2002.

20. Levine, Susan. "Cadaver Dogs Sniff Out the Clues." Washington Post 13 June 2002.

21. Ritchie, William. Interview with Bill O'Reilly. The O'Reilly Factor. Fox News. 28 May 2002. Transcript.

22. "Rock Creek Park" at http://www.mdbirds.org/dcbirds/ccorridor.html, 2000.

Bolen, Mandy. "Condit's brother has Key West record." Key West Citizen 18 July 2001.

Bolstad, Erika. "Condit's brother nabbed in S. Florida." Miami Herald 21 July 2001.

Bryan, Susannah and Rafael Omeda. "Congressman Condit's brother arrested in Dania Beach." Sun-Sentinel 21 July 2001.

"Cops Search Park for Intern." Newsday 17 July 2001.

"Darrell Condit." Star 22 July 2001.

DePaulo, Lisa. Talk Magazine article on Chandra Levy. Excerpt. London Times U.K. 12 Aug. 2001.

Doyle, Michael. "Condit denies Levy report." Modesto Bee 8 June 2001.

Fields-Meyer, Thomas, Champ Clark, Michael Fleeman, Macon Morehouse and J. Todd Foster. "Searching For Chandra." People 25 June 2001: 87.

"Gary Condit's brother jailed for missing court." St Petersburg Times 12 March 2002.

Hartman, Brian. "Repeat Offender Condit Brother Wanted for Parole Violation." ABC News 19 July 2001.

"I don't know intern, fugitive tells police." Miami Herald 22 July 2001.

Johnson, Kevin and Tom Squitieri. "D.C. police retrace steps in their search for Levy." USA Today 17 July 2001.

Kennedy, Helen. "Cops on Intern Net Trail: Computer shows Levy may have been lured to path." New York Daily News 16 July 2001.

Lathem, Niles and Andy Geller. "Investigators believe Chandra Levy was lured to her death by someone she knew or slain by a predator who methodically stalked her, police sources said yesterday." New York Post 26 May 2002.

Lengel, Allan and Sari Horwitz. "Levy Was on Internet on May 1, Police Say Intern Looked Up Rock Creek Map, Other Sites." Washington Post 16 July 2001.

"Levy case opens door on secret life: The search for missing former intern Chandra Levy has focused the spotlight on U.S. Rep. Gary Condit." CNN 1 June 2002.

Sale, Jon. Interview with Greta Van Susteren. The Point. Fox News. 23 July 2001. Transcript.

Sweet, Lynn. "Police: Missing intern no 'trollop'." Chicago Sun-Times 19 July 2001.

Grand Jury

1. Schmidt, Susan and Bill Miller. "Closer Look at Roles of Condit, Aides Debated: Discussion of Possible Obstruction of Justice, Witness Tampering as Leads Dwindle." Washington Post 6 Aug. 2001.

2. Lathem, Niles. "Condit Finds Crucial Day Forgettable." New York Post 2 Aug. 2001.

3. Dunleavy, Steve. "NYPD Would Crack Condit." New York Post 30 July 2001.

4. Aley, Terry. "Condit Retracts Action On EBay Art Auction." aleydesign. 8 Aug. 2001. <www.aleydesign.com>.

5. Ibid.

6. Ibid.

7. Larry King Live. "Panelists Discuss Gary Condit's Interview With 'Vanity Fair'." 23 August 2001. Transcript.

8. Dvorak, Petula and Allan Lengel. "Condit Met by Avalanche of Criticism: Democratic Colleagues Rebuke Congressman." Washington Post 25 Aug. 2001.

9. Flammini, Vince, George Lewis, Ed Rollins, Julian Epstein, Wendy Murphy, Candice DeLong, Don Vance, Dominick Dunne. "Backfiring of Congressman Gary Condit's media blitz." Rivera Live. CNBC. 27 Aug. 2001.

10. "D.C. police chief says Condit 'difficult'." CNN 30 Aug. 2001.

11. Dvorak, Petula and Allan Lengel. "Absent evidence, Levy probe stalls." Washington Post 9 Sept. 2001.

12. Ibid.

13. Dvorak, Petula and Lengel, Allan. "Levy Family Reflects on How 'World Changed'." Washington Post. 29 Oct. 2001.

14. Doyle, Michael. "Condit mulls month old subpoena." Modesto Bee 11 Dec. 2001.

15. Doyle, Michael. "Levy case still puzzles police." Modesto Bee 28 Apr. 2002.

16. Keary, Jim and Matthew Cella. "Grand Jury subpoena for Condit records." Washington Times 16 Dec. 2001.

17. Lengel, Allan. "Grand Jury Looks at Condit Material." Washington Post 19 Jan. 2002.

18. Kennedy, Helen. "Redemption or Final Bow: Voters to decide fate of Condit in primary." New York Daily News 4 Mar. 2002.

19. Sager, Mike. "The Final Days of Gary Condit." Esquire 1 Sep. 2002.

"April grand jury subpoenaes Condit." Washington Post 26 Mar. 2002.

Blomquist, Brian and Devlin Barrett. "Condit Dumped Item Before Search." New York Post 20 July 2001.

"Condit delays grand jury appearance in Washington." Sacremento Bee 5 Apr. 2002.

"Condit gets GJ subpoena." Reuters Washington 16 Nov. 2001.

"Condit's lawyer, Mark Garagos, lashed out at cops." New York Daily News 23 May 2002.

Isikoff, Michael; Klaidman, Daniel; Clift, Eleanor; Murr, Andrew. "An Affair to Remember." Newsweek 16 July 2001: 20.

Kennedy, Helen. "Levy pushed for Condit to divorce, friend says." New York Daily News 4 Aug. 2001.

Lengel, Allan. "Condit Had Appointment With Grand Jury: Data Was Kept Secret To Minimize Leaks." Washington Post 13 Apr. 2002.

Moraes, Lisa de. "'PrimeTime Prize': Connie Chung Gets Condit Interview." Washington Post 21 Aug. 2001.

Sherman, Mark. "A year later, no breaks in Chandra Levy's disappearance." Associated Press 27 Apr. 2002.

Squitieri, Tom and Kevin Johnson. "Lawyer starts investigation of intern's disappearance." USA Today 21 June 2001.

Wiegand, Steve. "Facts are few in Levy mystery." Sacremento Bee 3 Sept. 2001.

Found

1. Twomey, Steve and Sari Horwitz. "With Levy case going nowhere, chance stepped in." Washington Post 26 May 2002.

2. Twomey, Steve and Sari Horwitz. "Skeletal Remains Found." Washington Post 23 May 2002.

3. Williams, Ted. "Was Chandra Levy Sexually Assaulted Before She Died?" Interview with Greta Van Susteren. On the Record. Fox News. 31 May 2002. Transcript.

4. Cella, Matthew and Jim Keary. "Police believe Levy's body was put at site." Washington Times 24 May 2002.

5. Horwitz, Sari and Allan Lengel. "Levy Possibly Bound By Leggings: Knotted Garment Sharpens Suspicion of Foul Play." Washington Post 25 May 2002.

6. Smalley, Suzanne and Mark Hosenball. "You've Just Got Bones." Newsweek 3 June 2001.

7. "Police Search For Chandra's Ring." CBS News 29 May 2002.

8. "Medical examiner says Chandra Levy was murdered." Detroit News 28 May 2002.

9. Lathem, Niles. "Grim Park Site Is Reopened But Chandr Investigators Aren't Out Of The Woods Yet." New York Post 1 June 2002.

10. Williams, Ted and Michael Baden. Interview with Greta Van Susteren. On the Record. Fox News 4 June 2002. Transcript.

11. Lengel, Allan and Sari Horwitz. "Police Again Scour Park For Remains: Ramsey Says Animals May Have Moved Tibia." Washington Post 8 June 2002.

12. Lengel, Allan and Sari Horwitz. "Grand Jury Hearing From Condit's Aides: More Levy Bones Identified As Lipstick Is Also Found." Washington Post 12 June 2002.

13. Ibid.

14. Doyle, Michael. "No new developments in investigation into slaying." Modesto Bee 18 May 2003.

15. Moreno, Sylvia. "Hope for 'Closure' Follows Discovery." Washington Post 23 May 2002.

16. "Thread Archives" at www.justiceforchandra.com/forums, 5 Sep. 2002.

17. Ibid.

18. "Modesto mourns Levy as homicide is confirmed." San Jose Mercury News 29 May 2002.

19. "Thread Archives" at www.justiceforchandra.com/forums, 5 Sep. 2002.

20. Ibid.

21. Doyle, Michael. "Medical examiner can't tell how ex-intern was killed." Modesto Bee 29 May 2002.

22. Taylor, Guy. "Picture of Levy ring released." Washington Times 30 May 2002.

23. Kennedy, Helen. "Condit Lawyer: Lie Test OK: If FBI asks, congressman should do it, he's advised." New York Daily News 30 May 2002.

24. Ibid.

Cella, Matthew. "Levy death may be classified as homicide." Washington Times 25 May 2002.

Doyle, Michael. "A second opinion for Levy bones." Modesto Bee 20 July 2002.

Doyle, Michael. "Levy family left waiting for daughter's remains." Modesto Bee 1 Sept. 2001.

Doyle, Michael. "Levy's remains to be returned to Modesto, godparents say." Modesto Bee 22 May 2003.

Horwitz, Sari and Allan Lengel. "Levy May Have Been Strangled, Official Says" Washington Post 14 July 2002.

Horwitz, Sari and Allan Lengel. "Police Take New Look at Man as Potential Suspect in Levy Case." Washington Post 29 Sep. 2002.

Kennedy, Helen. "No clue in FBI tests to Chandra's killer." New York Daily News 15 Aug. 2002.

Lengel, Allan. "Dyed Cash Found Near Levy Site." Washington Post 10 June 2002.

Lengel, Allan. "Unfinished Business." Washington Post 5 May 2003.

Twomey, Steve and Sari Horwitz. "Park Slope Went Unsearched: Area Where Levy's Remains Were Found Fell Between Sweeps." Washington Post 24 May 2002.

Horse Trail

1. "Thread Archives" at www.justiceforchandra.com/forums, 5 Sep. 2002.

2. Lathem, Niles. "Grim Park Site Is Reopened But Chandr Investigators Aren't Out Of The Woods Yet." New York Post 1 June 2002.

3. Horwitz, Sari and Allan Lengel. "Levy May Have Been Strangled, Official Says" Washington Post 14 July 2002.

4. "Thread Archives" at www.justiceforchandra.com/forums, 5 Sep. 2002.

5. Wecht, Cyril. Interview with Bill O'Reilly. The O'Reilly Factor. Fox News. 23 May 2002. Transcript.

6. Williams, Ted and Michael Baden. Interview with Greta Van Susteren. On the Record. Fox News 4 June 2002. Transcript.

7. "Thread Archives" at www.justiceforchandra.com/forums, 5 Sep. 2002.

8. Horwitz, Sari and Allan Lengel. "Levy May Have Been Strangled, Official Says" Washington Post 14 July 2002.

9. Williams, Ted. "Was Chandra Levy Sexually Assaulted Before She Died?" Interview with Greta Van Susteren. On the Record. Fox News. 31 May 2002. Transcript.

"A local murder mystery." Sacramento Bee 25 June 2002.

Guandique

1. Doyle, Michael. "Investigators try to tie suspect to Levy's death." Modesto Bee 5 Oct. 2002.

2. Cella, Matthew and Jim Keary. "Police believe Levy's body was put at site." Washington Times 24 May 2002.

3. Lathem, Niles and Andy Geller. "D.C. Cops Want to Grill Condit for 5th Time." Washington Post 24 May 2002.

4. Horitz, Sari and Allan Lengel. "Police Take New Look at Man as Potential Suspect in Levy Case." Washington Post 29 Sept. 2002.

5. Doyle, Michael. "Investigators try to tie suspect to Levy's death." Modesto Bee 5 Oct. 2002.

6. Cella, Matthew and Jim Keary. "Police believe Levy's body was put at site." Washington Times 24 May 2002.

7. Kennedy, Helen. "Chandra Cops Stymied." New York Daily News 24 May 2002.

8. Horitz, Sari and Allan Lengel. "Police Take New Look at Man as Potential Suspect in Levy Case." Washington Post 29 Sept. 2002.

9. Doyle, Michael. "Investigators try to tie suspect to Levy's death." Modesto Bee 5 Oct. 2002.

10. Horitz, Sari and Allan Lengel. "Police Take New Look at Man as Potential Suspect in Levy Case." Washington Post 29 Sept. 2002.

11. Ibid.

12. Ibid.

13. "Housemate tips police to Smith after seeing video." CNN 5 Feb. 2004.

14. "Man's Friends Face Levy Case Grand Jury." Washington Post 4 Oct. 2002.

"Girl's family wants to know why suspect was free." CNN 8 Feb. 2004.

"Sister of missing student suspect asked to keep tabs on him." CNN 7 Dec. 2003.

Stacy, Mitch. "Man Questioned in Girl's Taped Abduction." Associated Press 4 Feb. 2004.

Woman Missing

1. Levy, Robert and Susan. Interview with Greta Van Susteren. On the Record. Fox News. 12 Dec. 2002. Transcript.

2. Doyle, Michael. "Levy's remains to be returned to Modesto, godparents say." Modesto Bee 22 May 2003.

3. Doyle, Michael. "No new developments in investigation into slaying." Modesto Bee 18 May 2003.

4. "Unsolved Cases: Chandra Levy Investigation." NBC4.com 6 Nov. 2003.

5. Chan, Sewell. "Morgue Again Takes Turn for Worse." Washington Post 27 Sep. 2003.

6. Hayes, Heather. "The Long Arm of the Law." fcw.com 6 Dec. 1999.

Lengel, Allan and Sari Horwitz. "Grand Jury Hearing From Condit's Aides: More Levy Bones Identified As Lipstick Is Also Found." Washington Post 12 June 2002.

0-595-31847-9

CPSIA information can be obtained
at www.ICGtesting.com
Printed in the USA
LVOW10s2259220117
521823LV00001B/66/P

9 780595 318476